D1499740

TRANSFORMATIONAL LEARNING

Also by Daniel R. Tobin

Re-Educating the Corporation: Foundations for the Learning Organization

TRANSFORMATIONAL LEARNING

RENEWING YOUR COMPANY THROUGH KNOWLEDGE AND SKILLS

DANIEL R. TOBIN

John Wiley & Sons, Inc.
New York • Chichester • Brisbane • Toronto • Singapore

This text is printed on acid-free paper.

Published by John Wiley & Sons, Inc.

Library of Congress Cataloging-in-Publication Data:

Tobin, Daniel R., 1946–
Transformational learning : renewing your company through knowledge and skills / Daniel R. Tobin.
p. cm.
Includes index.
ISBN 0-471-13289-6 (alk. paper)
1. Organizational learning. 2. Reengineering (Management)
I. Title.
HD58.82.T63 1996 95-39107
658.4'063—dc20

Printed in the United States of America

10 9 8 7 6 5 4 3 2 1

For Susan and Molly

ACKNOWLEDGMENTS

This book would not have been possible except for the willingness of so many people to share their ideas and experiences with me. At Ace Clearwater Enterprises, CEO Kellie Dodson and Vice President Gary Johnson spent a lot of time telling me about their experiences in renewing their company. Leila Mozafarri and Joan Carvell at the California Manufacturing Technology Center also provided me with vital information about the Ace Clearwater story.

Dr. Joseph Giusti was very gracious in providing me with information about engineering education programs at AMP, Inc., as well as sharing his long experience in the education field.

Dr. William Clover at the Amoco Management Learning Center provided me with useful information and innovative ideas that he has used in his outstanding programs.

Ed O'Brien and Bryan Lanahan told me the fascinating story of Corning's innovation process and the role of learning and training in establishing a new standard for product innovation and development throughout the Corning world.

Donna Hutter of Lab Safety Supply shared with me LSS's experience in doing process mapping and how the business was changed as a result.

Joe Slezak of Mercury Marine provided me with material about his outstanding Learning Center and shared many other ideas with me during my visit there.

Tim O'Brien of PHH University taught me a lot about learning and training in a multiunit business and the challenges of spreading learning among disparate business units.

Steve McIntosh, currently president of Tartan Consulting, hosted my visit to PPG Industries while he was still its Director of Training, Development, and Education. He and his staff provided me with excellent information about their approaches to building a "virtual training organization"—a term we each coined independently several years ago. Steve has been a great support over the past several years. Steve also generously gave me a copy of PPG's "Professional Development Sourcebook," one section of which is reproduced in Appendix B.

Steve Kirn from Sears was very generous with his time and in sharing his experiences with the "Phoenix Group," which has been driving the company's renewal process.

Lew Jamison and his staff at Sun Microsystems were very helpful in sharing the excellent approaches to building and sustaining action learning teams at Sun. Lew was kind enough to share with me SunU's list of Team Competencies, which appears in the book.

Ann Batal, Director of Human Resource Development at Biogen, was generous with her time and in discussing the challenges facing the biotechnology industry. She also shared with me Biogen's statement of values and the story contained in this book about how the company's leaders made the values real.

Britton Manasco, editor of *The Learning Enterprise*, a newsletter on corporate use of learning technologies, has been very helpful in exchanging ideas and views on the role of technology in creating learning organizations. He also reviewed and commented on my ideas about the concept of the "knowledge network."

David Hogg, Vice President of Quality Improvement at J.W. Mercer & Associates, and James Marchant, Vice President of Human Resources at Avenor, Inc., both graciously acted as in-process reviewers of this book and offered many useful insights and suggestions.

In addition to all of these people, I owe a great debt to my many consulting clients and the hundreds of people who have attended my presentations and workshops. These people not only have shared their own extensive experience with me but also have acted as sounding boards for many of the ideas contained in this book, forcing me to sharpen my concepts and to make my recommendations much more practical.

I am also grateful to my agent, Michael Snell, who helped me develop the ideas in this book and provided much support in making the transition from the original publisher, Omneo, to the new publisher who purchased Omneo. Jim Childs, publisher at Omneo, moved to a new position as Publisher of Business and Trade Publications at John Wiley & Sons and eventually brought this book with him. Thanks are also due to my new editor at John Wiley & Sons, Jim Bessent, who provided many excellent suggestions that make this book more solid and interesting.

Finally, my enduring thanks go to my wife, Susan, and my daughter, Molly, for their ongoing support.

CONTENTS

LIST OF TABLES AND FIGURES

TABLES

FIGURES

INTRODUCTION

London may have the best taxi service of any major world city. Not only are the taxis themselves scrupulously clean and free of dents, but the drivers know where they are going. Give a London driver an address, the name of a public building or monument, a hotel, or a major business establishment, and you get there without fuss or bother (although first-time American visitors are often confused by the cars driving on the "wrong" side of the road and the drivers sitting on the "wrong" side of the front seat).

To become a London cab driver involves more than buying a cab, installing a meter, and picking up fares—to qualify as a driver, a person must first acquire "the knowledge." As one writer describes it:

> The knowledge refers to knowing not only the streets of London, a skill equal in difficulty to learning Chinese as a second language, but also the fastest and cheapest way to go from a given point A to a selected point B.[1]

On my first trip to London in the mid-1980s, I happened to tune in to a movie on BBC television entitled "The Knowledge." It told the story of a group of people who yearned to earn a London taxi license. Their greatest challenge was to master "the knowledge."

The knowledge is contained in a published handbook containing several hundred routes through the London streets. By following and memorizing each of these routes, a driver candidate will traverse every street in the city of London, pass every public building and monument, see every hotel and business establishment, learn every one-way street and every exit off the motorways, and so on. It is an ingenious method of presenting the information that candidates must master to earn their taxi licenses.

Taxi driving in London is a *knowledge-based business.* And although the task of mastering the knowledge is a daunting one, once learned, the knowledge remains relatively stable. The streets of London are relatively immutable—the city may occasionally add a new street, may set up detours around construction sites, or may change a one-way street to bidirectional, but the basic layout of the city does not change much over time.

Would it be possible for every employee in every business to be given a book of knowledge that includes every destination, every task, every challenge the employee will ever face? I think not. In today's global business environment, products, technologies, markets, competitors, and customers change constantly. To respond to the ever-changing business environment, employees at all levels must acquire a set of knowledge and skills that will not only allow them to accomplish the work they face today but will also enable them to respond to changing business conditions to meet today's goals and to create new opportunities for their own and their companies' future success.

Just as the characters in the movie transformed their lives by mastering "the knowledge," so employees in every company can transform their own lives by acquiring the knowledge and skills they need to take command of their careers, to see how their own work is part of, and contributes to, the larger work of their companies. This is *transformational learning* that enables employees to renew their careers and their companies to renew their businesses.

LEARNING AND TRAINING

As demonstrated in the movie, people learn in many different ways. Some walk the routes; others ride them on mopeds or in cars, with the book and maps spread in front of them. Others study the book, trying to memorize the routes. Still others have people recite the routes to them repetitiously until they have committed them to memory. There isn't a formal training program to teach the knowledge. Each person learns in the way that is most natural and comfortable. The average driver candidate requires several attempts at the examination and *four years* to acquire the knowledge before earning a license.

The knowledge and skills required for company employees cannot be viewed solely as a "training problem." Training is one path, but many others also exist. Learning methods must be tailored to the individual employee, to the requirements of the job, to the goals of the company. Following the path to transformational learning does not automatically require that a company increase its training budget. Indeed, as learning is tailored more precisely to individual and company needs, a company may find that it does not need to invest as much in formal training activities as it has been doing.

PEOPLE: THE KEY TO COMPANY RENEWAL

As the American economy has staggered along over the past decade, many companies have sought to renew or transform themselves from old, slow, ungainly bureaucracies to newer, more agile organizations that can compete effectively in the global business environment. Many of these companies started by investing millions of dollars in new technologies and methodologies, betting that these investments would magically transform them. But technologies and methodologies cannot transform a company. They can enable change, that is, make it possible. They can facilitate change, that is, they can make it easier. But they cannot cause change—they cannot make change happen. People make change happen.

Today's successful companies have recognized that only by investing in their most important assets—their people—can a true company transformation become a reality. People, using their knowledge and skills, are the only effective change agents for any company.

Whether working from crisis and seeking a transformation or turnaround, or working from current success and seeking to renew the company to create a brighter future, leaders are finding that they must invest in learning, in helping employees at all levels acquire the knowledge and skills they need to fuel the transformation or renewal efforts. This is the basis for transformational learning.

In this book, I present a number of success stories, from companies large and small, that have undertaken their renewal initiatives by investing in transformational learning, and practical advice on how you can undertake your own journey to company renewal.

Unlike the streets of London, there is no stable body of knowledge that you can master to ensure ongoing success. But by mastering a set of skills and knowledge, by setting up a healthy learning environment, you can equip yourselves and your employees to meet each new challenge head-on and to keep everyone in the company headed in the right direction, pulling together to meet long-term and short-term goals.

OVERVIEW

In Chapter 1, "The Art of the Possible," we will examine how companies must define their renewal efforts, how they must recognize that the key to company renewal is through the skills and knowledge of employees at all levels. A model for knowledge and skill acquisition and a basic model for company renewal initiatives are presented.

The story of Ace Clearwater Enterprises (ACE) is discussed in Chapter 2. ACE is a prime example of a company that went from crisis to stability to bright prospects for the future by following the path of transformational learning for every employee, from the executive suite through the shop floor.

To accomplish a company's renewal goals, all employees must understand those goals and must align their individual and collective work with those goals. Chapter 3, "Define, Then Align," presents some ideas around the planning process and discusses common barriers to effective planning efforts.

In Chapter 4, "Forming the Partnership with Top Management," the stories of Sears, Amoco, and Corning's efforts to set new directions and to ensure that all parts of the company were aligned with those directions, are presented. This chapter also includes valuable lessons from these companies' efforts.

Chapter 5, "Starting at the Top: Getting Everyone Moving in the Same Direction," offers practical advice for company managers seeking to start their own renewal programs. This chapter also contains practical advice for business unit and departmental managers who want to start their own renewal efforts even when they have no clear direction from top company leadership.

Before starting any journey, you must define the point from which you are starting. Chapter 6, "Finding Your Starting Point," presents a set of "five foundations" that together form a strong basis for any renewal effort. This chapter contains methods of assessing the presence and strength of your organization's foundations and advice on methods of building or fortifying your foundations.

Once you have defined the knowledge and skills needed for your renewal effort, you must determine how to acquire them. Chapter 7 focuses on three key knowledge acquisition strategies: buying, renting, and developing.

Acquiring knowledge and skills are not one-time activities. The next three chapters focus on three key programs designed to maintain the momentum of the company's renewal program. Chapter 8 focuses on "Learning from the Best" or how to use internal and external benchmarking as a learning method. Chapter 9, "Building a Knowledge Network," provides methods for ensuring that the company can take advantage of the vast reservoir of knowledge and skill resources available both within and without the company to continually renew itself. Chapter 10, "Action-Oriented Teamwork," demonstrates how effective teamwork always has a "bias for action."

In most companies, learning activities have traditionally been the province of formal training and development or human resource development groups. Chapter 11, "Bridging Two Worlds," defines the role that these organizations must play in enabling and facilitating company renewal efforts and discusses why traditional training models are not able to meet these requirements.

Finally, in Chapter 12, we examine how companies and individuals "value learning," that is, how to measure the impact of learning on the attainment of individual and company goals.

PLANNING YOUR OWN JOURNEY TO COMPANY RENEWAL

As you will see throughout this book, there is no one path to company renewal that will work for all companies. Each company must select its own destination. Each company must determine its own starting point. And each must examine the many paths available to get from here to there.

But for all companies, for all destinations, no matter where the starting point may be, the journey is possible, the destination attainable only through the optimal utilization of the company's most important assets—the knowledge and skills of all company employees. Transformational learning provides the means for undertaking your renewal journey. It is my hope that this book facilitates your planning and makes the road you choose easier to travel.

ONE

THE ART OF THE POSSIBLE

Many companies have experienced various degrees of crisis during the past decade. New stories about layoffs, downsizings, rightsizings, and plant closings costing hundreds of thousands of jobs appear almost daily. Increased global competition, ineffective management, unproductive investments, strategies gone awry—all are cited by spokespeople for the downturn in the companies' fortunes.

Many of the programs that promised to redeem American industry (TQM, Business Reengineering, the Learning Organization, etc.) have more often than not failed to deliver the expected results in performance. As reported in a *Business Week* feature on "Quality: How to Make It Pay":

> Countless . . . managers have heeded the siren song of total quality management, or TQM, only to discover that quality doesn't necessarily pay. At Johnson & Johnson, quality teams for several product lines criss-crossed the country, benchmarking against other companies, but costs skyrocketed. In 1990, Wallace Co. won the Malcolm Baldrige National Quality Award. Two years later, the oil equipment company filed for Chapter 11 as the cost of the quality programs soared and oil prices collapsed.[1]

In fact, according to industry studies in the United States, Canada, and Great Britain, few companies that have undertaken TQM initiatives have realized any substantial business results.

> In a 1991 *Electronic Business* survey, only 13 per cent of CEOs surveyed said that their quality efforts paid off in higher operating income or higher profits. A study of British industry by *TQM Magazine* and A. T. Kearney concluded that 80 per cent of Total Quality Management (TQM) initiatives ultimately fail.
>
> A similar A. T. Kearney study of Canadian TQM efforts concluded that while 80 per cent of companies had total quality processes in place or were planning their implementation, only one-third of those companies with processes in place had tangible results such as improved market share, lower production costs, documented improvement in customer satisfaction or higher profitability to show for their efforts.[2]

Preliminary surveys of companies' business reengineering efforts have shown similarly dismal results. At the same time, many companies are succeeding, and others are rising from the ashes to renew themselves and find new prosperity. These organizations have discovered that the key to future success is in their people and the knowledge they use to help to achieve their goals. Successful companies cannot invest solely in plant and equipment, in new technologies and methodologies. They must invest in their most important assets—their people.

Knowledge is no longer the sole province of management; all employees, at all levels, must be charged with the responsibility for their own learning and for applying that learning to their jobs. Employers must take responsibility for creating a suitable learning environment, an environment that encourages and provides opportunities for learning and its application, for all employees at all levels.

LOOKING IN THE RIGHT PLACES

A midsized (450 employees, $60 million in sales) manufacturer in the Northeast had a problem. Eighty percent of the company's business came from a single product made for a single customer. At the start of the second year of its three-year contract, the company turned out 150 units per month.

One day the customer called: "Could the company increase production to 200 or more units per month?" The vice president of operations said that he would check out the plant's capacity and get back to the customer with an answer within a week. Analyzing his operations, he found a single bottleneck that would prevent the increased production level—a high-tech milling cell where operators took a piece of metal about 24″ by 12″ by 9″ and, putting it through a number of processes, created the frame onto which all other product components were attached. This cell appeared to be working at capacity—150 units per month.

Loath to go to his CEO with a $600,000 capital request to replicate this cell, the vice president called a summit meeting. On Thursday afternoon he assembled a team consisting of his own two industrial engineers, two engineers from the manufacturers of the milling machines, and a consultant from the customer. He sent the operators off to another part of the plant while the team spent the afternoon searching for a way to increase the capacity of the cell. At the end of the afternoon, the team reported back: "We might be able to get 165 or 170 units per month out of this cell, but 200 is out of the question."

The vice president decided to sleep on the problem over the weekend before going to the CEO with the capital request. On Friday morning, as he was walking through the plant, he was stopped by the lead operator from the cell. "What was all the hubbub yesterday? Who were all the big shots?"

The vice president explained the situation. The operator stood in deep thought for a minute and then spoke again. "I think we might be able to get 200 units a month out of this cell . . . with some changes."

"Oh, really!?!" replied the vice president, half wanting to believe and half not believing.

"You know," said the operator, "last week I was down at the sporting goods store at the mall. They'd just gotten in some gorgeous new baseball jackets. Do you think, if we got capacity up to 200 units a month, you might spring for new jackets for all of the operators in the cell? Maybe with the company logo and name embroidered on the back?"

"I could handle that," replied the vice president.

Early Saturday morning the six operators descended on the cell. Four of them spent the weekend tearing down the entire cell, fine-tuning each piece of equipment, and completely reconfiguring the cell layout. The other two hunched over their terminals, rewriting the numerical control programs for each piece of equipment.

On Monday morning the cell was up and running. And in the next 30 days, the cell turned out 230 units!

The vice president tried to solve the problem with knowledge rather than capital investment, but he looked in the wrong place. When you need to solve a problem, the first and most likely source for the solution lies with the people who have been doing the job, who have been facing the problem head-on. We have passed the point where knowledge can be the sole possession of management, where workers at any level can be expected to just follow orders and not think for themselves.

KNOWLEDGE: THE KEY TO RENEWAL

The knowledge of individual employees and the collective knowledge of the organization is the only real competitive advantage that any company can hope to develop. In the past, specialized equipment, information technology, and other "tangible" assets were thought to be primary sources of competitive advantage. But in today's global economy, these assets can be replicated quickly and relatively easily almost anywhere on the globe. What cannot be easily or quickly reproduced are a company's knowledge assets—the knowledge held and used by its employees, its suppliers, and its customers. These knowledge assets are the key to current and future success and must be nurtured for both managerial and technical employees.

> The new power [of knowledge workers] . . . is not only liberating employees from the monotony of the industrial age, but it is also providing companies with the know-how to alter their destiny—to make competitive leaps, to break into new markets, and to offer their employees wider ho-

> rizons and far more opportunity than any generation of workers has encountered before.[3]

To use knowledge as a key to renewal, companies and their employees must first determine what they need to know in order to succeed, and then set a course for learning. They must move from ignorance or partial competence to full competence, from unconscious to conscious knowledge.

THE PURSUIT OF KNOWLEDGE

The pursuit of knowledge takes many forms and happens in many ways. In the second quadrant of Figure 1.1, people "don't know what they don't know."

Many companies, which have been doing "business as usual" for many years, don't know what they don't know. American automobile makers operated in this quadrant for decades, listening only to themselves and not to their customers. The knowledge they needed was available—Japanese car makers had it—but their own arrogance prevented the American companies from learning from their customers.

Figure 1.1
The Pursuit of Knowledge

	Ignorance	**Competence**
Unconscious	UNCONSCIOUS IGNORANCE "I don't know what I don't know." Quadrant II	UNCONSCIOUS COMPETENCE "I don't know what I already know." Quadrant III
Conscious	CONSCIOUS IGNORANCE "I know what I don't know." Quadrant I	CONSCIOUS COMPETENCE "I know what I know." Quadrant IV

In this same category falls blind adherence to TQM or other "hot" methodologies—following the latest management fashion without really asking whether it is what the company needs, whether it will really solve the company's basic problems, whether there is a real return on the program investment.

The study of markets and the understanding of customers' needs and desires enables companies to set goals to meet the demands of the marketplace. This principle applies equally to a small manufacturer, such as Ace Clearwater Enterprises, and to large companies such as Sears, PPG Industries, and others that we will discuss in later chapters.

At the same time, most companies have within their employee base a huge, untapped reservoir of knowledge. This reservoir may contain "unconscious competence" (Quadrant III in Figure 1.1), where employees have already solved problems or found better ways of doing things that they don't share with others. This lack of sharing may sometimes be caused by selfishness, that is, if I do my job better than others do theirs, I'll get a better raise the next time around. More often it results from not recognizing that they have something unique that could add value to the work of others.

Also swimming around in this reservoir is a lot of "conscious competence" (Quadrant IV) that isn't shared because no one ever thinks of asking. This was the case in the story told earlier, where operators knew how to increase production, but management didn't think to ask them.

The goal of all this learning is to increase the individual's and the company's stock of "conscious competence" (Quadrant IV) and to create an environment where this stock is not only increased but also shared regularly and openly. Knowledge is a unique commodity—you can give it away without reducing your own supply.

KEYS TO COMPANY RENEWAL THROUGH PEOPLE AND KNOWLEDGE

The keys to pursuing knowledge as a renewal strategy include setting goals, aligning the entire organization behind those goals, assessing your starting point, and actually starting the journey (see Figure 1.2).

Figure 1.2
Keys to Company Renewal

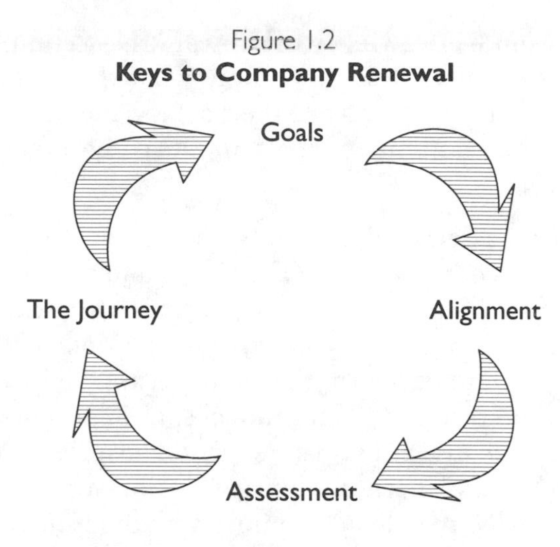

Determining Company Goals

The pursuit of company renewal starts with determining a set of goals for the entire organization. Before setting its goals, a company must overcome its "unconscious ignorance," that is, discover what it needs to learn to achieve the desired business results. This may involve developing a better understanding of the company's current and potential customers, of competitors, and of the full scope of its value chain, including suppliers, distributors, and so on. It also relates to future technologies and methodologies that may affect the company's operations and markets.

Goal setting is an ongoing activity. Customers, competitors, markets, technologies, methodologies, and many other variables constantly change. If the future holds one constant, it is that the rate of change in these and other factors will continue tc increase.

Aligning Your Value Chain with the Company's Goals

Once goals are set, they must be shared through all levels, divisions, and functions of the company, across the company's entire internal and external value chains, that is, all internal functions, all suppliers, distributors, and customers involved in the planning, production, distribution, and use of the company's products or services. People cannot effectively work toward the accomplishment of the company's goals unless they know what those goals are and how they can contribute toward their achievement. The company must also be honest about its goals and its commitment to them.

A CPA firm assembled a team to reengineer its process of preparing client tax returns. The long-standing process had each return assigned to a novice preparer for initial review and input, taking some five staff hours. Some 70 percent of returns had to be held at this point because of incomplete information received from the client. Supervisors then spent another five hours per return for inspection and revision, a process that was done twice on average for each return. Finally, the client administrator did a final inspection and approval. The reengineering team found that over 65 percent of returns had to be revised at least once, and over 50 percent needed a second revision.

The team's sole recommendation was to eliminate making triplicate copies of each return until after final approval. This saved the firm approximately $15,000 per year. What the team didn't calculate was the approximately $500,000 per year that could have been saved if the returns were completed correctly the first time, eliminating much of the review and revision work. "This would require reexamining the use of charge time as a performance measure, something the culture of this CPA firm couldn't allow."[4]

True progress begins with identifying and examining the organization's "sacred cows." It may be that there are real, legitimate reasons for their status, or it may be that they are true impediments to progress toward stated goals, in which case they should be sacrificed.

Once goals are set, the company must also examine all aspects of its internal and external value chains to ensure that employees, suppliers, distributors, and customers all understand the company's goals and are marching in step. Progress toward those goals is made much more quickly and efficiently if everyone knows where they are heading and is pulling in the same direction.

Assessing Your Starting Point

Once you have identified your company's goals and directions, but before setting out on your journey, you need to locate your starting point. No matter where your starting point, you can get to your destination from it. Begin by assessing exactly where you are in relation to your goals.

Making the Journey

Once through the first three stages, you have already done a lot of work; you are now ready to start your journey. Most road maps offer many alternate routes to get from any one place to another. In this stage you must examine alternate paths, choose the one that best fits your situation, and prepare to overcome the inevitable detours and roadblocks and, perhaps, disarm a few land mines along the way.

Midcourse Corrections

The major difference between this type of journey and your typical vacation trip is that the journey for company renewal never ends. Even as today's goals may come into sight, the constant reexamination of markets, technologies, and so on will require that you change your destination en route. Learning is a continuous process, and the renewal of your company through this process can never end. For this reason, evaluation is not included as a separate step in the process but must be an ongoing exercise within each stage and across all stages of the process (see Figure 1.3).

THE ACQUISITION OF KNOWLEDGE

The acquisition of knowledge is a multistep process (see Figure 1.4). This model starts with data and ends with wisdom, that highest end product of learning.

Whether generated within or without the organization, most companies are swamped with data—many are literally drowning

Figure 1.3
Midcourse Corrections

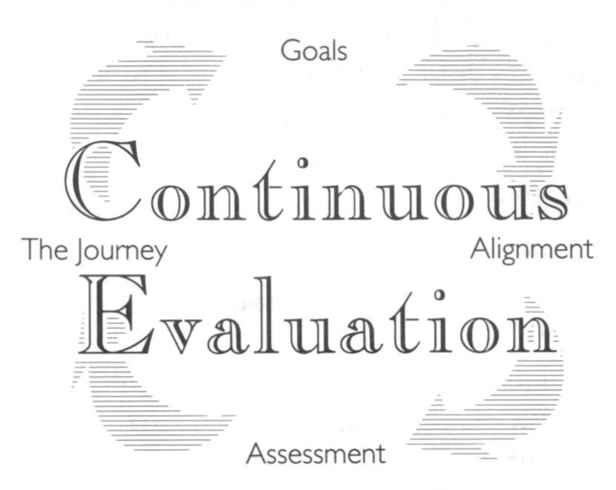

in it. The first stage in the learning model is to sift through these data and utilize only those data that are *relevant* to your organization, its work, and its goals.

Management guru Peter Drucker defines *information* as "data endowed with relevance and purpose."[5] In Stage I of this model, we are seeking relevance—information that can add value to the organization and to people's work within the organization.

Information may be relevant to the organization and its work, but it cannot add value unless it is *applied* to that work. People may have volumes of information, but until they apply it to their jobs, they cannot claim that they have any new knowledge. For example, statistical process control (SPC) programs may generate a lot of data about a manufacturing process, but having statistics and graphs piling up on someone's desk adds no value unless they are used to improve that process. Only when a person has applied information to his or her job and used it to add value to his or her work can that person say that *knowledge* has been acquired:

Information + Application = Knowledge

This stage can be thought of as the development of "conscious competence."

The final stage of the learning model, the development of wisdom, adds experience and intuition to the knowledge base. It represents the movement from unconscious competence, which has

Figure 1.4
The Four Stages of Learning

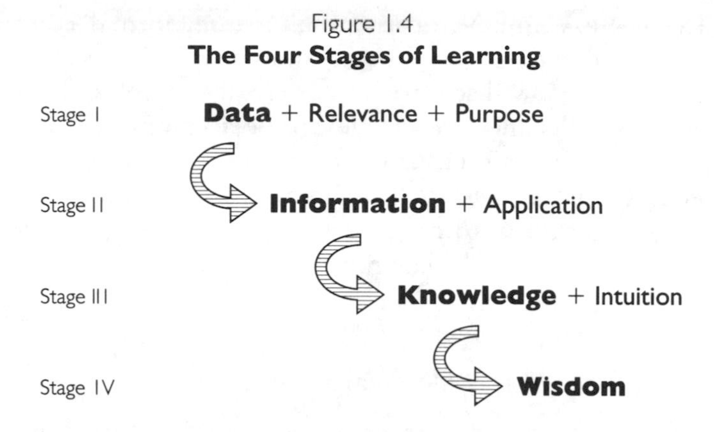

developed with experience, to conscious competence. That is, as people do their jobs over time, they develop experience and "gut feelings" about what will or won't work in a given situation. These "feelings" can be classified as unconscious competence from the Ignorance/Competence Model (see Figure 1.1). When this type of knowledge is captured by the individual and made part of his or her knowledge base, it becomes conscious competence and can be classified as wisdom.

TRANSFORMATIONAL LEARNING

If knowledge is the key to company renewal, then *transformational learning* is the means to that end. Transformational learning is *the identification, acquisition, and application of information that enables an organization, and the people within that organization, to reach their goals.* To undertake transformational learning, you must:

- Discover what you need to know, that is, uncover your areas of unconscious ignorance.
- Locate the information you need.
- Apply that information to your work.

The key to transformational learning is that all learning activities are strongly focused on specific organizational renewal goals.

Learning takes many forms, ranging from formal education and training activities to mentoring and coaching to reading and observation. As we will see from a variety of examples, the acquisition of new skills and knowledge can be accomplished in many ways, from formal training programs to the hiring of consultants to attending conferences to hiring new people who bring new knowledge and skills into the company. For learning activities to enable corporate renewal, they must:

- Be aligned with company goals.
- Be relevant to people's real and perceived work.
- Be applied to address today's problems and tomorrow's opportunities.
- Add value to people's work.

Aligning Learning Activities with Company Goals

Unfortunately, in most companies the training and development (T&D) or human resources development (HRD) functions, the very groups that should be leading the charge toward establishing and facilitating transformational learning, are themselves misaligned with their companies' strategic business directions. Most of these groups sit off in a corner of the human resources department, offering individual skills courses from a catalog. These courses have some value to individual employees and, indirectly, to the company, but they have no real impact on the company's renewal efforts unless they are aligned with company goals and tailored to directly contribute to the attainment of those goals. In the companies we will examine in this book, T&D/HRD are closely aligned with top company management:

> At the highest level, training is perceived as a direct, bottom-line business intervention. In the same way that product changes, platform reconfiguration, staffing changes, and new pricing strategies are seen as business interventions, impacting the competence levels of employees is also a business intervention.[6]

Throughout this book, we will see how forward-thinking T&D and HRD professionals are ensuring that their major efforts are designed to facilitate their company's renewal and growth.

Relevance to Real and Perceived Work

Only when employees see the relevance of their learning activities to the work they are doing and immediately start applying the lessons they have learned can real progress be made. Too often people return from a conference or training program full of good ideas but don't see how what they have learned applies to what they are doing. As we will discuss in later chapters, many employees spend their work lives doing their jobs but never really understanding how what they do relates to their companies' business.

Application to Today's Problems and Tomorrow's Opportunities

Employees too often are given new skills and knowledge but never are allowed to apply their learning to their jobs. In the case of the CPA firm mentioned earlier, the reengineering team had the tools to make a real difference in how the company processed its clients' tax returns, but the sacred cow of billable hours barred the team from attacking the real problem. Unless employees are allowed to apply their new skills and knowledge to their work and their planning, there is little point to even starting the learning activity.

Adding Value

Before undertaking any learning activity, or any renewal effort, companies must ensure that their investments will yield a return, that the activities actually add value to what the company is doing. Many times companies hop on the bandwagon of TQM or other hot transformation initiatives only to make the sad discovery that there are few returns on their investments.

Varian Associates, a scientific equipment maker, put 1,000 of its managers through four days of quality training and made other major quality investments, only to find profits dwindling while quality soared. "All of the quality-based charts went up and to the right, but everything else went down," says Richard M. Levy, executive vice president for quality.[7]

If any of these four key elements are missing from a learning activity, it cannot be classified as transformational learning. This is not to say that pursuing learning as an end in itself has no benefits, but only that companies should ensure that these elements are present if the learning activities they undertake are to have a direct effect on company renewal.

THE ART OF THE POSSIBLE

Industry trends, business conditions, pools of talent, available capital—so many factors play on a company's fortunes that no single solution or methodology will work for all companies in all situations. This book focuses on helping you find ways of identifying the knowledge resources that can help you move from where you are today to a better tomorrow. Not every idea presented here will apply to, or work for, every reader. But you should come away from this book with a variety of ideas and methods that will work for you. The focus is not on some "ivory tower" ideal, but on *the art of the possible.*

Toward this end, we will examine how virtually all of a company's business processes are really learning activities and how, by applying the principles of transformational learning, a company can energize its renewal or transformation programs to achieve its business goals. Companies must build strong foundations around organizational design and management practice to accomplish this. With these foundations in place, three key programs ("Learning from the Best," "Action-Oriented Teamwork," and a "Knowledge Network") will help change the company's, and its employees', learning experiences into true transformational learning and enable the company and its employees to reach new levels of achievement.

We'll start with the story of Ace Clearwater Enterprises, a company that used transformational learning as the means for company renewal.

TWO

FROM TWO STRIKES TO A HOME RUN: THE RENEWAL OF ACE CLEARWATER ENTERPRISES

Ace Clearwater Enterprises is a small sheet metal assembly company in Southern California. In 1991 it was on the brink of failure but renewed itself through transformational learning. At that time ACE had won the largest contract in the company's history; however, it was soon swamped by crises, with the customer threatening to cancel the contract that represented more than half of the company's revenue. Rather than admit defeat, the company president undertook a program of learning that saved the Boeing contract and laid the groundwork for a very bright future for the company and its employees.

FLASHBACK: FROM START-UP TO GROWTH TO COMPLACENCY

Ace Clearwater Enterprises began as a welding shop in 1961. Its first major job was welding bicycle frames, and it did its job very well. More and more jobs followed as the shop's reputation for quality work spread. Quality, at that time, was the personal mission of the owner and founder: "What's that scratch? The customer didn't pay us for that scratch, so I don't want to give it to him."

Over the years the company grew in orders, revenues, customers, capability, and reputation. Several large aerospace contractors located near the company's Torrance, California, location started ordering parts that they lacked either the capability or the capacity to make in-house. These started out as small, relatively simple part orders and, as ACE proved itself, grew into more complex, more expensive orders for such items as pilot seats, infrared suspension systems, and gas turbine ducting. By 1990 the company owner and president, Tim Dodson (the founder's son-in-law), could boast of an impressive list of aerospace customers and 170 employees in three plant locations.

In that same year the Boeing Commercial Airplane Group was working hard to find the outside suppliers it needed to keep its production lines going. Although the commercial airplane industry had fallen on some hard times, Boeing was still turning out fifty planes per month, requiring tens of thousands of parts from thousands of suppliers. Dodson's sales staff at Ace Clearwater saw this as an excellent opportunity to snag an impressive new customer and almost double the company's revenue.

By the end of 1991, Ace Clearwater negotiated $5 million in contracts with Boeing to produce more than 170 different part numbers. To satisfy Boeing's requirement that ACE focus high-level attention on the contract, Tim Dodson asked his daughter, Kellie, to take over the day-to-day management of the Boeing account.

THE WAKE-UP CALL

Kellie Dodson's grandfather and then her father had both tried to convince her to come into Ace Clearwater, but she had other ideas. First, she wanted to enter the foreign service and earned her bachelor's degree in international relations. Later she became interested in working with drug rehabilitation and earned a degree in social work. Not long after that she started her own video production business. After a few years, her father convinced her that her place was in the family business.

With no background in manufacturing, Kellie set about learning the business. Being a woman and the boss's daughter in a male-dominated industry wasn't easy. She remembers being sent to a four-day statistical process control (SPC) seminar at Allied Signal Aerospace, a large customer who insisted that Ace Clearwater attend. "I was lost. This wasn't the way we did things. And the alphabet soup of methods meant little to me. When I got back to Ace Clearwater, the management team all smiled at me. I knew then that I had been set up."

When the Boeing contracts were signed, Kellie was made the account manager—what better commitment could Boeing seek than having the daughter of the company owner as its account manager? The first program review at Boeing in Seattle was brutal. "I brought along a few organization charts and a few production reports," Kellie said. "It wasn't what they wanted or expected."

> "You don't even know how to make a proper overhead," complained Boeing, which was used to having presentation slides oriented horizontally, rather than vertically. "I didn't even know what 'landscape' meant," Kellie confessed.

This was only the beginning of Kellie Dodson's education.

> "When I walked into that first program review, I had no idea of the severity of our problem. It amazed me that Ace Clearwater could be holding up [our customer's] production line. Some of the detail parts we were making seemed so trivial, but those planes are designed with a lot of small, detail parts—everything matters. Just like every person in our organization matters, we are all small parts of a greater whole. When you see the parts installed on the aircraft, or watch a shear operator complete a detail for an assembly, you realize that it all matters."

According to its contract with Boeing, if Ace Clearwater's lack of performance held up the Boeing production line, they could be charged the actual cost of the production stoppage, amounting to thousands of dollars per hour. This was a harsh new reality in an industry whose standard operating procedure was to book orders and worry about delivering them later. Virtually every plane Boeing was building relied on at least one of the 170 different parts being manufactured by Ace Clearwater Enterprises. And Kellie and her company needed to face other harsh realities:

- Ace Clearwater was late on more than a third of its shipments to Boeing.
- Boeing was rejecting nearly one-fifth of the parts produced by Ace Clearwater. The Boeing target for rejects was a *maximum* of 1.9 percent.
- Ace Clearwater was losing substantial amounts of money on the Boeing contract.

BOEING AND THE BIRTH OF SUPPLIER CERTIFICATION

The Boeing Commercial Airplane Group started changing the way it did business with its suppliers back in the mid-1980s. Gone were the one-year, low-price contracts where Boeing squeezed every cent of the supplier's profit and then changed suppliers the next year based solely on price. Boeing required suppliers to seek its D1-9000 certification, adhering to the standards of Boeing's Advanced Quality System (AQS). To accomplish this, Boeing produced training programs and licensed them to community colleges throughout the United States. But the change in supplier processes and relations caused a lot of strain and pain throughout Boeing's huge supplier base (several years ago, a Boeing vice president said that the new Boeing 777 would involve a base of nearly 15,000 suppliers around the world). As reported in *Air Transport World*:

> Boeing is taking a meat cleaver to its supplier base and companies that cannot or will not make the commitment to quality are the first ones to go. Boeing has cut profit margins to the bone and it expects suppliers to make up the difference through process improvements. Far more than in the past, suppliers are being asked to accept an element of risk in Boeing programs. They have become more dependent on Boeing. Relations are better but the stakes are far higher. Fail today and you won't be asked back tomorrow.[1]

What this meant to suppliers like Ace Clearwater Enterprises was that the short- and long-term stakes were huge—perhaps not by Boeing standards, but the $5 million in Boeing contracts represented half of Ace Clearwater's revenues. At the same time, Kellie Dodson could see the number of empty buildings and folding businesses in the industrial area surrounding Ace Clearwater, an area that grew with Southern California's aerospace and defense-related industries—and went bust with it also.

In the last several years, Boeing's Southern California supplier base had shrunk from nearly 800 suppliers to 500, and Boeing made it clear that it would shrink further, to a base of 300 key suppliers, over the next several years. Some of the reductions were a function of Boeing's shrinking business, but most resulted from Boeing's goal of building stronger relationships with a smaller number of suppliers.

At the end of its first program review, Boeing was convinced that Ace Clearwater was not going to be one of that smaller group. Several Boeing employees pulled Kellie into a separate room and told her: "This isn't going to work. It's not going to happen." She made up her mind right then that it would work, that she would make it work.

LEADERSHIP FOR A NEW BEGINNING

Kellie Dodson returned from the Boeing program review and reported the bad news to her father. Tim Dodson had grown up doing business the old way, and he knew that it would not be easy for him to change. He recognized that the person to change Ace Clearwater Enterprises was Kellie, not him. Tim went into semiretirement and appointed Kellie as company president. Kellie agreed: "If I was going to be going up to these program reviews and making commitments on behalf of the company, I needed to put a team together to support me. To do that, I needed the authority."[2]

Kellie's first task was to discover what she and the company had to learn—what they didn't know. A lot of advice was available—Boeing had more than a half dozen personnel working in the Ace Clearwater plants on a full-time basis, expediting the Boeing orders, checking the quality of the parts being produced, and generally looking out for Boeing's interests.

Kellie reviewed her resources, mostly old-timers who had grown the business with her father, and found that she needed to assemble a new team if she were to have a chance of succeeding. One of her first new hires was a director of manufacturing. Dick Forsythe was an experienced manufacturing manager who had worked in many larger companies. With half a dozen years left before retirement, he was looking for one last challenge.

"He started educating me the minute he arrived," Kellie said. "His first request was to see the backlog report. My response was: 'What's a backlog report?' Dick was someone I could learn from—there were lots of people in the company who could teach me the craft, but I needed someone to teach me the business. Dick was that person."

Over the next year, Kellie also hired a human resources manager, a materials and logistics manager, a plant manager for the company's Paramount, California, operations, a comptroller, and a director of manufacturing engineering. Tim Dodson resisted these hires. It was understandable that he, having built the business without a large staff, would question the need for all these people. As Kellie Dodson would later comment:

> Often in the past, the successful organization revolved around a single person with an *intuitive* sense of what had to be done, and who could do it. This person was clearly the thought leader and the engine that drove *everything*. As the company grew beyond the scope of a single individual, things just stopped working.[3]

It is much to his own credit that Tim Dodson realized the limitations of his own view and was willing to entrust his company to his daughter's vision and leadership.

LEARNING WHAT SHE DIDN'T KNOW

Kellie Dodson realized early on that she had a lot to learn. But without a real manufacturing background, she couldn't even list the subjects she needed to learn. One giant step was her insight that she herself would never be able to learn everything. Her program of hiring key individuals into new and important functions was one method of increasing the total knowledge base within the company. She was also receiving a lot of advice from Boeing and from the Boeing employees who were working full-time in her company. She also realized that while the Boeing employees were trying to be genuinely helpful to Ace Clearwater, their first priority was the delivery of parts to fill Boeing's current production needs, not the long-term viability, growth, and profit of Ace Clearwater Enterprises.

The Boeing schedule and contract, of course, had to be Kellie's top priority.

> "The first thing was getting on schedule and supporting our customer," Kellie said. "The way that we were doing things, all manually, putting people onto tasks for which they hadn't been trained, just didn't work—people had no idea what their responsibilities were. If we were going to give them this huge task, to get us back on schedule, they needed to have the proper tools. What kind of tools had we provided? Not much except tribal knowledge, and a lot of the old tribe wasn't around any more. We had brought in all these new people. Plus, there were a lot of new part numbers, parts we had never built before, so we couldn't rely on tribal knowledge. We went from about 170 employees to about 240 employees just by throwing people at the problem, people who weren't well-disciplined, weren't well-trained, who didn't know what was expected of them or how to go about doing it. We were in a panic situation. We just did a bad job."

Once the immediate crisis was over and Boeing deliveries were back on schedule, other problems arose. First, the "throw-people-at-the-problem" approach was consuming a lot of resources and making the Boeing work unprofitable. Second, Boeing was insisting that Ace Clearwater begin instituting statistical process control and total quality management and that the company work toward receiving Boeing's D1-9000 quality certification.

These were all new concepts to Kellie and to Ace Clearwater, and Kellie knew that it would not be enough for just her to learn about them. Everyone in the company needed to learn new ways of working, new ways of thinking, new ways of managing and leading. Some of the new hires that Kellie was bringing into the company already had some of this knowledge, but everyone, all 200+ employees, needed it.

EXTERNAL EXPERTISE, ADVICE, AND TRAINING

Kellie Dodson knew she was on the right track when she started bringing additional knowledge resources into the company through key external hires. But she also knew that this step would not be sufficient to get ACE positioned for the future. New knowledge could not be the sole possession of a few key individuals; everyone in the company, from herself to the shop floor, had a lot to learn.

She approached the Center for Applied Competitive Technologies (CACT), located at nearby El Camino College, for assistance. One of eight such centers associated with community colleges throughout California, the CACT at El Camino had responsibility for helping manufacturing companies with fewer than 500 employees throughout the state to use technology to become more competitive. The CACTs were also the delivery arm for courses sponsored by the California Supplier Improvement Program (CALSIP).

CALSIP is a consortium of 10 major aerospace companies, including Boeing, working with the California Department of Commerce, the California community colleges, and the California Employment Training Panel, designed to provide "Training in total quality management, designed by the aerospace industry, especially for small supplier companies." The state of California subsidizes these training programs for suppliers to the aerospace industry. The CALSIP curriculum includes training on:

- Total quality management (TQM).
- Statistical process control (SPC).
- Cycle time reduction and just-in-time manufacturing (JIT).
- Teamwork, leadership, and communication (TLC).

So Ace Clearwater's source of assistance was originally the CACT and, through it, CALSIP. Later, when the California Manufacturing Technology Center (CMTC) was formed with funding from the National Institute for Standards and Technology (NIST) and state agencies, some of those programs were included under its umbrella. Kellie Dodson also became a member of the board of directors of the CMTC.

These associations brought two key programs to Ace Clearwater Enterprises: training for all personnel and a "manufacturing assessment."

Cramming to Survive

During a one-year period, the community college, through its various programs and affiliations, provided 154 hours of training to more than 100 Ace Clearwater employees. Training included statistical process control, total quality management, just-in-time manufacturing, and other related topics. The 10 top managers in the company received more than 100 hours of training on these topics as well as on management and leadership.

The sponsoring prime contractors of the California Supplier Improvement Program originally nominated suppliers they wanted to be included in the CALSIP training. Ace Clearwater Enterprises was *not* on Boeing's nomination list, a reflection of Boeing's dissatisfaction with Ace Clearwater and its feeling that ACE couldn't be saved. When Kellie Dodson discovered this, she successfully pushed Boeing, CALSIP, and the CACT to include her company in the program.

Even considering that most of the cost of this training was subsidized by the state of California and federal programs, this was a massive investment for a company the size of Ace Clearwater. Many major corporations, with outstanding reputations for employee training, have a goal of providing employees with 40 hours of training per year. Ace Clearwater was clearly making a major investment in its people and their knowledge. As Kellie Dodson told me: "[Our employees] are the ones who make it happen. They need to be given the tools."

It is also unusual to find a company under such immense pressure to deliver product on time that takes the time to do this massive amount of training. "At the time we went through the training," Kellie told me, "everyone was saying 'How are we going to keep up with production and still have training at the same time?' But really, morale went up. Production was high. People realized that we were investing in them so that they could have a future here at the company. We were increasing their value to the organization."

This training was not just a one-time investment for Ace Clearwater, but an ongoing one. Today more advanced training on these techniques is being implemented, and plans are in the works for English as a Second Language and other basic skills training to help improve the skill levels of Ace Clearwater's multiethnic, multilevel workforce.

Another important step for Ace Clearwater was to hire a Director of Change. This individual, King Lum, known as "DOC," had responsibility for working with individuals and teams throughout the company as they started to implement what they had learned in the more formal classes. This type of reinforcement and coaching of new skills taught in the classroom is often overlooked, resulting in the quick demise of new approaches once employees return from the classroom to the job. Kellie Dodson views this as a key position in the growing company: "He's the mentor of each team, giving them opportunities to vent, providing training and coaching. King is amazing. We've had two companies try to steal him from us, and he's only been here for three months!"

The Manufacturing Assessment

Although Ace Clearwater had approached the community college solely for training, CACT personnel working with the company sold Kellie on the idea of conducting a "manufacturing assessment." The CMTC describes the benefits of this program as follows:[4]

> A manufacturing assessment provides vital information for your company's leadership. Your managers will obtain a better understanding of the company, how it is functioning, and what issues are affecting its productivity and competitiveness. The assessment will provide your company with

a yardstick for comparing itself to industry peers. In addition, your management will learn about growth opportunities both for the company itself and within its competitive market. Finally, assessments and issue specific query activities highlight specific areas for improvement resulting in:

- WIP reduction
- Cost reduction
- Product quality
- Decision making
- Scrap and rework minimization
- Technology upgrades/implementation
- Throughput maximization
- Design for manufacture
- Productivity
- Competitiveness

Kellie Dodson describes the process in this way:

> When the CMTC did our manufacturing assessment, they came in and spent about a week interviewing our management, our operators on the floor. Then they came up with an interim debrief to validate what their findings were. Then they did a final debrief and that put together for us a whole business scenario—this is Ace Clearwater, this is where you are and where you are going, these are your strengths and these are your weaknesses. These are some quick-hit projects we recommend that you can do with minimal resources, and here are some longer-term projects that require more resources.

This type of impartial assessment is important to companies like Ace Clearwater. While it is vital that small suppliers listen to their customers, the customer does not always have the best interests of the supplier in mind. In discussing all of the changes being mandated for Ace Clearwater by Boeing, Vice President Gary Johnson said:

> At that time, Boeing was experimenting on how to "flow down" these requirements to suppliers. ACE as a company was a guinea pig. They had these D1-9000 requirements, but they didn't have it going on in their own shop. And they needed to see how far they could push suppliers, how much change could be effected on these suppliers.

Similarly, when small companies bring in vendors to assess how they can improve operations, the recommendations are often biased in favor of the solutions sold by those particular vendors. This is one of the reasons that the CMTC manufacturing assessment program is so valuable to the small manufacturing concern: The advice is keyed to the needs of the company, not to any vendor-specific or customer-specific solution.

CMTC executive director Joan Carvell said that an important function of the CMTC is also to help small suppliers like Ace Clearwater do benchmarking, not against industry giants whose resources they cannot hope to duplicate, but against other similar firms with whom they will be competing. The CMTC and the other Manufacturing Technology Centers around the country provide excellent information bases that can be used by small manufacturers like Ace Clearwater for these purposes.

THE TALLY FOR THE FIRST SCORING PERIOD: ACE GETS AN A+

The most notable indication of the renewal at Ace Clearwater Enterprises occurred in 1993 when the company was named Boeing's Supplier of the Year. This would be a major accomplishment for any company, given Boeing's huge supplier base. But given that Boeing had threatened to cancel the Ace Clearwater contracts for nonperformance only two years earlier, the turnaround effort is all the more remarkable. The improvements in Ace Clearwater's performance in this two-year period are summarized in Table 2.1.

In more concrete terms, some of the results of these programs for Ace Clearwater Enterprises have been:

- The company returned to profitability.
- Manufacturing teams were created, resulting in improved communications and productivity.
- Boeing awarded the company its D1-9000 certification for its Advanced Quality System and, further, follow-on contracts.
- Rework and reinspection were reduced, improving on-time delivery.
- Customer relations with Boeing and other customers improved.
- Overtime was reduced.
- Plant morale improved, and absentee rates declined dramatically.

RAKING IN THE FRINGE BENEFITS

Let's look at a few of these results more closely. We'll start with the improvement in communications. Two long-term shop employees, Larry Moore and Bob Amour remarked:

> [Before all the training,] we weren't really involved with other groups. We were pretty much in the dark. There was the shop and there was the office. Now, we work more with

Table 2.1

Ace Clearwater Enterprises Performance on Boeing Contracts 1991–1993

Performance Measure	Boeing Requirement	ACE 1991 Performance	ACE 1993 Performance
Late Deliveries	0%	36%	0%
% of Parts Rejected	<2.0%	18–19%	<1.0%

each other. We know who to go to with our problems now. The training brought us all a lot closer together. It used to be we didn't even know where to go. If I went to the boss and said "I have a problem." He'd say: "Do the best you can." We got a lot of communications skills out of those meetings.

One example of the benefits of this new level of communications and the empowerment of workers to find solutions to the problems facing them came from a job ACE was doing for General Dynamics. This job required particularly strong welds, which would be inspected by X ray. Because of this requirement, the materials were expensive, and the cost was many times the company average of $600 per part. Of the first seven parts produced, only one passed the X-ray inspection—a scrap rate that made the customer very unhappy and the job highly unprofitable.

A cross-functional team diagnosed the problem as resulting from too much moisture in the gas lines. For most work, this level of moisture didn't make a difference, but for this particular job, the moisture created a major problem. The long-term solution was to replumb the gas lines at a cost of $15,000, money that Ace didn't have available. The welders came up with a more cost-effective solution. Working with the gas supply company, they had several tanks of very pure mixtures brought to the welding booth. For the General Dynamics job, the welders used these tanks instead of the normal supply. The result was perfect welds that passed the X-ray inspection every time, saving the company large sums of money.

As Larry and Bob put it: "They now encourage us to work with each other, to find solutions to problems, to call in help from the customers and suppliers if necessary."

Another example of benefits from the new approach is being on customers' "short lists" when they start paring their supplier base, as well as referrals for new business. Kellie Dodson gave this example:

Allied Signal has gone from 200 sheet metal suppliers to 50 and will be reducing that to 25, and we'll be part of that

> small group. Allied Signal's commodities team came in here and saw our documentation and our improvement plans and said that ACE should be used as a benchmark. That's a real compliment to us.

Gary Johnson, Ace Clearwater vice president, who manages the sales department, continues the story:

> They are also introducing us to other parts of Allied Signal. They're supporting us financially by getting us more work within their own company. Allied Signal is also showing confidence in us by giving us bigger-ticket items to make. Our average part costs $600. We just completed work on a piece for Allied Signal that costs $20,000 per item. That's a big step for us. We're stepping up to a whole new level of manufacturing.

So the results are coming in, and the future is looking bright for Ace Clearwater Enterprises. But what are the effects on the company's employees? What benefits are they seeing from all the training they have received and the new work methods that have been instituted? According to Bob Amour and Larry Moore: "Just having a job in this day and age is a big reward. Just having someone say thank you is what we want. It means a lot."

WHAT DOES THE FUTURE HOLD FOR ACE CLEARWATER?

Putting the Future in Writing

Ace Clearwater Enterprises grew up like many small companies, revolving around the abilities of a single person. For many years that person was the company owner and president, Tim Dodson. The traditional way in which business was done was "to just book orders and get around to it when our customer hollered loud enough." When Kellie Dodson took the reins, she realized that her father's methods just weren't going to work in the future.

> I realized that if our company was to become successful, it couldn't revolve around just one person. I was going to lead

> it. I was going to have the vision for it. I was going to help motivate it and give it the energy that it needed. But we were becoming too sophisticated, too many demands and requirements were being placed on us, that one person couldn't have all the answers. My brain couldn't possibly hold all that information. I had to start relying on other people.

But other people couldn't follow unless the leader could articulate the goals. The company had never had a strategic business plan. In 1993 Kellie Dodson and Gary Johnson spent a long weekend developing that plan, which they presented to an all-employee meeting. It was the first time that everyone in the company really had any idea of what they were working toward. "And the wonderful thing, too," according to Gary, "is that we have accomplished many of the things we wrote in that plan, and virtually 100 percent of them are in the works."

In 1994 Kellie set out the broad goals for the company and asked her management team to build the plan. This was a big step for a company that always had revolved around a single individual, and managers and shop employees alike felt more empowered and more engaged in the company's plans and efforts.

Contracts manager Mike Feldberg looks to a great future for Ace Clearwater and its employees:

> The future here is unlimited. When I worked for other aerospace corporations, the future brought plant closings, layoffs, pay cuts, aggravation. At this company, with orders going up and shipments on time, with profits obviously being invested back into the company, constantly updating and modernizing—it's a pleasant place to work. It's just really unlimited.

SOME WORDS OF ADVICE FROM THE PRESIDENT

Given her obvious success at renewing her company, I asked Kellie Dodson to offer some advice to others who might find themselves in a similar situation. How should you start your renewal efforts?

What are some key considerations for other companies? Here are a few of her key points:

- "*Create your own niche.* Whatever it is you want to do, have it clearly defined, and be the best at what you do. Be very focused on what it is you do best.
- "*Listen to your customer.* Customers define the price and quality for the parts they want. What other value can you add to your customer that no one else can give? It could be service, it could be somehow enhancing their product—something other than quality and price—those are givens.
- "*Listen to the people you employ*—you depend on them so much. When you bring together a team, make sure they have the same values, the same goals, the same type of energy."

She summarizes: "At ACE, there are good days and there are bad days. But on some days, the energy level is so great that the shop is just humming! That's our role as leaders—keeping that energy alive."

BOTTOM-LINE LESSONS FROM THE ACE CLEARWATER ENTERPRISES STORY

Let's look at the Ace Clearwater Enterprises story from the perspective of the models for knowledge acquisition and company renewal presented earlier.

Kellie Dodson started out with a substantial store of "unconscious ignorance," that is, she didn't really know what she didn't know. Having no real background in manufacturing, the requirements being laid down by Boeing didn't mean much to her, other than raising a large red flag. Her first actions were to move from unconscious ignorance to conscious ignorance—to be able to recognize what she and her company needed to learn. She did this in three ways:

1. She listened to her customer. Quality is defined by the customer, and if she wanted to keep Boeing as a cus-

tomer, Ace Clearwater would have to meet Boeing's requirements.

2. She recognized that the job extended well beyond her own learning, and beyond her capacity to learn. She therefore hired a number of key personnel who could bring their own knowledge stores into the company and help spread the learning load beyond the one person at the top.
3. She sought expert advice from an unbiased, external source, the Center for Applied Competitive Technologies, whose staff had more experience and knowledge related to the Boeing requirements than anyone inside Ace Clearwater.

At the same time, she recognized the need for learning at all levels of the company and brought in massive amounts of training for all personnel, to help everyone in the company move toward conscious competence. By hiring a director of change, she also recognized that changing long-used methods and introducing new technical processes and new ways of working are not easy tasks. They require reinforcement and coaching on a regular basis as people try out their new skills and knowledge on the job.

Kellie also tapped into the reservoir of conscious and unconscious competence already resident in her employees by empowering them to solve their own problems and make their own decisions. One of her most empowering actions was open and public admission of her own errors. Several times she spoke candidly to company teams, saying: "I was wrong. I screwed up. I thought it would work, but it didn't. Now, how can we fix this situation?" By this example, she showed employees that they too could try their own solutions, and if they didn't work, they could come back to their teams to seek help.

Keys to Company Renewal at Ace Clearwater Enterprises

Looking at the four-stage process ("Keys to Company Renewal"—see Figure 1.2), it is easy to see how Ace Clearwater Enterprises moved through each stage. Starting with "Goals," Kellie Dodson listened to her customer, got the help she needed, both through building staff capabilities and through importing external expertise, and set new goals for the company. At first she and Vice President Gary Johnson wrote the company's strategic plan. Later her executive team set the goals and asked the various teams that ran the company to develop plans to meet those goals.

At the second stage Kellie worked to ensure that all parts of the company were aligned with the company's overall goals. A key to this stage was the development of real communication, not only from her to the various teams and individual employees through such devices as all-company meetings, but also from the encouragement of cross-functional and cross-plant communication. This strategy helped to break down long-standing barriers between "the shop and the office," between the Torrance plant and the Paramount plant, between shop workers and engineers, and so on. Without this type of communication, the turf battles that had plagued the company for years would continue, and little alignment with the overall company goals would be accomplished.

The CACT's manufacturing assessment gave Kellie a clear picture of the company's starting point, both its strengths and its weaknesses. Once the goals were in place, all parts of the company were aligned with those goals, and the starting point was identified, Ace Clearwater was able to set out on its renewal journey with the assistance of a wide variety of internal and external resources.

PLANNING YOUR OWN JOURNEY

The story of renewal at Ace Clearwater Enterprises is presented as one example of how companies can use transformational learning to renew themselves through people and knowledge. It is not meant to serve as the sole methodology that all companies should follow. Every company is unique. Each has a history, a culture, a set of embedded work methods, and a reservoir of knowledge and skills unique to its own workforce.

In the following chapters, we will look at how other companies have undertaken the same journey using a variety of methods. We will also look at how your company should evaluate those methods and choose the methods and the path most suited to its unique situation. But no matter what your goals or what path you choose to take, the key to your company's renewal lies in its people and knowledge.

THREE

DEFINE, THEN ALIGN

If you don't know where you're going, any path will do.

Northern Telecom Inc. (NTI) is the U.S. arm of Canada's Northern Telecom Limited. NTI was started in the early 1970s to take advantage of the new market opportunities created by deregulation of the U.S. telephone industry. The company was very aggressive in pursuing those opportunities, acquiring new plants and personnel. But, through its inexperience, the company also encountered many problems.

> By 1980, when Desmond Hudson arrived from Toronto to take over as president and CEO, the company was growing rapidly and losing money. Goals were fuzzy; organizational structure was weak. Senior management realized that all levels of management urgently needed a thorough retraining process.[1]

Every organization is concerned with progress. But lacking a sense of direction, there can be no progress. The first requirements for any organizational renewal effort are to define a set of goals and to ensure that all parts of the organization are aligned with those goals. Without this sense of direction, companies too often find themselves, like NTI, with "some business units . . . going off in different directions—in some cases competing with one another—creating both inefficiency and confusion."[2] The first task in organizational renewal is the setting of goals and the alignment of all parts of the organization with those goals. The goal-setting process, properly planned and executed, is itself an element of transformational learning.

THE DEFINING

The process of goal setting must be based on knowledge: knowledge of the organization's capabilities and limitations, its core competencies, its customers, its suppliers and competitors, major trends in the global economy and in technology, and the myriad factors that will affect the organization's business today and in the future. Employees involved in the planning process must also learn the techniques of planning, how to use the newly gained knowledge to create alternative scenarios and test those scenarios, and how to weigh alternatives and make decisions about the directions the organization should take.

Since no one can predict the future with certainty, much of this "knowledge" must be classified as "educated guesswork." Because no one person can be the sole source of knowledge about the organization's current capabilities, the current state of the organization's business, and the organization's relative placement among its field of competitors, planning must be a collaborative effort involving many people with different sets of skills, expertise, and experience.

The process of setting goals must be one of learning. And since conditions and knowledge will continually change over time, this learning must be continuous. Without continuous learning, effective management today and effective planning for tomorrow cannot take place.

PLANNING FOR THE LONG TERM, FOR THE NEXT YEAR, AND FOR BEING HERE TOMORROW

American companies engage in three common types of planning:

- *Visionary planning:* setting long-range goals, based on a vision of the future of the organization developed by the organization's leadership.

- *Regularly scheduled annual planning:* setting annual goals that lay out the game plan for the organization's next fiscal year.
- *Crisis planning:* correcting annual and longer-range goals, reacting to a sudden downturn in business or an immediate threat of such a downturn because of the actions of a customer or competitor.

Let's look briefly at each of these three types of planning.

VISIONARY PLANNING

The best way to ensure a prosperous future is to create the future you want. But because the future is uncertain, no organization can paint a precise picture of where it will be in 5 or 10 or more years. The best that an organization's leaders can do is to study all of the factors affecting its future, paint one or more general scenarios of what they believe the future holds, and then define where they want the organization to fit within that future. Visionary planning involves not so much putting a stake in the ground as setting a direction for the organization.

Visionary planning requires the acquisition of both knowledge and the skills to apply that knowledge. An organization's vision cannot consist solely of platitudes about customer responsiveness and return on stockholder's equity but must be based on research (the search for knowledge) and realistic views of what is possible for the organization to achieve. University of Michigan professor C. K. Prahalad describes it this way:

> Foresight requires probing for underlying trends and then synthesizing their implications for the set of businesses that you have or the businesses you want to get into. It is not some vague statement like, "We will serve our customers and shareholders and communities."[3]

Plans must be stated in terms that people, both internal and external to the organization, can understand and respond to. When was the last time you had a good idea and suggested to your manager: "This is sure to boost our shareholders' return on equity!"? Goals must be real and tangible.

The long-range planning process must be based on *learning*, and this learning must be accomplished by top company management and everyone involved in the planning process. What needs to be learned? To form even the most rudimentary long-range plan, an organization must understand:

- *Customers:* Who will be buying the types of products and services we offer? Where will they be located? What will they be seeking—price, features, locations, delivery options, and so on? How will we sell our products and services? How will customers learn about us? How will they buy from us?
- *Products and Services:* How should our products and services change over time? Will customers be seeking the products and services we now provide, or will they be seeking new solutions? How will new products and services be manufactured and delivered?
- *Competitors:* Who will be our competitors at that time? Will they be the same ones we now face? Will new competitors come into the market? What will our competitors offer to our current and potential customers to lure them away from us? What will be the sources of competitive advantage in the future?
- *Means of Production:* How will we create our products and services in the future? What new technologies must we adopt or adapt? What other capabilities will these technologies offer us? What technologies will our competitors be using?
- *Human Resources:* What types of skills and knowledge will be needed in the future? Will these be available in the marketplace? How can we best utilize or develop the knowledge and skill bases we already have to meet future requirements?
- *Organization:* How will we need to be organized to respond most effectively to our customers? How will

we manage our organization? What will our value chain look like? Which business functions will we do ourselves and which will we subcontract to others? Who will be our partners and suppliers?

- *Finances:* What will it cost? How will we pay for it, for example, out of working capital, stock issue, bonds?

Any vision of the future, any set of long-range goals, to be believable, must be accompanied by a plan of how the company is going to achieve those goals. The effective leader paints a picture of the future, saying "Here's what we plan to become, and here's how we can get from here to there."

Preparation for Planning

How does a company ensure that it has all of the information it needs, or at least all that is available, for the purpose of long-range planning? To ensure that planning is done well, the following conditions must be met:

1. The organization's leaders must *define the parameters* that will shape the organization's future, that is, which of the preceding factors will be critical to the company's future.
2. The people who are doing the planning must be those who will have responsibility for effecting those plans. Inversely, the people who have responsibility for effecting plans must themselves do the planning.
3. The people who are doing the planning must have, within the constraints of the organization's resources, all available information as well as a methodology for creating the plan.

Each of these three conditions requires learning.

First, to define the parameters, organizational leaders must leave their egos at the door and take a hard look at what the future holds for the economy, the industry, and the organization. They must uncover their own areas of unconscious ignorance by seeking inputs from all sectors, internal and external. The worst mistake that organizational leaders can make is to assume that they already know everything they will need to know in the future.

Second, planning is often done in a vacuum by an organization's top management or, in some large organizations, by a formal planning department. Virtually everyone in the organization should have some role in the planning process.

- When planning efforts are left to the few, the organization loses the benefit of the knowledge held by the many. The head of research and development, for example, knows more than others about what is happening inside a company's laboratories, but she may not have knowledge of an important development at a university laboratory where a recent hire worked while earning his graduate degree. The head of market research may have a lot of data about the organization's customers but may not have the new product ideas that a customer recently shared with a salesperson.

  Valuable knowledge exists throughout the organization, and organizations must learn to tap into *all* of it—to capture the large stores of both conscious and unconscious competence that already exist.
- People are more likely to buy into plans they have helped to create than those from which they have become excluded. Participation in the planning process creates "our" plans, rather than "their" plans.
- The people who actually do the work are generally more knowledgeable about what it will take (e.g., knowledge and skill requirements, technologies, plant and equipment, etc.) to get from here to there than top management or people in a planning department.

Third, relevant information should be gathered from every available source, internal and external, limited only by the resources and time available. Although there are too many potential sources for many organizations to tap into, critical sources of relevant information should be identified and selected. Potential sources of information are listed briefly in Table 3.1.

Table 3.1
Sources of Planning Information

Customer Information.
- Market research firms.
- Industry, trade, and professional associations.
- Industry and market journals and periodicals.
- University research centers.
- Current customers, both those who buy from your organization and those who buy from your competitors.
- Surveys.
- Focus groups.
- Census and other government data.
- Your own salesforce and customer service reps who spend time with your customers.

Product and Service Information
- Market research firms.
- Industry, trade, and professional associations.
- Industry and market journals and periodicals.
- University research centers.
- Current customers, both those who buy from your organization and those who buy from your competitors.
- Focus groups.
- Your own salesforce and customer service reps who spend time with your customers.
- Suppliers and partners.

Competitors
- Market research firms.
- Industry, trade, and professional associations.
- Industry and market journals and periodicals.
- University research centers.
- Current customers, both those who buy from your organization and those who buy from your competitors.
- Your own salesforce and customer service reps who spend time with your customers.
- Suppliers and partners.

Means of Production
- Industry, trade and professional associations.
- University research centers.
- NIST-sponsored Manufacturing Technology Centers.

(continued)

Table 3.1 *(Continued)*

- Suppliers and partners.
- Technology vendors.
- Research and development departments and consultants.
- Manufacturing departments and consultants.

Human Resources

- Industry, trade, and professional associations.
- Industry and market journals and periodicals.
- University research centers.
- Current customers, both those who buy from your organization and those who buy from your competitors.
- Census and other government data.
- Suppliers and partners.
- Technology vendors.
- Local educational agencies.
- Industry education associations.

Organization

- Industry, trade, and professional associations.
- Industry and market journals and periodicals.
- University research centers.
- Suppliers and partners.
- Technology vendors.

People at all levels of the company must participate in conducting this research. Too often research tasks are assigned to planning departments, market research groups, and others at relatively low levels in the company. Later, when top management reviews the research reports, they often are so tied to their own beliefs about what is "really happening" that they cannot or will not accept other realities. People at all levels should take the time to understand what is happening in the market.

> For a weeklong learning program for a Fortune 500 company's sales and sales support organization, a speaker was hired from a well-known market research firm in the company's industry. Working with the company's market research director, the consultant had put together an excellent presentation on the company's markets, customers, competitors, technology trends, and so on. A typical reaction

> from the audience was: "Where was the company's top management? We know most of this stuff—we face it daily in the field. The people who need to hear this are the company's president, the vice president for engineering, the sales and marketing vice presidents. Where were they?" The complaint was not with the consultant, but with the company's top managers who weren't taking enough time to understand the market and the challenges being faced by the company's sales force.

CEOs and other top managers need to undertake their own learning activities to keep up with what is really happening in the marketplace. Table 3.2 includes some ideas for nontraditional types of learning activities for senior organizational managers.

Planning Methods

Many planning methodologies are available in the marketplace—dozens of books on planning, proprietary methodologies sold by every major consulting firm, formal and informal methods developed by university professors and independent consultants, and those developed over time by many companies for their own use. I won't present a new one here.

No matter which method you choose for developing your organization's long-range plan, the planning process should be a real *learning experience* for everyone involved. Too often planning is done by a chosen few following a long-standing methodology. "Nobody really cares what's in the plan," said one executive. "It's just an annual exercise we do, changing the baseline to reflect last year's results and applying the standard formulas to make projections. Once its done, it will get filed away with the rest of the plans. The only time we'll look at it is next year when we start all over again."

If you are seeking to renew your company, to create a better future, you cannot take this mechanistic approach. Whichever method you choose for planning, you must make it a *real* learning experience, a *real* opportunity to create the future rather than to extend the past. To accomplish this, your planning methods should include at least the following elements:

Table 3.2
Learning Activities for CEOs and Other Top Management

- Make a sales call with a sales rep.
- Make a service call with a service rep.
- Be briefed by your Research & Development department.
- Be briefed by your Market Research department.
- Be briefed by an industry analyst.
- Attend an executive education program sponsored by:
  - a university business school.
  - a technology vendor.
  - a market research firm.
- Speak at an industry conference and attend other sessions.
- Speak at a university program and participate in discussions with students, faculty, and other speakers.
- Spend a day with a customer to see how your products or services are really used.
- Spend a day with a competitor's customer to see how their products or services are being used.
- Visit retail stores or trade shows where your wares and your competitors' wares are being shown side by side.
- Participate in a university-based, multicompany consortium on topics of interest (technology, management, education, etc.).
- Do formal and informal benchmarks with other companies.
- Read.
- Invite speakers of interest into your company to share ideas.
- Serve on industry or market association boards and committees.

1. An explicit statement of assumptions, boundaries, and methodologies to be used in the planning process.
2. The systematic collection of information from a wide variety of sources, both internal and external.
3. The involvement of as many people as practical in the data collection.
4. A systematic review and synthesis of all collected data by all relevant departments, rather than just a few planners.
5. Testing of at least several alternative future scenarios before settling on a direction for the organization.

6. Widespread sharing and discussion of the plans, once developed.

We have already discussed several of these items, that is, the need to collect planning information (#2), the desirability of including many people in the process (#3), and the benefits of sharing plans widely so that people know where the organization is heading and can therefore contribute more easily to its success (#6). Let's consider the others.

Any methodology for planning must start with an explicit statement of assumptions and boundaries (#1). Many times these are well known but never explicitly stated. For example, in the earlier example of reengineering the tax return preparation process of a CPA firm, there was an implicit barrier to any change that would reduce billable hours. Often there are real, legitimate reasons for some bounds. But too often people on planning committees operate on a set of implicit constraints that are not real and on hidden agendas that are not intended by the company's top management—for example, "the company will never build a new plant, even though we need it" or "they'll never let us bring in the sales force for retraining"—and these constraints limit real future possibilities. The only way to avoid these types of problems is to put the constraints explicitly on the table.

The planning process should involve people from many functions working together (#4). In many organizations, where planning is done by rote, each function and business unit does its own projections and the planning committee simply rolls up all of those numbers into an organization-wide plan. Although this approach might have made sense in an earlier time, the future cannot be limited to what has been done in the past; it will rely on the breaking down of the barriers between functions and business units. As C. K. Prahalad put it:

> Many of the issues that impact the future cut across many business units. There may be no natural home for thinking about them. So the business units may be thinking about what happens to their business as they see it over the next 5 to 10 years. But they do not see looming, large changes that may totally undercut the businesses as we know them today.[4]

When the planning process has become so routinized that only one possible plan emerges, the organization has lost the whole point and benefit of real planning. The planning process is a real opportunity for the organization to consider alternatives for its future and to make real choices about that future (#5). To consider only a single alternative limits possibilities for the future. Whatever planning method you choose, you must see it as an opportunity to introduce new information and new skills into your organization, and to increase the knowledge assets of your employees and the organization. As Karl Albrecht puts it:

> There is no divinely inspired truth to be discovered in charting the destiny of any enterprise. There is only the most enlightened concept for success that is possible given the information, energy and talent applied to the issues. It requires a certain degree of humility, a willingness to question one's own certainty and, at the same time, the willingness to commit fully to a common cause and get on with it.[5]

PLANNING FOR THE SHORT TERM

Every organization must plan for its immediate future. What resources will be needed to meet immediate and short-term requirements based on today's business and the business projected for the next fiscal period? How will business be conducted over the next year? How many people will be employed? What new investments will be made, and so on? Without effective short-range planning, myriad problems will arise and the organization may soon find itself out of business. We need to fill those orders, meet our customers' needs, provide the services for which we have contracts, keep new business coming in to replace completed work, and so on.

But, for many companies, the annual planning process has become so routinized that employees fill out the forms, attend the meetings, and negotiate the budgets without really thinking about what they are doing or whether the plans have any basis in reality.

For other companies, which actually rely on these plans to run their operations, the annual plan can actually limit opportunities for innovation and growth. How many great ideas are squelched by managers who tell their employees, "It's a great idea and I wish I could help you, but it just isn't in the plan"? How many opportunities for real progress in quality, new business, or cost savings are lost simply because they "aren't in the plan"?

A manager in a consumer products company told me: "I've lost track of how many times I've had a new idea turned down because the cost savings or the new business that would result wouldn't show up until the next fiscal year. My boss would say: 'It's a great idea, but our budget is fixed for this year. Unless we can at least recover the costs in this fiscal year, we can't justify the expense. Maybe we can consider it next year.' "

This happened time after time, she told me, "even when there was an almost perfect guarantee of a 10-times return in the next fiscal year, even when there was a clear window of opportunity and waiting until next year would make the idea near worthless."

Managers sometimes spend so much time figuring out how to get a bigger share of the pie that they never have time to consider how to make the pie bigger. Too often the annual operating plan becomes not a guiding light for the organization, but a millstone used to crush creativity and new opportunities.

The annual plan deserves the same care as is given to the long-range goal-setting process. This is the time to look closely at how work is being done, what opportunities are likely to emerge over the year, how the plan can be structured to allow for unforeseen opportunities. If preparing the organization's annual operating plan is done in a "business-as-usual" mode, the chances are that the organization will be unable to respond to any unusual business opportunities, barring progress during the year.

The other major problem in the business-as-usual approach to annual planning is that it regularly ignores longer-range goals. If next year's plan is simply a repeat of this year's plan, adjusted for inflation, how is the organization ever going to achieve the longer-range goals that have been set?

The lack of real planning efforts in developing annual operating plans and the resultant inflexibility of such plans are the major cause of the third common type of planning effort—crisis planning.

CRISIS PLANNING (OR, AS SMOKEY SAID: "ONLY YOU CAN PREVENT FOREST FIRES")

Crisis planning is what makes headlines:

> "Reacting to a sudden downturn in business, the XYZ Corporation today announced massive cuts . . ."
>
> "Faced with a major loss in market share to overseas competitors, Acme Amalgamated laid off 25 percent of its workforce . . ."

Crisis planning is most often the result of poor long-term and short-term planning. Having failed to examine long-term trends, not having paid attention to what customers were asking for and what competitors were delivering, organizations "suddenly" face a crisis. The reaction to that crisis, or crisis planning, often takes the forms of large reductions in the workforce, selling off parts of the business, closing plants, and other drastic measures.

These crisis interventions also make it very difficult for the people who remain in the organization to maintain any optimism about the future. Burdened with now doing not only their own jobs but also those of their departed fellow employees, they often have little to look forward to—no rosy projections for future company growth and the attendant promotions and salary increases, little value left in stock options and stock investment plans, a generally dismal atmosphere in which to work every day.

Crisis planning is *reactive* rather than proactive. So much attention is focused on overcoming the crisis that planning for the future is laid aside. The goal is no longer "what can we become in the future?" Now it is "how we can survive until tomorrow?"

The problem with this type of planning is that with no vision of growth, employees will inevitably become more and more demoralized and, resultantly, less and less productive.

> "If we are downsizing all operations, where is my chance for job growth and promotion?"
>
> "If we have to do the same work with fewer people, how will new management jobs ever open up for me?"

"If we are stripping out layers of management, where's my career path?"

Short-term crisis planning is sometimes necessary, but once the immediate crisis is over, organizational leaders must quickly turn their attention to longer-range planning. They must set goals with which employees can identify and in which employees can find a future. Otherwise, today's crisis is very likely to spawn still more crises, from which employees will retreat into more and more defensive positions.

If your company's planning processes are in order, the next challenge is to ensure that all parts of the organization align their own plans with the overall direction of the company.

GOAL: COMPANY-WIDE ALIGNMENT

Select any one of the top 10,000 companies in the United States today. Look at its plan for the year 2000. The odds are that the company's projections will place it firmly in the Fortune 500 at the turn of the century. If you were to revisit that company's financial statements at the end of its fiscal year 2000, the odds are that its results will more resemble 1995 than the original plan.

The reasons for this failure to meet the organization's goals and expectations can be many, but very often it will have resulted from failure to align the work of individuals, functions, and business units with the stated goals of the organization. Progress is much more likely when all parts of the organization are pulling together toward the stated goals than if each person, function, and business unit is headed in a different direction.

Xerox faced a common problem—the misalignment of its research and development community with the company's business directions. The problem was solved, according to CEO Paul Allaire, by involving the R&D community in the planning process. ". . . [W]e have a strategy now that the research-and-development community is totally supportive of. They are focusing their energies on implementing the strategic direction of the company . . . The way we've done that is by engaging [them] in the development of the strategies."[6]

HOW ORGANIZATIONS BECOME MISALIGNED

Start-up companies are never misaligned. In a start-up, a small group of entrepreneurs works closely together to plan, produce, and market that first new product. But as the start-up grows, this close-knit group expands, departments form, and misalignment starts to become evident. In most companies, misalignment is a major barrier to renewal efforts.

Misalignment of an organization's long-range goals and business activities emerges from five root causes:

- Lack of leadership.
- Functional myopia.
- Playing by the wrong rules.
- Rewarding the wrong behaviors.
- Not knowing how to change.

Lack of Leadership

Strong, committed, visible leadership is required to ensure that all parts of the organization are aligned with the stated goals. Leaders must visibly communicate those goals as being important and must keep them in front of all employees at all levels: "Here's what we are striving to become, and we're not going to get there unless we all work together." This cannot be a one-time statement or, worse, memo, for this approach will only hasten the return to business as usual. Leaders must be seen as personally guiding the effort and must hold themselves and their organizations accountable to those goals.

AN EXAMPLE FROM TEXAS INSTRUMENTS

Several years ago at Texas Instruments, a senior planning committee developed a set of 16 goals for its division. At a high-level meeting, company leaders asked one of the committee members to list the goals, without looking at his notes. The person did very well—he got 14 of them. The committee was then told that 16 goals are too many for anyone to remember. The list was reduced to four major goals, and these were communicated widely throughout the organization so that everyone in the division knew what the goals were and, if asked, could list them. More importantly, every group and every employee was required to write into their own work plans how they would support those goals.

Alignment will be a much easier task if all parts of the organization are involved in setting those goals, thus ensuring early buy-in. Mark Hoyal, a consultant with Hewitt Associates, puts it this way:

> If you give people a plan, they will find three or four things wrong with it. If you involve them, they will understand the issues, and you build acceptance as you go along. The more they are involved, the more ownership they will take and the more they will understand the new vision.[7]

Functional Myopia

Functional myopia occurs when a function, group, or business unit is so focused on its local goals that it loses sight of the overall goals of the organization and, often, finds itself suboptimizing overall organizational performance while optimizing local performance measures. Examples can be found in every corporate function:

- The purchasing agent who buys raw materials in large pieces because the cost per pound is cheaper, only to greatly increase scrap rates as those large metal blocks are milled down to make small parts.
- The legal department that holds up a major partnership agreement arguing over minor language changes.
- The engineering department that insists on the most elegant design even though it hasn't been requested by customers and it prices the product out of the market.

- The salesperson who discounts goods so highly that she wins the sales contest but wrecks the company's profit margins in the process.
- The business unit manager who resists adoption of a new practice because it wasn't invented within his own department.

To correct functional myopia, management must ensure that all employees understand the overall organizational goals and align their own work toward the achievement not only of local goals but also of the larger goals of the organization. The process starts with a shared vision of the future. Northern Telecom vice president Graham M. Palmer states the requirement this way:

> Creating a global, end-to-end business process vision and communicating this dynamic picture of tomorrow, across all major functions, is mandatory to ensure alignment of visions between multiple business units, across all functions, and across all employee groups.[8]

Once they have seen the "big picture," employees can do their jobs, and make their daily decisions, keeping in mind not only their personal responsibilities but also how each action and decision will affect the organization's overall results.

Functional myopia occurs not just within well-defined business functions, such as purchasing, legal departments, and engineering groups, but also among independent business units that often end up competing with each other, rather than cooperating to create a better future for the overall organization. For many organizations, the future cannot be created within current business units but must be conceived and built by cross-unit cooperation and collaboration.

Xerox has solved this problem, in part, by creating a Market & Technology Development unit, charged with evaluating Xerox-developed technologies that aren't aligned with any existing business division. "If the group finds a promising technology that the business divisions aren't interested in, it can conduct market research and then put together a business proposal to create a new separate venture."[9] In recent months this unit has been responsible for bringing two new products to market that otherwise would not have been adopted by existing business units.

Playing by the Wrong Rules

As organizations grow, they have a tendency to establish policies and procedures that become more and more rigid. Although these rules are originally developed to ensure fairness, to make people's jobs easier, and to ensure consistency, they tend to become like organization charts, blocking the types of creative solutions that are required in today's marketplace. A former Sears executive talks about how restrictive such set policies and procedures can be:

> "You start focusing on *how* decisions are made rather than on what you decide. At Sears, the problem was compounded by a whole library of 'bulletins' that spell out procedures for dealing with almost any problem. God forbid there should be a problem that comes up for which there isn't a bulletin. That means the problem's *new!*" [10]

Any organization that is trying to renew itself must take time to examine the organization's policies and procedures. Are they supportive of the new directions of the organization, or are they going to obviate the kinds of changes being mandated? Will they allow people to try new, creative approaches, or are they going to restrict people to applying the old solutions? Are they going to encourage a broad view of the business and employees' responsibilities within the overall business, or are they going to reinforce functional myopia?

Rewarding the Wrong Behaviors

If you want employees to practice new behaviors, you cannot continue to reward the old ones. If you are asking people to add value to the business, you must design measurements and rewards to reflect those new requirements. These types of changes are not easy to make and cannot be made without integration into the overall plan for organizational renewal. According to Dr. Edward Lawler III, director of the Center for Effective Organizations at the University of Southern California School of Business Administration:

> The underlying phenomenon here is that people will no longer be paid for what the job is worth, but, in essence, for the value that they can bring to the corporation and what they are capable of doing. Set pay made sense in a world with standardized work tasks. But what we are now seeing is more flexibility in organizations and more and more emphasis on skills and portability of skills. The rigid box-like structure of traditional organizations is dissolving, and all that matters is what skills an individual has.[11]

Progress has been slow in adapting measurement and reward systems, but there are some notable exceptions:

- Polaroid Corp. recently put all its managers on skill-based pay.
- Frito-Lay Corp. rewards its managers for core management skills such as leadership, group process facilitation, and communications ability.
- One aerospace company has developed a contract with its managers that leads to a bonus if learning objectives are met.
- Motorola, Inc., since late 1991, has been testing peer review for pay. Work-team members at its Cellular Infrastructure Group facility at Arlington Heights, Ill., are asked to vote at year-end on team members' performance to determine part of their pay . . .
- Levi Strauss & Co. has implemented a new performance-management- and-pay program—with individual and team pay components—for its salaried workers. And it is working on altering the piece-rate system it has used for 50 years in its manufacturing plants.[12]

Again, the lesson to be learned is that all parts of the organization, all policies, procedures, measurements, and rewards must be closely aligned with the goals of the organization's renewal effort if optimal progress toward those goals is to be achieved.

Not Knowing How to Change

Changes in how work is to be done must be accompanied by changes in the skills and knowledge of the people doing the work. No matter how much has been invested in plant and equipment, no matter how much new technology has been introduced, the work is done by, and competitive advantage will come from, your people. People can't change long-held work methods without learning. For example, many companies have invested millions of dollars in technologies to enable manufacturing and engineering groups to work together in developing new products. "Concurrent (or Simultaneous) Engineering" programs, as they are known, are designed to improve time-to-market, raise quality, reduce costs, and so on. But unless people learn how to work together, unless they learn how to negotiate product changes that cannot be decided on strictly technical criteria, no amount of technology will enable those goals. In later chapters, we will examine learning requirements and methods more deeply.

ONCE GOALS ARE SET

After planning processes are in place and the short-and long-range goals have been decided for the organization, the next step is to start communicating these goals and aligning everyone with them. People at all levels, across all functions and business units, must form a partnership with top management and with each other to start work on those goals. Unless this is done up front, any company renewal effort, any investment in transformational learning, will at best never reach its full potential or, at worst, fail. In the next chapter, we will examine how three companies, Sears, Amoco, and Corning, are working on these tasks.

FOUR

FORMING THE PARTNERSHIP WITH TOP MANAGEMENT

Company renewal efforts, to be most effective, must start at the top. To ensure that all employees are contributing the most they can to the company's renewal, top management must first make everyone aware of the company's directions and then work to ensure that everyone's efforts are correctly aligned with short- and long-term goals. The planning process itself, the acquisition of the knowledge needed to set the company's direction, can be used to start the process. Once goals are set, this process of education must be continued down through the various layers of the company, until everyone has gained the knowledge necessary to set organizational and individual goals that will support the company's direction.

In this chapter, we examine how top leaders in companies such as Sears and Amoco are working to ensure that managers throughout their widespread organizations keep abreast of company directions and the methods they utilize to ensure proper alignment. These methods include:

- Creating widespread knowledge of the company's directions.
- Involving managers below the operating committee level in planning how to achieve the company's goals.

- Giving managers the skills and knowledge they need to align their own efforts with the company's overall directions.

In these companies, top corporate executives are leading the charge toward company renewal and have instituted formal programs to equip managers at lower levels to participate effectively in the renewal process and to ensure that their organizations are pulling in the right direction.

Not every company has such strong leadership. In many companies that are attempting to renew themselves, the goals for the effort are not so explicitly stated, the directions being taken are not so clear for the rest of the organization. In such companies, where there is not such strong visible leadership for the renewal effort, there are still ways for managers to determine the overall company direction and to work to ensure that their groups' work will support that direction, even if not explicitly stated. Partnership with the company's top management does not have to be led by the company's top management but can start with the efforts of lower-level managers. We will examine how this was done at Corning later in this chapter.

THE BIRTH OF THE NEW SEARS

Sears ruled American retailing for many decades. In 1963 Sears revenues exceeded those of its next four rivals *combined.* By 1993, however, Sears had lost its shine. According to a *Fortune* article, Sears had become a "dinosaur" and was described as "not extinct, only painfully and wheezingly gasping for breath."[1] Sears became a dinosaur through its own arrogance—assuming that its size and position would protect it from predatory rivals.

Starting in the 1960s, the dinosaur was attacked by discount stores, first by Kmart and later by Wal-Mart. While failing to focus adequately on the changing needs and tastes of its customers, it built the Sears Tower, "an opulent monument to greatness, completed in 1973."[2]

In twenty years, from 1972 to 1992, Sears slipped from #6 on the *Fortune 500,* with a market valuation of $18.2 billion, to #81, with a market value of not quite $16 billion. By 1992 Wal-Mart was #3 on the list with a market value of $73.5 billion. During the same two decades, the Standard and Poor 500 was up 269 percent. Even harder for Sears management and employees to swallow was the fact that it had become identified with the low end of the retail market.

> [Sears] was once known as a family department store. But the only families that seemed to shop there—for anything more than paint and ceiling fans—were named the Clampetts. Things got so bad that some industry folks suggested changing the chain's name and starting again from scratch.[3]

Enter Arthur Martinez

In 1992 Arthur Martinez was appointed the CEO of Sears. Like many other crisis managers, Martinez began by slashing costs. He closed the Sears catalog operation, an American institution that had outlived its usefulness and was losing tens of millions of dollars a year. He also closed a slew of stores and eliminated thousands of jobs to stop the company's hemorrhaging.

But Martinez knew that this first aid would not be enough to ensure the company's future success. Along with these crisis interventions, Martinez created a vision for the future of Sears, a vision around which the remaining employees could rally. He set long-range goals, not just in monetary terms, but also in terms of what Sears would be in the future, the types of merchandise it would sell, the look of its stores, and the customers it hoped to attract and serve.

Martinez realized early on that creating a new vision for Sears was not a one-person job but required the active buy-in and involvement of his entire top management team. In the old Sears, the goals and related management decisions would have been distributed as a series of memos or bulletins, both on paper and through the company's electronic mail system. Martinez had the wisdom to realize that when you are trying to accomplish fundamental change, you need to do it in person. To this end, he created "the Phoenix Group."

The Phoenix Group

Named after the city in which it first convened, the Phoenix Group is composed of Sears's operating committee and its direct reports—the company's top 90 managers. Started with a weeklong meeting in 1993, the group continues to meet in the Chicago area *one Saturday per month* for a half- or full-day session. The purposes of these monthly sessions are many, including:

- To ensure that everyone in the top management group understands the company's vision and goals.
- To ensure that all company functions and operations are aligned with the vision and goals.
- To report on results, both from Sears and from its major competitors.
- To discuss short- and long-range program efforts and, where necessary, to make midcourse corrections.
- To discuss new ideas and make decisions on those ideas.
- To communicate important news.

Although these functions were critical to the company's renewal agenda, Martinez recognized that his management team would need other help in its quest to rebuild the company. To refocus on the company's grassroots business, managers would have to spend more time in the field to better understand how the stores themselves operated and the challenges being faced at the local level. And to lead the renewal process, all members of the Phoenix group would themselves need improved leadership and management skills.

Other major goals for monthly Phoenix Group meetings include both sharing information on store-level strategies and tactics and periodic leadership and management-development activities. According to Steven Kirn, director of education and human resource development for the Sears merchandising group, and a member of the Phoenix Group, little attention was paid to the development of the company's executives and managers during the several years of crisis management. The focus was elsewhere—on stopping the hemorrhaging in the company's balance sheets. Therefore, the Phoenix Group's agendas include executive-development activities. To foster greater cross-functional teamwork, the agendas often contain opportunities to discuss new ideas across product groups, and team-based assignments. In "the new Sears," development of people's abilities has become as important as development of new merchandising techniques. Training and development is also provided through programs of Sears University.

The monthly meetings of the Phoenix Group are held on Saturdays because its members spend much of the week on the road, visiting their own and their competitors' stores. Kirn and his staff, for example, spend a significant amount of time in the stores and "walking the malls," even though their responsibilities are focused more on the development of headquarters personnel. They need to understand the company's business and the challenges being faced not only at headquarters but also in the field. If they didn't know the business, if they didn't know the challenges facing their clientele, how would they ever be able to address them through training programs and other types of learning activities? Kirn feels that he and his development group have to align their work with goals of the company as closely as any merchandising group or store manager.

Empowering Sears's Store Managers

Martinez felt that any renewal effort at Sears, to be successful, had to have the *full involvement of all Sears employees.* In particular, he saw a greater role for its store managers. Under the old regime, store managers had been cut out of the decision-making loop. They were "shopkeepers who opened the doors and swept the snow off the sidewalks," said Martinez. "I was amazed at how uninvolved they were."[4]

One of Sears's problems was that there were too many chains of command. Although the individual store manager had ultimate responsibility for the success of the individual Sears store, the merchandising arm of the company, located at Sears headquarters, decided which products to produce, the prices they would charge, and even how products would be displayed. This company's product line organization, which made all of these decisions, extended from the company's merchandising headquarters right down into each store. Store managers were "out of the loop" when it came to merchandising.

LESSONS FROM THE SEARS EXPERIENCE

The Sears experience contains several important lessons. First, even when facing a crisis that requires drastic actions, such as store closings, layoffs, and so on, you must start building a new future. Without a vision of the future, Sears employees would have remained shell-shocked. People need goals to work toward. The psychological damage from just reacting to crisis after crisis will eventually take its toll if there is not a new rallying cry or, as Kirn puts it, "a new vision and mission to compel commitment and create positive energy."

The second lesson from the Sears experience is that people need to see their leaders and know that their leaders recognize and feel both their suffering and how hard they are working to rebuild the company. They need to hear about the new directions from the top. By spending so much of his own time in the stores, and by insisting that every member of the Phoenix Group also spend time every week developing a true understanding of the company, Martinez provided that visible leadership and brought the feeling of hope to the entire organization.

Third, Martinez recognized that to succeed, the company's management team needed to start working *together,* breaking down the product-line barriers that traditionally prevented cross-functional teamwork. The Phoenix Group helped to start breaking down the boundaries and barriers that had evolved over many years between the various product groups by itself working as a team, and by making group members work together cross-functionally. The result has been greater intergroup communication and cooperation and is reflected not only at the company's merchandising headquarters, "Prairie Stone," but also in the stores themselves.

The Phoenix Group is itself an exercise in transformational learning, where the company's entire top management team is actively engaged in developing the skills and knowledge needed to renew the company. The Phoenix Group was so named because of the location of its first gathering. With improving business results, the name should also represent the renewal of Sears, and the rising of this once-great company from its near ashes. The job at Sears is starting to show positive results but is by no means complete—in the competitive retail environment, it will never be complete.

Next let's look at how another company, Amoco, is carrying its renewal program down another level.

AMOCO'S RENEWAL PROGRAM

Like many other giant corporations, Amoco went through its own crisis in the mid-to-late 1980s. And, like many others, it slashed expenses and jobs, reducing its workforce from 46,000 to 37,000 to try to get revenues and expenses back in line. But even as cuts were being made, then-president and now-chairman Larry Fuller conceived the Amoco Renewal Program.

As with many other companies, Amoco's renewal efforts started with leadership meetings for the company's top 10 to 12 executives in which the top management team determined the key issues that the company needed to address. This led to a series of executive education seminars with Amoco's worldwide management team (about 100 executives) and covered topics ranging from leadership to strategy, from globalization to diversity.

As with most executive education sessions, participants took away many meanings from what they heard and discussed. The results were general, in that the ideas discussed created new approaches for them to try within their spans of control. One specific outcome was that the reactions to the programs were so positive that the participants were eager to spread the ideas they heard throughout the Amoco management community.

The Amoco Management Learning Center

> The single most important task before us is to engage all the talent, all the teamwork and team spirit, all the en-

ergy and drive, all the initiative and all the commitment of everyone in the Amoco family.

Larry Fuller, Chairman
Amoco

The result was the creation of the Amoco Management Learning Center (AMLC) and the start of a very ambitious series of programs, begun in early 1992, that attempt to provide "continuous communication and definition of Amoco's renewal process while providing the conceptual and practical tools to help Amoco managers and leaders achieve "renewal" in their own parts of the business.

The AMLC's goals are listed in Table 4.1.

Table 4.1

Amoco Management Learning Center Goals

- Concentrate on "renewal" programs that *uniquely* add value.
- Evolve to be Amoco's core educational university for cross-company education.
- Deliver the "right" next material to drive the renewal process.
- Blend personal/team improvement and cutting-edge conceptual frameworks.
- Contribute to a better understanding of Amoco's Mission/Vision/Values/Strategies.
- Help frame what it means to be a "strategically managed company."
- Provide a two-way mirror between senior and middle management ranks.
- Model the behaviors we seek the corporation to emulate.
- Challenge individuals to build a "learning organization" ... network the corporation.
- Provide insight on how large-scale, systemic change processes work ... using the "Renewal Star" as the model.
- Find the best ways to extend the message and link with others.
- "Stretch the envelope" of relevant management education to the limits.
- "Stretch the use of technology" to deliver the message (e.g., Business TV, teleconferencing, etc.).
- Provide corporate dialogue without being seen as *the* vehicle for corporate propaganda.

The AMLC program is a very ambitious effort involving:

- Amoco's top 3,400 managers, worldwide.
- A five-day program every 12 months.
- 42 to 46 sessions every year.

Each year's program is based on the company's renewal process. Exact content is designed by conducting a multilevel needs assessment that, according to Dr. William H. Clover, Amoco's Manager of Training and Amoco Learning Centers, includes the following elements:

- Direct input from the company's operating committee.
- A needs assessment of the target audience.
- Participant feedback.
- Faculty input.
- Operating company input.
- Senior management feedback (from their experiences in previous programs).
- Experience with external and other special programs.

Based on these inputs, Clover and his staff design each program. Clover has three overarching goals for the AMLC programs:

1. A shared mind-set.
   - Common conceptual models / vocabulary.
   - The ability to explain Amoco's strategic direction efforts.
2. Alignment.
   - AMLC curricula consistent with operating sectors' and corporate initiatives.
3. Improved results.
   - Individual.

- Team.
- Organization.

Based on these goals and the results of the needs assessments, the topics selected for the three-year program are listed in Table 4.2.

The goal of these programs is for participants to take personal responsibility to act on relevant issues when they return to their offices. Bill Clover states the primary message of the program this way: "Creating our success requires urgency, courage, and action." According to Clover, the "Renewal series is not only a program about ideas; it is an experience about how we take ideas and work with them and each other to change the culture."

These are major challenges for any company. How do you set about designing program elements that can achieve these ambitious goals? Major elements of the Amoco program include:

Table 4.2
Amoco Management Learning Center Program Themes

Program I Themes (1992–1993)
- Understanding the Differences Between Leadership and Management.
- Experience 360-Degree Feedback.
- Managing Change.
- Continuous Improvement.
- Strategic Thinking.
- Globalization.

Program II Themes (1993–1994)
- Engaging Full Talents, Energy, and Commitment of Our Employees . . . through Diversity and Teamwork.
- Gain an External Perspective.
- Provide "Line of Sight" Examples.
- Leadership through Managing Dilemmas.

Program III Themes (1994–1995)
- Create a Sense of Urgency.
- Understand Financial and Nonfinancial Pressures on the Industry.
- Help People Gain the Confidence and Courage to Act (or Act Differently).
- Learn by Sharing Examples of Renewal throughout the Corporation.
- Create a Sense of Continuous Learning.

- Alignment of corporate, operating company, and individual goals takes place through sessions where company officials and faculty explain and discuss what the corporation is trying to do, what it means for the corporation, for the operating companies, and for individual employees.

- Top Amoco executives, using personal reflections, take time from their schedules to sit down with the participants and talk on a personal level about the company's renewal efforts, what it means to the executive, to the company, and to the participants. They engage in a no-holds-barred discussion of the issues with the participants. Participants always include at least one member of the company's Strategic Planning Committee. In the program's first year, the chairman kicked off 30 of the 42 weekly sessions, talking about "Why renewal?"

- New ideas and methodologies are introduced at each session, and multilevel, cross-functional, cross-company teams of participants go through intensive exercises to apply those ideas to the business challenges they are facing.

- Sharing of experiences through poster displays and individual and group presentations allow participants to see what others are doing in different parts of the company, to evaluate new ideas, and to bring new ideas back to their own parts of the company.

- Action planning requires the individual participants to take the ideas from each session and start planning how to use them once they return to their offices to make real change happen.

The program is designed to include in each weekly session a broad cross section of geographies, business units, and functions. The AMLC faculty has designed the program in this way to create energy through what Bill Clover affectionately calls the "Microwave Theory of Change"; when an item is placed in a microwave oven, he explains, it is charged with energy that continues for a time after the oven is turned off. So he sees the energy of the sessions carrying back to the participants' home offices. And even as one participant's energy level has started to diminish, another person from that office will be returning from another session and will add his or her energy, which will have more transference effects on the office.

Impact of the Amoco Management Learning Center

Clover summarizes the impact that the programs have had on the company:

- The creation of a new energy throughout the company.
- The creation of a unified culture.
- The generation of a common language.
- The modeling of what "renewal" means for the company and the individual.
- The creation, acceleration, and deepening of business relationships across levels, functions, and operating companies.
- The generation of new ideas.
- The creation of a forum for the sharing of successes, failures, and learning.

The company has generated no "hard data" on the returns from its investment in the AMLC programs. The program is valued because company management and individual participants see it as a key enabling activity for the company renewal program. This is not to say that there have not been real business results. The crowning achievement, according to Bill Clover, was the creation of a new, multimillion dollar business:

> "We are pleased to announce the formation of a new cross-subsidiary business unit dealing with power co-generation . . . This business unit was conceived by three participants during their April 1992 AMLC class."

The three participants, from three different operating companies, met at a 1992 AMLC session and, during discussions, conceived the idea for this new business. It is very unlikely that these people would ever have met, that the new business would ever have been created, without the opportunities afforded by the AMLC program.

Amoco's Approach to Change

Clover and his staff realize that many possible approaches can be taken to create change, some perhaps more dramatic than the approach taken by the AMLC. For example, as staff members plan Round 4, to begin in the second half of 1995, they are considering bringing in intact work teams. For the first three years of the program, however, Clover states that the primary goal of the program was "to break down the barriers between operating sectors and business units in different businesses. We felt this could best be done with a stratified random sample of the top 3,400 managers from across operating sectors. When we go to teams, we will change this dynamic in ways we don't fully understand."

Insights from the Amoco Experience

The single factor most responsible for the success of the AMLC program has been the leadership of Amoco chairman Larry Fuller. Fuller created the renewal program in 1988:

> To assure that we . . . engage in corporate renewal, we need to develop and reassess our mission, values, goals and strategies. We then must define this direction in clear language and communicate it to the organization with the intent of creating understanding and ownership.
>
> Larry Fuller
> Key Largo, Florida
> January 1988

Fuller created his vision four years prior to the first AMLC program. Indeed, the AMLC did not exist in 1988 but was created to help implement his vision for the company. A major change in a company's culture takes time, and it takes committed leadership that sticks to its goals and insists that every part of the organization similarly persevere.

The AMLC program is remarkable for its commitment to directly reach almost 10 percent of the company's total population; for not only its impact on creating understanding of the company's renewal process but also its effectiveness in crossing functional, business unit, and hierarchical boundaries; and for its effectiveness in pushing change down the organization, beyond the immediate participants.

WHAT YOU SHOULD LEARN FROM THE SEARS AND AMOCO EFFORTS

A number of key lessons can be learned from the Sears and Amoco programs:

- Even in the midst of crisis, companies need to spend time building a vision of the future that will inspire and challenge their employees. Sears started from a crisis situation, with eroding profits and parts of its business losing substantial amounts of money. But along with the necessary cuts in operations and staff, Sears created a clear vision for a brighter future—goals that could inspire the company's employees. Amoco did not face the same type of crisis but started from a perception that there would be a crisis if the company didn't take action to build a different and better future. Faced with flat and eroding profits, Amoco's leadership felt it was time to "jump to a higher curve," to use Charles Handy's concept.
- Companies undertaking renewal efforts must have strong, committed, and visible leadership. Both Arthur Martinez at Sears and Larry Fuller at Amoco worked to ensure that all employees understood where their companies were headed. Both led the charge at their companies; they didn't issue a policy statement and then become invisible.

- Renewal efforts require a long-term commitment to change and an effective plan to ensure that the leaders and managers (1) understand the new directions, (2) are aligned with the new directions, and (3) are equipped to lead the changes within their respective organizations. A single weeklong session is not sufficient to build and sustain momentum. Sears's Phoenix Group continues to meet on a monthly basis a year after the initial weeklong session in Phoenix. The AMLC program was designed for a three-year period, and even as the company approaches the program's third year, further follow-on activities are being planned.
- Overcoming functional, organizational, and business unit myopia is a prerequisite to any renewal effort. Both Sears and Amoco are working to break down long-held barriers between various functions, operating units, and levels, by including cross-functional participation and intergroup work assignments in their program activities, to ensure that opportunities are not lost due to any one individual's or group's myopia.
- Renewal efforts require that people at all levels in the company be equipped with the skills and knowledge needed to change. In both companies, the programs created to help managers deal with the changes implicit in the new directions are *learning* programs, rather than training programs. Certainly, both programs contain some training activities. But, more important, both companies are creating regularly scheduled, long-term opportunities for their staffs to learn—from top company management, from noted external experts, and from each other.
- Learning must be an integral part of the renewal effort. In both companies, the learning programs are viewed as part of the corporate renewal efforts. Steve Kirn at Sears and Bill Clover at Amoco both report through the companies' human resources departments, but neither Sears's Phoenix Group nor the Amoco Management Learning Center are viewed as human resources

or training programs—they are viewed as an integral part of the companies' renewal programs.

Table 4.3 provides a summary of the lessons we've just examined.

STARTING WITHOUT A CLEAR VISION

Few companies have renewal or transformation goals stated as explicitly as those of Sears and Amoco. The press of day-to-day business often consumes so much of the time of top company managers that they may not have developed an explicit statement of the company's direction.

If the company's top management has not created and communicated a clear vision of the future, how can functional, organizational, and business unit managers ensure that their own and their groups' work addresses important company issues?

J. Edwin O'Brien, director of human resources at Corning, tries to ensure that the programs he and his group develop support the company's strategic business initiatives. According to O'Brien, Corning's top management has a vision for the future but hasn't translated that vision into a set of top priorities or strategic busi-

Table 4.3
Lessons from the Sears and Amoco Experiences

- Company renewal efforts require a real vision for the future of the company, beyond the immediate response to the company's business crisis.
- Strong, committed, visible leadership is a prerequisite to fundamental change.
- Renewal efforts require a long-term commitment and effective planning.
- Overall company renewal requires the breaking down of barriers between functions, operating units and levels.
- Ongoing learning programs are needed to equip employees with the skills and knowledge they need to work toward the company's vision.
- The learning programs must be viewed as an integral part of the companies' renewal efforts, not as a human resources or a training and development program.

ness initiatives. O'Brien determines the company's key business issues by examining the meeting agendas of the company's senior management committee, composed of the top 150 managers from across the company. What issues keep appearing week after week, month after month? What issues get the most attention, the most time allocated? After doing this analysis and developing his own list, he takes the list back to a few key executives. Are these the right issues for us to be working on? How would you prioritize the items on this list?

O'Brien feels that it is vital to get sponsorship for any new program from a member of the company's management committee. He differentiates between a program *sponsor* and a program *champion*. A sponsor is a senior company official who can give an official "blessing" to a program and can foot the bill for the program's design and implementation. A champion, on the other hand, is someone who will "pick up the ball and run with it"—someone who will drive the program and make certain that what needs to get done does indeed get done. "This person," says O'Brien, "must be the real fanatic on the issue." Without both a sponsor and a champion, no program has much chance of success. O'Brien gives an example of the type of strategic program developed and implemented using this procedure: Corning's "innovation process."

INNOVATION AT CORNING INC.

Thomas MacAvoy had been the Corning president for a number of years. When he retired from that job, he became the company's vice chairman for technology, and his real hot button in this position was how innovation was handled at Corning, how new products were brought to market, and ensuring that more of the company's new products would be winners in the marketplace.

As part of his new role, MacAvoy sponsored a two-day conference on innovation, which included top academic authorities and expert practitioners from other companies along with Corning people. According to Bryan Lanahan, Corning's director of marketing, "they ended up with a mass of good information. The question then was what they were going to do with it." MacAvoy went to his human resources people and asked them to make certain that this knowledge wasn't lost, that it was kept and used.

A committee was formed to examine Corning's innovation process and to use the information from the conference to improve that process. The committee also did benchmarks with other companies known for their innovation, such as 3M. One of the great problems with Corning's process, according to Ed O'Brien, was that the three groups most heavily involved in the process—R&D, manufacturing, and marketing—each had its own language and culture, each had its own methods, and all felt that it was the key link in the process. The challenge was "to get them to work together, exchanging the information they needed to exchange to make the right decisions for the company."

Over the course of several years, they decided on a "stage-gate" approach, taking every new idea through a series of five "diamond gates," at each stage deciding to either go ahead to the next phase or to kill the project because the probability of success was too low. As the process evolved, Corning's Education and Training Directorate was asked to become involved because, according to O'Brien, it was "a teachable process."

At that time O'Brien was the head of the Education and Training Directorate, and he recruited two well-respected, longtime Corning employees to take on the project. Both were selected on the basis of the credibility they had developed in the company over time. Neither was a professional instructor. Bryan Lanahan, one of those instructors, told me, "I'd never taught anything before in my life."

The process was first taught to the company's top six operating officers; once they had blessed it, it was rolled down to lower levels. People were taught as intact teams; that is, to attend the training, the entire development team for a new product had to sign up. Each team was taught the process and then provided with ongoing consulting and coaching until it mastered the process. Within a few years, more than 2,000 people had completed the training and were actively using the new processes, and Corning could say that the innovation process had become institutionalized.

The development of Corning's innovation process, like every major change effort in a large corporation, took a long time. The initial idea for examining how Corning developed new products and for looking at how they could improve that process started with Tom MacAvoy in 1983. The first courses were taught in 1988, and it wasn't until at least 1990 that the innovation process could be called the standard operating procedure for new product development throughout the company.

Lessons from the Corning Experience

Even in the absence of a strong corporate vision and stated long-range goals, managers can discover what is important for the company if they examine the issues that consume the time and attention of top management. They can determine what they think those issues are and then check back with top management to reach agreement on the list. Before starting a new program based on those priorities, they need to find a high-level sponsor—someone who believes in the issue strongly enough to both fund it and publicly state its importance. Each program also requires a champion, a person with the necessary passion to drive the issue and make change happen. Both sponsor and champion must have credibility within the organization. They must be people whose reputations make people take notice: "Well, if Barbara and Fred are driving this, we know it's important and we know it's going to be done right."

A second lesson from the Corning experience, emphasized by both O'Brien and Lanahan, is that the cultural issues will almost always prove to be more formidable barriers than technology or process issues. The need to develop a common language among the participants on a cross-functional team is of prime importance. A one-shot training effort is not going to solve this type of problem. Ongoing consultation and coaching are absolutely necessary to ensure that the content of the training is applied and that the ongoing cultural issues are continually addressed.

The third lesson, and one that is reflected in the Sears and Amoco stories as well, is that major change takes a long time to accomplish. In Corning's case, the innovation process took a full 7 years to be fully implemented, and it is still being refined today, 10 years after Tom MacAvoy's initial mandate.

FORMING THE PARTNERSHIP WITH TOP MANAGEMENT

A major corporate transformation or renewal requires strong leadership from the top. Nothing can take the place of a strong leader with a clear vision of the future who communicates the vision enthusiastically and who "lives the vision." Conventional wisdom says that with this type of strong, committed, visible leadership, a total organizational renewal can be effected in three to five years. Without such leadership, it will take at least a decade, if it ever gets accomplished.

All three companies described here saw clearly that their transformation efforts were tied intimately to the stock of skills and knowledge resident in the company's employees. All of the efforts described were to develop *people.*

In all three companies, human resources and training and development groups acted as change agents. Sears's Kirn, Amoco's Clover, and Corning's O'Brien did not just sit in their corners of the company doing their standard functions of employee relations, recruitment, individual skills training, and the like; they became deeply involved in using their expertise to develop innovative approaches to enabling the types of changes that corporate leaders were seeking. In all of these cases, their work was seen as so critical to the success of the company that they were never asked to provide a separate financial justification for the programs they developed. The programs were seen not as "just another training program" but as an integral part of the companies' renewal efforts.

If you are seeking to help your company's renewal, you need to start by forming a partnership with the company's top management. No matter in what function or capacity you serve your organization, you need to make certain that what you and your group are doing is directly aligned with the company's strategic business directions. In the next chapter, we will examine alternative approaches you can take in forming this partnership.

FIVE

STARTING AT THE TOP: GETTING EVERYONE MOVING IN THE SAME DIRECTION

No single approach to renewal will work for every company. Not every company faces the same situations as Amoco or Sears nor does every company have the same resources for the renewal effort. But if your company is seeking to renew itself, some important lessons from these companies' experiences can guide your efforts. In this chapter, I will present a set of recommended procedures for how a company can ensure that the work being done by various functions, departments, and business units is aligned closely with overall company directions.

Company renewal is much easier to accomplish if there is strong, committed, visible leadership, with the company's leaders working hard to ensure that everyone in the company knows the direction the company is taking—both short and long term—and that every person, every function, and every business unit is closely aligned with that direction. The first approach to company renewal that is discussed is a process that can be used to maximize *individual and organizational learning opportunities,* that is, to help people learn what they need to know in order to meet today's business challenges and to create the company's future success. It is not strictly an educational or training experience, although it will have some of those components. The recommended process is designed to help companies develop a learning environment where people can acquire the knowledge and skills they need for their individual and collective success. This process relies on strong, committed leadership.

Since not every company has the leadership needed to develop the first set of processes, the latter part of this chapter provides a process to help managers in such companies identify the company's strategic directions and then to start aligning their work with those directions. Even in strong companies like Corning, the company's priorities may be buried in the day-to-day work of top management.

STARTING AT THE TOP

To effectively lead a company, its top managers need to ensure that the entire top management team, not just the company's board of directors and operating committee, knows what is happening and where the company is heading and is part of all major decisions. If this is not being done on a regular basis already, managers should consider starting with a weeklong off-site meeting, as Sears did with its Phoenix Group. This should be followed by regularly scheduled meetings, ranging in length from a half-day to two full days, to be held monthly at best or quarterly at worst.

The Initial Top Management Team (TMT) Meeting

What needs to be covered in the initial TMT meeting? The following list of topics can provide a starting point, but no subject should be barred from discussion:

The Current State of the Company:

- Financial results and projections.
- Numbers of employees and near-term employment projections.
- News of upcoming events, for example, new sites, reorganizations.

- Planned major programs, for example, TQM, business reengineering, refitting of an old factory.
- Other major news, for example, updates on labor negotiations, partnership agreements, and so on.

Product/Service and Competitive Information:

- Recently introduced and soon-to-be-introduced products and services.
- New or upcoming announcements from major competitors.
- Announcement and analysis of recent major wins and losses in the marketplace.
- A presentation by a major customer and/or an industry analyst.
- A good sense of what's happening today, and what is projected for the future, in your industry.

The TMT meeting should set overall company directions and provide opportunities for honest questions, answers, and discussions. Suitable amounts of time should be included and structured for both formal and informal discussions. The presentations on the topics listed should not be of the formal "read the charts, thank-you, and good-bye" type. Company leaders should encourage questions, provide explanations that go deeper than the annual report, and engage in a frank and open discussion of where the company is heading, what major roadblocks lie ahead, and how the company plans to overcome or detour around those roadblocks.

In discussions with top executives in some firms, I've noted some strong objections to sharing strategic information with lower levels of management.

"What you're asking us to discuss is highly confidential information. We can't just give it out to everyone, for fear it will end up in the wrong hands."

My response: "We are talking about the top management team in your company—the people who are being charged with making it successful. They need this information to do their jobs effectively. If you feel you can't trust them with the information, you should replace them with people in whom you can put your trust."

Yes, there may be an issue that is at such a sensitive stage, for example, a critical industry partnership negotiation that may be so confidential that any leak could sink the effort, that you dare not discuss it openly. If this occurs, you should state the reasons that you cannot discuss the issue and promise an update at a later meeting.

You may also occasionally have someone on your top management team who indeed cannot be trusted, and you may not know who that person is until sensitive information gets out. But the greater risk is in not giving your management team your trust and the information they need to do their jobs properly.

The initial meeting is also the time to start getting people from various functions, business units, and locations to work together (if you have not already been doing so). Don't structure the meeting so that all of the communication is one-way, from top executives to the audience. If the plan is to have strictly formal presentations, a memo or videotape will save the company and its employees a lot of money and time (but not accomplish your objectives).

Split the group into cross-functional, multilevel teams, and give the teams real problems to work on rather than hypothetical case studies. Team membership should include every level present at the overall meeting, including the CEO. This is not a meeting where top company executives fly in, make their formal presentations, and catch a limousine back to the airport.

What should the teams do? Whatever team assignments are given, they must not be just an exercise but must be reviewed and acted on. For example, team assignments could be to:

- Analyze major competitors, what effects their newest campaigns will have on your business, and what measures you can take to counter the competitors' efforts.
- Plan a new product/service introduction, or review plans that have already been drafted.
- Look at how various functions, business units, or locations have been handling issues such as team-based

pay, quality improvement teams, and employee development; that is, do some internal benchmarking.

- For new business development, brainstorm ideas that cross locations or business units.
- Plan for local announcement/introduction of a major new business initiative, for example, a new market, the introduction of TQM, or activity-based costing.

Teams should report back to the larger group, and the ideas generated should be openly considered and discussed with top managers, who themselves should have been part of the groups. The idea is to get people to know each other, to break down the functional and business unit stovepipes that have been erected over the years, to start creating some synergistic effects in the company's planning, and, yes, to get some real work done.

To get this process started, you will probably have to provide some training during the week. The training may include teamwork skills, management-style assessments, a planning methodology, or other topics that will enable the participants to carry out their team-based assignments. You should also have resource people (internal or external consultants) available to guide the teams' efforts, to provide coaching on newly introduced skills and methodologies, and to facilitate the overall meeting and the team working sessions, if the company's top management does not have these skills.

If this type of meeting—this type of participation and openness—is new to your company, you need to demonstrate your commitment to the new approach. Most people will appreciate your candor in telling them that top management needs their help. But for this to work, you have to play by the ground rules:

- If you want candor in the meetings and want really productive working relationships to result, you cannot stop discussions if they touch a nerve. Telling people that you want to change the way the company works will quickly be seen as a sham if you immediately stop the discussion when it touches on a sensitive issue. *How top management acts during this initial weeklong meet-*

ing will prove to be a better indicator of long-term success than the actual content of the meeting.

- The planning exercises undertaken as part of this initial meeting must be seen as making a difference. If at all possible, decisions should be made on the spot: "Yes, that's a good idea and we will make the changes you have recommended." And there must be follow-through.
- Assignments must be given so that the new working relationships started at the initial meeting, and the new methods introduced, are not forgotten until the next meeting. Give assignments. Set deadlines that are challenging but realistic. Make things happen.

Another objection to this approach that is sometimes heard: "We're talking about a massive investment of time and talent. We can't afford to take the entire top management team out of the office for an entire week. It would be a disaster!"

The response: "If these are the people who are going to determine the future success of your company, you have to invest in their development, just as you invest in new plant and equipment. What is more important to your company than having your entire management team working toward the same goals, working together as a team, and together building the company's future?"

The response to the idea that the company will fall apart if the top team is away from the office for a week is: "If the company is really going to fall apart because the top managers are away from their offices for a week, you have much deeper problems than the lack of coordinated planning. If your company is going to end up in ashes because your top management team cannot be absent from the fire fighting for a week, you had better start a very good fire prevention program immediately—before starting the TMT meetings."

This initial meeting should have a few more ground rules:

- Everyone on the top management team must be required to attend. A few people may have pressing *per-*

sonal reasons that they cannot attend, but, in general, no exceptions should be made. Experience at many companies shows that the initial meeting will be attended with a lot of grumbling and complaints. But if the week is planned and executed properly, you will create a tremendous energy and participants will clamor to attend the next meetings.

- The meeting must be held off-site to minimize distractions. Companies that have tried to hold the meeting at their headquarters offices find that the sessions keep getting disrupted by secretaries delivering messages, by field personnel who "take a few minutes" to check in with one office or another with those few minutes turning into hours, and by home office personnel who go back to their offices at breaks to check messages and aren't seen for the rest of the day. Holding the meeting off-site delivers the message that the meeting is important and that the participants' focus is to be on the meeting and not on "business as usual."

- No matter how well planned the program's content, no matter how excellent the speakers and their messages, at least half of the value to participants will come from the informal interactions they have outside the formal activities. It is therefore vital that you allow time for these informal actions to take place—over meals, during breaks, after hours, and so on. You should also structure some informal or recreational time during the latter part of the week so that people have time to talk, to explore ideas, and to build personal relationships outside the meeting's formal structure.

Continuing the Work of the Initial Meeting

After the initial meeting, the work of the group needs to continue. This is best accomplished by reconvening the group on a regular (monthly to quarterly) basis for sessions ranging from a half-day to two full days, depending on what needs to be handled in each session. These periodic sessions should cover:

- Updates on information given at the initial meeting.
- New developments.
- Follow-up on action items taken at earlier meetings.
- Planning for new actions.
- Further developmental activities for the group (see Table 5.1 for a list of possible topics).

The best way of ensuring that these TMT meetings will be valued by the participants is to include them in the planning of the meetings. As participants get to know each other, they will develop relationships and will have their own ideas for the meeting agendas. If the initial meeting went as planned, you will find a large store of enthusiasm for the process and a wealth of valuable ideas for future meetings.

Table 5.1

Possible Topics for Top Management Learning Activities

■ High Performance Teams	■ Motivation
■ Empowerment	■ Change Agents
■ Learning Organizations	■ Personal / Work Life
■ Alliances & Partnerships	■ Continuous Improvement
■ Creativity	■ Globalization
■ Technology	■ Systems Thinking
■ Leadership	■ Organizational Design
■ Strategy	■ Diversity
■ Interunit Planning & Cooperation	■ Team Learning
■ Customer Focus	■ Environmental Concerns
■ Coaching	■ Health & Safety
■ Communications	■ Constructive Conflict
■ Negotiations Skills	■ Benchmarking
■ Planning Methodologies	■ Strategic Thinking
■ Visioning	■ Managing Change

Adapted from Amoco Management Learning Center materials.

Another vital aspect of this whole process is to enable communications among the participants between meetings. Do you have an internal electronic mail system? Do you have teleconferencing facilities? What about computer-based bulletin boards and conference capabilities? These can be important tools to enable participants to continue their work together between meetings.

Moving Learning through the Organization

If the TMT meetings prove successful, their value to the participants and to the company as a whole will be plainly evident. The next step is to spread the benefits of this approach across the company. This can be done in many different ways.

Participants in the top management group should be encouraged, if not expected, to share their newly acquired learning with their own employees. Knowledge and learning are not the sole province of top management; every employee will benefit, and the overall company will benefit, from learning about the company's strategic business directions, about the company's competitors, about new plans and opportunities. New ideas and the solutions to current business challenges can and should come from all levels of the company.

One of the topics of the TMT meetings should be how to move the learning from its sessions down to lower levels of the organization. This can be done on a group-by-group basis by each member of the top management team or, better, can be done collectively, as with the programs of the Amoco Management Learning Center. Just as the TMT had goals of breaking down functional and business unit stovepipes, so a cross-functional, multilevel learning approach can do the same at lower levels of the company.

The Amoco model presented in Chapter 4 is outstanding for this purpose. Its major elements include:

- An annual weeklong program for the top 7 percent of the company's managers.
- Participants from every function and business unit, including major business partners.
- Each year's program built on the company's major directions and themes as well as on the content of the previous year's program.

- Top company management participation in the program through formal presentations along with informal discussion and personal reflections.
- Each program's learning elements related to understanding the company as well as skill building to enable participants to share in building the company's future.
- Participants assigned to multilevel, multifunctional teams and given real work to do during the week.
- Coaching and reinforcement of skills taught in the formal sessions provided to work teams during the week.
- Communications systems established to enable participants to continue their work, and the relationships they have built, after they return to their offices.

Let's add a few more elements to the Amoco model that will make it even more effective:

- Participant Selection: Amoco selects participants to allow for a broad representation of functions, business units, and geographies in each group of 70 or 80 participants. Groups that are starting to work together or are already working as a team should be allowed to attend as an intact group. During the weeklong program, they can be split up for the various team assignments. The groups and the company will benefit more if all members of an individual team receive the same instruction at the same time and, therefore, can start applying their learning together at the completion of the session.
- Coaching and Reinforcement: During each weeklong session, Amoco staff members are available to provide coaching and reinforcement for new skills and behaviors while participants are practicing their newly acquired learning in the group exercises. Coaching and reinforcement should continue to be available after the completion of the program. Newly acquired skills take time to master, usually more than a week of practice.

The chances of success will be greatly improved if the types of assistance made available during the program continue afterward through the use of internal or external consultants.

- Follow-Through: The Amoco Management Learning Center has received a lot of feedback from participants: how valuable the sessions have been, how participants have used their newly acquired skills and knowledge back in their home business units, and how new relationships formed during the program have led to new business ideas. But these results, although impressive, have been mostly serendipitous, resulting from the enthusiasm and good intentions of the participants. Follow-through will be more likely to happen if participants negotiate an informal contract with their managers, as part of their job plans—before or immediately after attending the program—which states exactly how each participant will use the learnings from the session to improve individual, group, or company performance.

Needed: Strong, Committed, Visible Leadership

These approaches cannot be successful without strong, committed, visible leadership. If the company's leaders have not recognized that the future of the company lies not just in their own hands but in those of every employee, if they have not recognized that the transformation of the company can only come from learning by all employees at all levels, there is little point to starting the TMT meeting process. Nothing will sink the company's collective ship faster than to promise a new approach only to abandon it before the hull is completely sealed and the engines installed.

If your company does not have this type of leadership, don't try to implement the programs just described. But this does not mean that you, as a senior or midlevel manager, cannot work to make a real difference in the performance of the group or function you manage. Next we'll explore some options you have even in the absence of strong company leadership and the TMT meeting process just described.

FINDING YOUR WAY WITHOUT STRONG, COMMITTED, VISIBLE LEADERSHIP AT THE TOP

Your starting point is developing your knowledge of the company's business and your role within that business. It doesn't matter whether you are managing a business unit or a function, whether you are in a line or staff job, whether or not you feel that your work is directly related to the company's finished products and services—if you understand how your work fits into the company's overall strategies, you will be better able to align your work with those strategic business directions.

Knowledge of the overall company will also help you establish your credibility with top management, your peers, and your employees. When it comes time to put ideas into action, to make a capital request, to propose a new product line or business unit, to suggest a new way of organizing, the chances of success will be much higher if you can demonstrate a rock-solid understanding of the company's business and can show how the ideas will positively affect the company's overall results.

UNDERSTANDING YOUR COMPANY'S BUSINESS

You can develop your understanding of your company's business in many ways. The optimal way of doing this is to consult the company organizational chart, which, ideally, the company has prepared to illustrate all of its business processes as well as its internal and external value chains. Such a chart makes it clear how the company runs its business; how it creates value for its customers; and how all functions, all business units, and all customers and suppliers fit into the picture. Once this has been done, the knowledge must be shared throughout the company so that all employees understand how they fit into the picture, how their individual and collective work adds value. With this understanding, employees can easily see whether the work they are doing, the decisions they are making, are adding value. With this broad view, employees will not suffer from functional myopia.

But what if your company has not invested in charting its business processes and its internal and external value chains? What if company leaders do not communicate their views of the future to the company's employees? Even then, there are many steps you can take to develop your own understanding of your company, how it works, and where it is heading. Sources for these types of information include:

- Public information.
- Internal training programs.
- Personal research within the company.
- Personal research outside the company.

Table 5.2 lists many of the activities that fall into each of these categories.

Some of these ideas may seem very obvious, but experience shows that few people ever take advantage of the many opportunities they have to learn more about their own companies.

How Companies Can Enable the Sharing of Company-Related Information

Becoming knowledgeable about your company is much easier if the company takes steps to make these types of information available to its employees (see Table 5.3). Does your company:

- Send its annual report to all employees? Don't employees need to know as much about the company as stockholders?
- Publish internal newsletters to share company news, for example, changes in organizations and personnel, new contracts?
- Have a company library stocked with all company literature? The library should be accessible to employees before, during, and after business hours. It should also include a wide range of industry and professional journals and competitive information.
- Maintain bulletin boards (real or electronic) on which it regularly displays company literature, press clippings, and so on?

Table 5.2
Gaining Knowledge about Your Company

Public Information Sources

- Read the company's annual report.
- Read the company's 10-K filing for the Securities and Exchange Commission.
- Read all available company literature.
- Attend the company's annual stockholders' meeting.
- Read the company's press releases and the items it receives from clipping services.
- Read professional and industry journals and magazines.
- Search databases at your local public or college library for articles about the company.
- Attend meetings at which company officials are speaking.
- Become a company spokesperson for community organizations and visiting groups.

Internal Training Programs

- Attend, or review materials from, company orientation programs. Look for materials from various programs developed by different functions and business units.
- Attend one of the company's sales training courses.
- Read the company's sales literature and its analyses of its competitors.
- Attend an industry trade show. Spend time at your company's exhibit and at those of your company's competitors.

Personal Research within the Company

- Have lunch with people from other parts of the company. Ask them about their work.
- Spend time with a salesperson, a customer service rep, a plant manager.
- Attend a staff meeting of another function or business unit.
- Invite people from other functions or business units to your staff meetings.
- Serve on a company-wide or business unit planning committee.
- Help plan a company-wide event: a picnic, a product announcement, the United Way campaign.
- If you have the necessary skills, volunteer to facilitate a planning meeting for another function or business unit.
- Become a mentor to people from other parts of the company.
- Coach a cross-functional team.

(continued)

Table 5.2
Continued

Personal Research Outside the Company

- Talk with a customer.
- Talk with a supplier.
- If you hear of a problem that a customer or supplier is having with the company, take personal responsibility for following up and resolving the issue.
- Volunteer to serve on a benchmarking committee visiting other companies.
- Volunteer to host a visiting benchmarking committee from another company.
- Attend an industry conference.
- Attend briefings by industry analysts.

Table 5.3
How Companies Can Share Company-Related Information

- Send the annual report to all employees.
- Publish internal newsletters to share company news.
- Establish a company library stocked with all company literature.
- Maintain bulletin boards to display company literature, press clippings, and so on.
- Involve a wide range of employees in public events.
- Invite a wide range of employees to important briefings being made to the company.

- Involve a wide range of employees in public events?
- Invite a wide range of employees, from many levels, functions, and business units, to in-house briefings by industry analysts? Does the company broadcast major company presentations to all employee sites, or at least make audio- or videotapes of such presentations widely available to employees?

Today's smart companies recognize that their near- and long-term success depends on the knowledge and skills of their employees. Therefore, they try to facilitate employees' access to the information they need. Unfortunately, many companies, rather than enabling employee learning, actually erect barriers to it.

Barriers to Learning about the Company

Barriers to learning take many forms, including:

- *Secrecy:* Some companies maintain an atmosphere of secrecy around what the company is doing. Although some types of information certainly demand secrecy, many companies won't even make information available to employees that is already in the public domain, for example, information reported on the company's SEC (Securities and Exchange Commission) filings, information contained in the annual report, or information released to stockholders at the annual meetings.
- *Control:* In companies whose management philosophy is to strictly control employees' time and activities, managers may not allow time or give opportunities for employees to even talk with each other, except in strictly controlled situations.
- *Paranoia:* "Why do you need to know that?" "Who do you work for? I don't work for her. I'm not going to help you."
- *Stovepipes:* By maintaining rigid hierarchies and stovepipe organizations, where the organization is so structured that communications can take place only at the tops of the various functions or units, many companies ensure that little learning will take place by those who are located further down the funnels.
- *Lack of Communications Tools:* If the company is widely geographically dispersed, and it provides no means for people to get to know each other or even find each other, many opportunities for sharing of knowledge will be missed.

(Table 5.4 provides a brief list of the barriers to learning.)

Table 5.4
Barriers to Learning about the Company

- Secrecy
- Control
- Paranoia
- Stovepipes
- Lack of Communications Tools

Many companies regularly conduct "employee attitude surveys." Usually conducted by an external consultant, these surveys ask employees a wide variety of questions relating to their satisfaction with their jobs and with their employers. I have yet to see a single one of these surveys where "poor communications" was not among the top two or three issues listed by employees—they feel that the company's management doesn't tell them what is happening in the company. Whether real or imagined, employee communications, that is, the spreading of knowledge about the company's directions, results, changes, and so on, remains one of the greatest challenges for virtually every company.

In companies where such barriers exist, they have probably developed over time and will take time and concerted effort to overcome. Again, this takes strong, committed, visible leadership.

Spreading Your Learning

Once you have succeeded in gaining the requisite knowledge about your company's directions and how your own and your group's work can contribute to company goals, *don't keep it a secret!* If company renewal efforts are to be successful, it will take a concerted effort by all employees. Knowledge that has value for other employees should be shared with them. Knowledge is unlike other economic goods: You can give it away and still keep it. If employees are expected to align themselves with overall company goals and their own group's goals, they need to know about those goals.

ALIGNING YOUR WORK WITH THE COMPANY'S STRATEGIC BUSINESS DIRECTIONS

Knowing where the company is headed makes it much easier to align individual and group work with those directions. Following the preceding methods should have provided the necessary information. The next challenge is to ensure that individual and organizational planning and action contribute directly to the achievement of the company's goals while also meeting personal and local goals. Doing this properly requires several different views of individual and group goals:

- Alignment with the stated directions of the parent company.
- Alignment with internal and external customers and suppliers.
- Alignment with other internal groups and business units.
- Internal consistency—ensuring that work is consistent with the stated goals.
- What other opportunities exist that might cross traditional boundaries but might contribute to group and company goals?

Alignment with Company Directions

Sometimes a functional or business unit manager will read the overall company goals and disagree with them. "We're doing fine. We're making our numbers. As long as we are making our required contribution to the company's bottom line, we really don't need to worry about the directions we receive from on high."

This is a surefire way of derailing your company's renewal efforts. If every function and business unit goes off in its own direction, no real forward progress can be made by the overall company. Differences of opinion on the company's direction should have been resolved during the planning process. Once the direction is set, it is your responsibility to align your function's or business unit's work with that direction. Ask yourself these questions:

- How do my group's (or function's or business unit's) goals align with those of the company?
- Are changes required in my group's goals to support the company goals?
- Are there new individual and group goals we should add to support the company's goals?
- Does my group have goals that will work at cross-purposes with the stated company goals?
- If we were to start from scratch in developing my group's goals, what would we do to support the company's goals?

If these questions have been answered, and there are still some goals that are vital to your group but that may be misaligned with the company's goals, you should negotiate with your superiors. Maybe company goals need some alterations. Maybe your group's goals will still need some changes. The alternative is to ignore the company's goals and follow your own path—and this is certain to defeat the whole effort to get everyone moving in the same direction.

Alignment with Internal and External Customers and Suppliers

You and your group do not work in a vacuum. You have customers and suppliers, whether these are internal or external to your company. How is the work done by your group, whether that results in a product or a service, used by your customers? How do your group's requirements affect the work of your suppliers? Although it is certainly a company responsibility to chart the overall value chains and business processes of the company, you can do things to better understand *your* piece of the business even if the company has not made the effort to develop the knowledge for you. When you talk to your suppliers, do the following:

- Explain what you are doing with the materials or services or information they supply to you.
- Ask them how their business works. How do they produce their goods, services, or information? How does the work they do for you fit into their overall business?
- Explore with them: Are there possible synergies where you can add value to each other's work?

Change hats. Ask these same questions of your customers:

- What are your customers doing with the goods, services, or information you supply?
- Ask your customers how their businesses work. Explain your business to them.
- Explore with them: Are there possible synergies where you can add value to each other's work?

People who start talking regularly with their customers and suppliers often find immediate benefits from seemingly small or inconsequential changes that can make a real difference in the workings and costs of both groups. And these minor changes can often have significant effects on the company's overall results.

Extending Your Reach

Once the analysis of how your work fits into that of your internal customers and suppliers is completed, you should extend this examination to other parts of your company with which you may not have direct links but with which nonetheless you may find synergies. In this way, you not only will be working to align your own group's work with overall company goals but also will be helping other units and functions accomplish this as well.

- How does your work and theirs fit together in terms of the company's overall goals?
- Do you have customers and suppliers in common? If so, could you possibly work with them jointly to find

new opportunities for efficiency or for new sales? Are there customers or suppliers in your sphere of influence that might be of interest and value to these other units?

- Do you understand the other units' goals and how they might affect your own? Do they understand yours?
- Are these other units having difficulties meeting some of their own or the company's goals, and could your group help in some way?
- Are there opportunities, within the company or in the market, that neither of you could fill individually but might be able to jointly?

The key, again, is to share your knowledge with others and for them to share theirs with you. Only by such sharing will you be able to uncover new opportunities that have never before been considered.

Matching Words and Actions

Just as individual functions and business units often pursue their own goals, even when these local goals may suboptimize the larger goals of their company, so this type of behavior may also be found within your own function or business unit. Too often business leaders make statements about how they want employees to work, but they don't look at how work is really being done, what behaviors are being measured and rewarded within the company, whether their management techniques will really accomplish the goals they have set out, or whether those techniques actually counteract the goals.

- Does everyone in your group understand not only their individual goals but also the larger group goals and the even larger company goals?
- Are internal measurements and rewards keyed to the larger goals? Are employees being measured and rewarded not only for achievement of their individual goals but also for contribution to the larger goals?

- Is your group, and the group's work, structured in such a way that employees are encouraged to share their knowledge with others? Do you provide opportunities for the sharing of knowledge?

Finding Other Opportunities

Many companies miss very important opportunities to serve their existing customers, or to sign up new customers, because emerging market demands do not fall easily into any single existing line of business. Business managers need to understand not only the capabilities of their own staffs but also the wealth of resources that exist throughout the company. They need to keep their eyes open for ways in which they can utilize other company resources in conjunction with their own to meet customer needs and to exploit market opportunities that are beyond the scope of their individual group's responsibilities or capabilities. Only in this way will they be able to address new opportunities that do not fall neatly into their existing businesses.

Companies must work to develop a spirit of entrepreneurship within their own ranks, encouraging employees to seek out new opportunities in the market and to respond to those opportunities even when they do not fit within the strict bounds of any existing line of business. To do this, employees must develop a broad understanding of their own businesses as well as the capabilities and resources available throughout the company.

STARTING AT THE TOP . . .

If you are part of your company's top management, there are many ideas within this chapter, and elsewhere in this book, on how you can ensure that your employees obtain the knowledge and skills they need to be effective in their jobs. But even while you work on strategies for disseminating knowledge throughout your company, you must also be aware of your own learning needs. As stated in an earlier chapter, this involves uncovering your "unconscious ignorance," that is, discovering what you don't know, what you need to learn. One of the things you can do, which can be very empowering to your employees, is to publicly state that you don't have all the answers, that the company needs to tap into the knowledge and skills of all employees.

If you are not in the top management tier of your company, you still need to learn where that top tier is headed in order to ensure that your own and your group's work is correctly aligned with the company's strategic directions. If you want to be really credible with your company's top management, ask yourself these questions:

- Do you understand the overall mission and goals of the company? Of the executives to whom you report? Do you know what keeps the boss awake at night?
- Do you know the company's markets? Why do people buy your company's goods and services? Who are your major competitors? What are your sources of competitive advantage? Uniqueness? Price? Service excellence?
- Is it "our company" or "their company"? Do you take ownership of the business issues for which you have responsibility? Is it "their problem" or "our problem"?
- Do you speak the bosses' language? Or are all of your memos and presentations full of the jargon of your own profession or specialty?
- Can you understand top management's perspective and not take all decisions personally?
- Can you foresee the principal issues that concern top management? Can you respond to those issues in ways that will satisfy those managers' business concerns?

Whether your acquisition of knowledge comes from learning activities designed or sponsored by top management, or whether you do it all on your own, the types of learning activities discussed in this chapter will help you build your own credibility with top management. And just as you work hard to develop your own knowledge, you should also be working hard to develop the knowledge of those who work for you.

. . . AND WORKING DOWN

Don't be selfish with your hard-won knowledge. A primary responsibility for managers at all levels today is the development of their employees. You should start by modeling the behaviors you are trying to develop in your employees:

- Do you want them to share their knowledge with one another? Start by sharing yours with them.
- Do you want them to read industry and professional journals? Show them that you are doing this type of reading and circulate articles of interest to others in your group.
- Do you want them to coach one another? Start by doing some coaching yourself, or, better, ask some of them to coach you.
- Do you want them to become more involved with your group's customers and suppliers? Show them that you yourself are becoming more involved. Invite customers and suppliers, internal or external, to make presentations to your group. Assign individuals to be liaisons with other groups/functions/business units and have them report back on what they have learned.
- Do you want them to work more closely together? Assign projects to teams rather than to individuals.
- Do you want them to work more cooperatively together? Cross-train them on various department functions and responsibilities.

At all levels of management, you must ensure that all employees—across all levels, functions, and business units—have knowledge of the company's directions, its short- and long-term goals, and how each individual's and each group's work contributes to the attainment of those goals. Only then can you expect employees to align their personal and group goals with the company's larger goals. Only then can employees judge whether the work they are doing and the decisions they are making are in the best interests of the overall company. Only then will employees work to not just optimize local goals but to balance their local needs with those of the larger organization.

SIX

FINDING YOUR STARTING POINT

Any journey to company renewal must start from where the company and its employees are today, but most companies have trouble finding that starting point. People tend to hide problems, knowing that their managers would rather hear good news than bad, often leading the company to imagine that things are better than they really are. In the case of a crisis, when someone pulls up the rug under which all the dirt has been swept, things may appear worse than they really are; for example, many of the skills and knowledge needed for company renewal may already exist but have never been identified or utilized. False assumptions on either side of the scale can lead to disaster—to win a race you must know where the starting line is located.

As you start your journey, you must know both your destination and your starting point before selecting the best route to get from here to there. With effective short- and long-range planning processes, the company's destination, or at least the direction in which it wants to head, has been defined. Before the optimal path can be chosen, you need to assess where the company is now; otherwise, you may choose an inappropriate path, may miss a crucial turn, or may retread paths that have already been traveled.

This assessment must be brutally honest. Too often companies have developed procedures and practices that, though they may have worked over the years, are consuming human and monetary resources that could be put to better use in other ways, or they are just so cumbersome that they prevent any real progress toward the company's renewal goals. Digital Equipment Corporation, IBM, and other high-tech companies, for example, grew so rapidly for decades that the easiest solution to many problems was to hire people and throw them at problems until they were solved. These tactics worked, so long as the growth rates continued—nothing hides problems better than a 20 percent annual growth rate. But when their markets stopped growing at these tremendous rates, and competitors ate into their market shares, many high-tech companies found themselves burdened with more personnel than they needed and systems and business practices that were neither efficient nor effective in meeting the needs of new market realities.

High-tech companies are not alone in suffering from these phenomena. With the coming of competition to formerly regulated industries, such as telecommunications and electric utilities, many companies found that although their long-held business practices worked, they could not compete effectively with new competitors who were designing their organizations, systems, and procedures from scratch to take advantage of the latest methodologies and technologies. Regulation was a two-edged sword: It limited the returns on investment allowed for these industries, but it also allowed returns on even unwise investments and cost-plus accounting for even the most outmoded business practices.

In doing research for this book, I had made an appointment with the director of organizational learning at one of the "Baby Bells." When I arrived for the appointment, in a 30-story downtown office building, I went to the receptionist to sign in as a visitor. I gave the person's name and was asked if I had her telephone number. I said that I didn't have it handy. The receptionist then spent nearly 30 minutes trying to locate the person—in an on-line directory, in multiple paper directories, and by making calls to various departments. We found the person only when I dug through my briefcase and found her number myself. No, the person had not just moved into the building; she had been in this same location for several years.

If I had called this same Baby Bell's directory assistance in this same city, I would have received the number for even a new listing in a matter of seconds. The company's internal directory assistance function was badly in need of help.

Where should companies start with their assessment process? Since the company's renewal is going to be based primarily on its people, and their knowledge and skills, then the assessment should start with looking at the practices that most directly affect the company's employees, with the knowledge and skill requirements of the company's people. Without paying primary attention to the "people issues," companies usually find that their strategies for dealing with technology and systems issues do not yield the hoped-for results.

REQUIREMENTS FOR THE FUTURE

Before starting to assess whether they have the knowledge and skill base needed for future success, companies must first define the desired end result—what knowledge and skills must the company have to succeed in the future? Only with this information can companies start to assess their current stocks and, as a result, determine what they need to do to get from the current state to the desired future state. Although some basic categories are prerequisites for future success regardless of industry, as will be discussed, each company's overall requirements will be somewhat different. To determine those requirements, companies must start with their stated goals, both for the short term and long term.

Translating Goals into Knowledge and Skill Requirements

To translate the company's goals into knowledge and skill requirements, you must ask questions such as:

- Is the company planning to "go global"? What new knowledge and skills will employees need to do business in the global community?

- Is the company planning to adopt "agile manufacturing"? What does this mean in terms of the skills and knowledge needed by workers and managers?
- Will customer service be a hallmark of the company's future goals? What knowledge and skills will employees need to differentiate the company's customer service from that provided by its competitors?
- Are the company's future products or services going to be based on new materials or technologies? What knowledge and skills will employees need to take advantage of technological advances?

Let's start by looking at some basic requirements that together form a solid infrastructure for a company's transformation or renewal efforts. In *Re-Educating the Corporation: Foundations for the Learning Organization,*[1] I described a set of five foundations that together form a strong basis for any organizational renewal effort.

Please note: The remainder of this chapter will summarize a much more extensive discussion contained in *Re-Educating the Corporation: Foundations for the Learning Organization.* Readers of that book may want to skim this chapter for some new examples. Others may want to move on to Chapter 7.

THE FIVE FOUNDATIONS

For any organizational renewal effort to succeed, these foundations must be in place:

1. Strong, committed, visible leadership.
2. Basic skills for "thinking literacy."
3. Overcoming functional myopia.
4. Building and sustaining effective learning teams.
5. Managers as enablers.

Let's briefly review these foundations and see how each may affect the company's renewal effort. If you find that your company is lacking one or more of the foundations, you must start your journey to renewal by building or strengthening them. As will be explained in the following discussion, fulfilling these prerequisites to the renewal effort can itself be classified as transformational learning.

TRANSLATING THE FIVE FOUNDATIONS INTO KNOWLEDGE AND SKILL REQUIREMENTS

The following discussion of the five foundations includes a series of questions or statements designed to provide an indication of the presence or strength of each of a company's foundations. We will examine each of these questions and the implications of a negative response for the company's learning needs as well as other collateral changes that may be necessary to build or shore up each foundation area. The procedure for this analysis is as follows:

- Step 1: Identify the goal behavior that is either missing or not being demonstrated sufficiently well.
- Step 2: Identify possible indicators of the deficit.
- Step 3: Identify the knowledge and skills requirements to attain the goal behavior.

Lack of knowledge and skill requirements may not be the only causes of the deficit. Other potential causes include:

- Managerial practice that bars the desired changes in behavior.
- Measurement and reward systems that support old behaviors instead of the desired new behaviors.
- Inappropriate organizational design.
- Policies and procedures that prohibit new work methods.
- Inadequate support systems and technology.
- Misalignment of local goals with company goals.

Each of these factors, as well as others, can inhibit or accelerate the company's renewal process. (See Figure 6.1.)

Figure 6.1
The Company Renewal Process

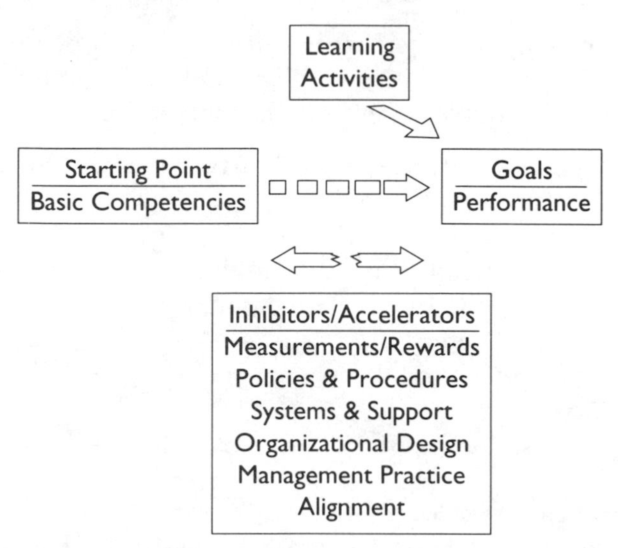

Although organizational renewal is primarily accomplished through people and knowledge, training is not the *only* potential solution to be considered. If the cause of the problem is not a "learning deficit," training, no matter how good, how long, or for how many people, will not solve the problem.

STRONG, COMMITTED, VISIBLE LEADERSHIP

Without leadership, no change is going to happen. Most people are willing to change old habits and work methods if they know that company leadership is serious and committed to making the change happen. How can you tell whether this foundation is present in your company? Without it, the changes you have made to your planning process will not have been successful. The following statements will provide a good indication of whether the needed leadership is in place:

- We have a well-defined, easily understood vision for the entire company.
- There is total agreement on the vision across all levels, functions, and divisions.

- All company leaders are committed to the transformation effort and are committed to seeing it through.
- Company management has developed thorough plans to implement the renewal effort and has committed sufficient resources to ensure the plan's success.
- The renewal effort spans all parts of the company with no group being exempt.

Does your company have the required leadership? Let's look at how one company, and one leader, built this foundation for his company's renewal efforts.

Leadership for Change at Ameritech

With the breakup of the "Ma Bell" monopoly of the telephone business in the mid-1980s, Ameritech was left as one of the regional operating companies, or Baby Bells, encompassing Illinois Bell and four other Midwestern Bell companies. Looking to the future, Ameritech chairman and CEO Bill Weiss saw that the future would have to be very different from the past. For several years he tried the old approach of incremental change, but he saw that it just wasn't going to achieve the results he knew the company needed. Going to the board of directors, he received the mandate he had sought—to remake the corporation.

Weiss started with an off-site planning meeting for his management committee, the company's top seven executives. He asked each one to write a vision statement for the company in the form of a magazine article that would appear five years later. The exercise revealed that there was little consensus on the future directions for the company or what needed to be done to succeed in the future. Weiss divided the group into teams and gave them a homework assignment—to "develop white papers on the company's most important strategic options. They were to form leadership agendas and also to speculate on what would happen if nothing was done."[2] The exercises were later expanded to include the company's top 30 executives. Weiss's agenda: "We are going to creatively disassemble and rebuild Ameritech."

The process was not an easy one for any of the participants, including Weiss. Many people left the company because they could not agree with the changes being made. Weiss acted as a leader, doing himself everything that he was asking of his employees. For example, he participated fully in an outdoor team-building program. As reported:

> In the wall-climbing exercise, Weiss was grabbed by the scruff of his neck and the seat of his pants and dumped unceremoniously over the top. He then leaned over and extended his hand to help haul the next person over. "When I saw Bill's ass go over the wall, that's when I knew this was for real," remembers one executive.[3]

Before Weiss started the renewal process with his radical agenda for change, Ameritech would not have been able to answer affirmatively to the leadership indicators listed previously. At the end of the process, they certainly could.

Was all the pain of change worth the investment? Weiss refers to a group of 120 executives who participated in a business planning exercise as part of the change effort: "Those people own this business in a way I have never seen before. They were so committed that they were unstoppable."[4]

Radical change often requires radical solutions. And radical change will not take place without the strong, committed, visible leadership typified by Ameritech's Bill Weiss.

Building the Knowledge and Skills Needed for Leadership

Table 6.1 lists the five desired behaviors that indicate the presence of a strong foundation of strong, committed, visible leadership. For each of these behaviors is listed one or more possible indicators of inadequacy in this behavior and how each might be translated into knowledge and skill requirements. Other learning-related barriers may well be present in your company. Your analysis should include whatever factors you see as inhibiting your own renewal.

Table 6.1

Assessing Learning Needs for Foundation 1: Strong, Committed, Visible Leadership

Desired Behavior	Indicators of Deficit	Knowledge /Skill Requirements
We have a well-defined, easily understood vision for the entire company.	1. Leaders don't understand the need for a vision.	1. Educate leaders on why a vision is needed.
	2. Leaders don't understand how to develop a vision.	2A. Skills to build a vision. 2B. Knowledge of factors affecting the company's future.
	3. Leaders unable to build a consensus around a vision.	3A. Skills to build consensus. 3B. Conflict-resolution skills. 3C. Negotiations skills.
There is total agreement on the vision across all levels, functions, and divisions.	1. Company employees don't understand the importance of a company vision.	1. Communications skills to demonstrate the importance of the vision.
	2. Leaders "talk" but don't "live" the vision.	2. Leadership and communications skills.
	3. There is little consensus on the company's direction anywhere in the company.	3A. Leadership skills. 3B. Consensus-building skills.

All company leaders are committed to the vision and to seeing it through.	1. Top company management has not involved leaders from all levels and functions of the company.	1. Leadership and communications skills.
	2. Actions don't follow words.	2. Skills to demonstrate commitment through action (walking the talk).
	3. Employees resist, or erect barriers to, change.	3A. Negotiations skills. 3B. Other methods of removing barriers.
Company management has developed thorough plans to implement the renewal effort and has committed sufficient resources to ensure the plan's success.	1. Implementation plans not included in vision development.	1. Learn the importance of implementation planning, and how to do it.
	2. Implementation plans missing critical elements, e.g., building employees' knowledge and skills needed to make the vision a reality.	2. Learn full range of factors that will affect the successful achievement of the vision.
	3. Leaders not willing to commit the resources necessary to enable the vision.	3. Learn that a vision without the means to accomplish it is as bad as, or worse than, no vision at all.

(continued)

Table 6.1
Continued

Desired Behavior	Indicators of Deficit	Knowledge /Skill Requirements
The renewal effort spans all parts of the company, with no group being exempt.	1. Exemptions from the vision and plans are given to particular groups, functions, or divisions.	1A. Learn the need for comprehensive planning. 1B. Learn consequences of granting exemptions.
	2. Lack of understanding of total internal and external value chains and how exempting some parts affects others.	2. Develop understanding of company's value chain and interrelatedness of various groups, functions, and divisions.

When Learning Isn't the Problem

The leadership and associated skill and knowledge requirements listed in Table 6.1 can enable and facilitate the development of the strong, committed, visible leadership required for the company's renewal effort. Other factors can also inhibit the company's renewal process.

- If leadership is pushing for new behaviors but measurement and reward systems continue to reinforce old behaviors, little progress will be made. For example, this often happens when companies introduce cross-functional teamwork to establish a concurrent engineering program or to implement TQM or other programs. If measurement and reward systems remain keyed to *individual* achievement, teamwork goals may be undermined as individual team members strive to demonstrate their personal achievements, so as to maximize their personal rewards.
- If policies and procedures continue to bar new ways of working, even the best-intentioned efforts may fail. For example, an external vendor may be able to provide a timely, cost-effective solution to a particular company need, but if company policy places so many legal requirements on the external vendor that it cannot afford to do business with the company, your need won't be met. Or if the company's procurement requirements burden the vendor with so many extraneous costs that it must raise its price, the solution may no longer be cost-effective.
- If systems and support services make cross-functional cooperation impossible or difficult, goals may not be achieved. For example, different technical systems being used by manufacturing and engineering departments may make timely sharing of information all but impossible. There have also been cases where a European division of a company lost a multimillion dollar sale because the person who could have closed the sale

belonged to a U.S. support group and was barred from overseas travel because it wasn't related to U.S. business goals.

- Finally, if one or more business units are moving off in their own directions, which may be at odds with corporate business directions, they may achieve their own business goals but may forestall the achievement of overall corporate goals. "The rest of the company may be yielding to the pressure to gain ISO 9000 certification, but we haven't had a single customer ask us about it, so why waste the time and resources?" This myopic view may bar other company units from winning business from customers who require the entire company to be ISO 9000 certified.

Related factors also can accelerate the renewal process, such as:

- If the company has cost-effective, easy-to-use communications systems (voice, data, video/image) in place to facilitate the sharing of information and ideas, team communications will be facilitated.
- If management encourages cross-functional collaboration and teamwork, and coaches employees on new skills learned in training programs, the change process will happen more rapidly and be more effective in its implementation.
- If employees are measured and rewarded not just on local goals but also on how much they contribute to overall company goals, alignment will be much more easily accomplished.

In many companies, the building of a company vision has taken a backseat to survival. If a company is constantly in fire-fighting mode, if each day's agenda is full of life-threatening emergencies, company leaders may never have the opportunity to sit down to discuss a company vision, even if they feel it is important.

> Former U. S. President Dwight D. Eisenhower once said that only two types of papers ever reached his desk, those

> marked "urgent" and those marked "important." He spent so much time on urgent matters, he complained, that he never got to what was important.

Building a vision for the company and getting all parts of the company aligned with that vision must be a top priority for company leaders.

Another common problem is that the company's leaders don't "live" the company's values and vision. Often, to make the vision real, leaders must make a notable "act of commitment" to demonstrate the importance and reality of the vision.

> Biogen chairman Jim Vincent decided several years ago that the company needed to have a "Values Statement" to guide the company's future. The company spent considerable time and effort involving employees in the development of the statement and finally published it, communicating it to all employees through a series of meetings. Despite all of the communications around the statement, it didn't become real until the fall of 1994. (The full text of the Biogen Values Statement appears in Appendix A.)
>
> One of Biogen's two major near-term research and development efforts didn't work out. Clinical trials of a new drug just didn't yield the results the company was hoping for. Despite the dedicated work of a group of 70 to 80 employees over a six- to seven-year period, Biogen had to make a difficult decision to abandon work on the new drug.
>
> When the decision was made, Chairman Jim Vincent and COO Jim Tobin called a company-wide meeting to announce the decision and to *honor* the team that had done the work. There were no recriminations, no announcements of firings or layoffs. In honoring the team, Vincent said he would like to read a few items from the company's "Values Statement" including: "Weigh risks carefully but do not hesitate to innovate or to encourage and reward innovation and initiative. . . . Accept that innovative approaches do not always succeed."
>
> With this one "act of commitment," the "Values Statement" became real and ingrained in every company employee.

Leaders must take a comprehensive view of all of the factors required to build and sustain the company's renewal efforts. Without such a comprehensive view, without strong, committed, visible leadership, transformational learning cannot take place.

BASIC SKILLS FOR THINKING LITERACY

Even as companies struggle to bring every employee up to basic skill levels, they are realizing that functional literacy isn't enough to ensure the success of the company's renewal efforts. The set of skills required for *thinking literacy* include:

- Communications Skills—to enable clear, open communications, including reading, writing, listening, and speaking skills.
- Math Skills—to at least the level of basic algebra, required to read and interpret such work-related documents as spreadsheets and SPC charts.
- Self-Management Skills—so that employees can plan their own lives and careers. In today's business environment, no company can give an ironclad guarantee of lifetime employment. In many companies that have gone through round after round of layoffs, the remaining employees spend so much time worrying about the next round that they cannot focus properly on their jobs. By giving employees these skills, they can better focus on their work knowing that even if their current company may not employ them forever, they can plan their own learning so that they will always be employable.
- Business Skills—Employees must understand the company's overall business and how their individual work contributes to the company's success. They must also develop other business-related skills, such as problem solving and decision making.
- Function-Specific Skills—Most jobs will, in addition to these generic skills, require additional, function-specific skills.

The following statements will provide a basic measure of whether this foundation is in place:

- The company has identified the sets of basic skills needed for all jobs within the company.
- The company has assessed the basic skills levels of all employees to determine training needs.
- The company sponsors needed remedial basic skills instruction for all employees, either in-house or in cooperation with local educational agencies.
- The company encourages all employees to exceed basic skills requirements and provides opportunities for such education, either on-site or by paying employees' tuition at local schools and colleges.
- The company invests in basic business, team, communication, and self-management skills training (in addition to the three Rs) for all employees.

Do employees in your company have the knowledge and skills required for thinking literacy? Have you defined the skill and knowledge requirements for workers into the next century?

Assessing Basic Competencies at Eastman Kodak

In 1993 Eastman Kodak published the results of a multiyear study entitled "Foundation Skills and Workplace Competencies—Profile of Tomorrow's Competitive Employee." The study was undertaken when a superintendent of schools met with a local plant manager: "As a major employer in this area, I consider you one of my school system's major customers. I need to know what skills my graduates need to succeed at Eastman Kodak." As a result, a task force was formed, consisting of both Kodak and school system employees. The group spent almost a year developing a list of competencies. Shortly after this work was completed, a second school system asked Kodak to help them with a similar study. Still later, another local study center asked Kodak to participate in a wider study with other school systems and companies. The "Profile," developed and validated through three studies, focuses on skills, knowledge, and attitudes in nine broad categories:

1. Dynamics of Change.
2. Quality Process Skills and Customer Focus.
3. Communication Skills.
4. Math, Science, Technology.
5. Workplace Behaviors and Teamwork.
6. Ethics.
7. Commitment to Organizational Excellence.
8. Personal Attributes.
9. Global Awareness.

Although it would be ideal for school systems to take full responsibility for turning out perfectly trained employees, this is not a realistic expectation. Kodak's inventory of skills, knowledge, and attitudes, however, can also serve as an assessment tool for measuring the basic skills of any company's employees. Just as the final study was published, Eastman Kodak went through its own crisis, which resulted in rounds of cost cutting and layoffs, so the next step for the company, the testing of its own employees for these competencies, is still awaiting execution.

Variability in Companies' Experiences in Basic Skills Assessment

While the statistics on functional literacy within the American workforce are shocking, they vary widely from company to company. At Mercury Marine in Fond du Lac, Wisconsin, Training and Development Manager Joseph Slezak found a very high employee literacy rate. He attributes the finding to being located in a small town that has excellent schools and a strong work ethic.

At Corning in Corning, New York, Vice President of Human Resources J. Edwin O'Brien says that fully one-third of its employees tested below the fourth-grade level on the "three Rs"—their basic measure of functional literacy—and another third tested above the fourth-grade but below the eleventh-grade level, the minimum level the company targeted for all employees. O'Brien said the company was shocked by the findings because, like Mercury Marine, Corning is located in a rural area with a strong work ethic and good schools.

Don't make assumptions about your employees' basic competencies; you won't know what your employees' basic skills levels are unless you measure them.

Overcoming Deficits in Basic Skills

The five indicators for this foundation are listed in Table 6.2 along with possible causes of deficits and knowledge and skill requirements to overcome each deficit.

Unless every company employee, from the board of directors to the shop floor, from the research laboratory to the sales office, has the basic skills for thinking literacy, the company's renewal efforts can never reach their full potential.

Relating Basic Skills to Employees' Work

To make basic skills training effective (whether to bring employees to a level of functional literacy or to move beyond functional literacy to thinking literacy), it must be related to employee's real work. This is a basic principle of adult learning theory. University of North Carolina professor Teresa L. Smith calls this a "functional context approach"—where employees "see the immediate practical value of what they are learning."[5]

The job of developing and delivering basic skills training can be aided by a variety of public and private agencies: community colleges, local schools' adult education programs, volunteer literacy groups, state economic development agencies. No company should have to develop this type of training from scratch. But these agencies must also work with the company to ensure that the instructional materials and methods relate to employees' actual work. Smith describes the methodology in this way:

> "By observing and interviewing workers and examining job-related materials, trainers will be able to better under-

Table 6.2

Assessing Learning Needs for Foundation 2: Basic Skills for Thinking Literacy

Desired Behavior	Indicators of Deficit	Knowledge /Skill Requirements
The company has identified the sets of basic skills needed for all jobs within the company.	1. The company has not realized that employees need additional skills to help the renewal effort succeed.	1. Company management must learn the importance of employee skills to the success of the renewal effort.
	2. Employees are told to do their work and leave thinking to management.	2. Managers must learn the importance of employee involvement and empowerment and the skills employees need to make these work.
	3. The company doesn't know how to assess the needed skills.	3. Knowledge of the research on workers' skills and benchmarks on other companies.
The company has assessed the basic skills levels of all employees to determine training needs.	1. Some companies don't want to know what needs exist—they're "afraid" of what they might find.	1–2. Learn that putting your head in the sand doesn't make the problem disappear.
	2. Company assumes that work experience and educational credentials of employees guarantee basic skills.	

	3. Companies don't know how to do this type of assessment.	3. Learn how to do an assessment or how to find the resources that can do it for the company.
The company sponsors needed remedial basic skills instruction for all employees, either in-house or in cooperation with local educational agencies.	1. Companies assume the expense of these programs will be too high.	1A. Learn what resources are available at little or no cost to the company. 1B. Learn the costs of *not* providing these types of training.
	2. Companies don't want employees leaving their jobs for this type of training—"Let them do it on their own time."	2A. Learn that sponsoring in-house programs doesn't require loss of work time. 2B. View training as an investment.
The company encourages all employees to exceed basic skills requirements and provides opportunities for such education, either on-site or by paying employees' tuition at local schools and colleges.	1. Arranging on-site education is too time-consuming.	1. Learn how to work with local educational institutions that will assume most of the responsibility for setting up and running the programs.

(continued)

Table 6.2
Continued

Desired Behavior	Indicators of Deficit	Knowledge /Skill Requirements
	2. Company can't afford the expense.	2. Learn about the benefits of investing in employees.
The company invests in basic business, team, communication, and self-management skills training (in addition to the 3Rs) for all employees.	1. "Employees don't need all this training."	1. Learn what skills employees will need to make the renewal effort successful.
	2. "We can't afford it."	2. Learn to view education and training as a necessary investment in the company's future.
	3. "All these soft skills aren't important to the company's success."	3. Learn about the full scope of knowledge and skills needed to ensure the success of the company's renewal efforts.

stand the demands of the job, which will allow them to teach the required basic skills."[6]

OVERCOMING FUNCTIONAL MYOPIA

Too often, as companies grow, the focus of individuals' work narrows to include only their local standards, goals, and measurements. When this happens people tend to suboptimize the overall goals of the company. People at all levels, in all functions, across all company locations must have a clear view of overall company goals and must be measured and rewarded not just on local or functional goals but also on their contributions to the company's overall success.

If your company can agree with each of these statements, this foundation is in place:

- All company business processes have been charted and analyzed.
- All employees understand the company's basic value chain and how their work fits into that chain.
- Cross-functional teamwork is common practice.
- Employees are measured not only by functional goals and standards but also by how much they contribute to the overall success of the company.
- Administrative policies and procedures encourage a wide view of the company's business.

Companies across the world are spending the time and resources to chart their business processes—before any improvement can be made to current processes, you need to understand how things are really working (or not working). The process charts specify the company's starting point.

Process Mapping at Lab Safety Supply

At Lab Safety Supply (LSS), a mail-order safety equipment company in Janesville, Wisconsin, the company's major business processes were charted and analyzed. According to LSS's Donna Hutter, the goal was clarity—to better understand how major business functions operated and how decisions were made. The results of the activity, according to Hutter, were that particular business processes were refocused, and resources were redeployed to support major processes.

For example, to focus more on customer service, the credit and collections function was moved from the finance department to customer services. In this way, customer service representatives were able to quickly access the information and help they needed to quickly respond to customers. Similarly, the accounts payable function was moved from finance to procurement, since the procurement function was the one that relied most heavily on, and generated work for, accounts payable. By analyzing the company's major business processes, Hutter says, "we were able to arrange our business functions to work more effectively in accomplishing our overall goals, reduce management loads, and were able to move some personnel from one area to another where they were needed."

Measurements and Rewards

It is human nature that people tend to focus their efforts on those factors their managers are measuring in order to maximize the rewards they will receive. But few companies have taken the time to review their measurement and reward systems to see whether they are actually encouraging the behaviors they are advocating with their rhetoric. If people are the most important assets of the company, attention must be paid to how those assets are utilized.

As one example, look at your company's performance appraisal system. If, as at most companies, the great majority of people get ratings of "excellent" or "above average," how come the company isn't reaching its goals? Consultant Ken Blanchard tells of a telecommunications company in which 80 percent of employees were rated as "excellent performers," yet the organization was missing its goals. According to Blanchard, "the evaluation system obviously had nothing to do with the established goals."[7]

In your measurement and reward systems, what are you measuring? Do these systems encourage people to contribute toward the company's goals or do they allow people to continue "business as usual" and still be rewarded? Do your company's standard performance appraisal forms contain questions such as: "Employee is a self-starter" or "Employee takes responsibility willingly"? Although these may be good characteristics for employees, do they really measure whether the employee is contributing to the achievement of the company's goals?

Overcoming Functional Myopia

Table 6.3 includes several statements designed to measure the presence and strength of this foundation, along with common practices and attitudes that indicate the need to build or strengthen the foundation and its associated learning needs.

Open-Book Management

One of the most recent programs to help overcome functional myopia is now called "open-book management." Jack Stack, CEO of Springfield Remanufacturing in Springfield, Illinois, is credited with starting this trend by introducing his employees to what he calls "The Great Game of Business."[8] In essence, he taught all of his employees how to read the company's financial statements, held regular meetings to explain those statements, and then goaled every employee to find ways of improving the company's financial results. This new focus moved each employee from the myopic view of his or her individual work responsibilities to a larger view of how each person could help improve the company's overall results.

In a new book, *Open-Book Management: The Coming Business Revolution,*[9] John Case gives many other examples of companies that have renewed themselves by using open-book management to widen employees' views of the business. Case cites three primary differences between open-book management and traditional business practices:[10]

- Every employee sees—and learns to understand—the company's financials, along with all the other numbers that are critical to tracking the business's performance.

Table 6.3

Assessing Learning Needs for Foundation 3: Overcoming Functional Myopia

Desired Behavior	Indicators of Deficit	Knowledge /Skill Requirements
All company business processes have been charted and analyzed.	1. "If it ain't broke, don't fix it."	1. Learn that old methods, though they may work, aren't always the best.
	2. "We don't have the time or resources to undertake such a massive project."	2. Learn the benefits and the real costs before making a decision.
	3. "Managers don't want others poking into how their work gets done."	3. Learn how to create a "safe" environment for change programs.
All employees understand the company's basic value chain and how their work fits into that chain.	1. "Employees don't need to know this information."	1. Learn the benefits of greater employee involvement in the company's business.
Cross-functional teamwork is common practice.	1. "We don't need it. We're doing fine the way we have always worked."	1–2. Learn about the benefits of cross-functional teamwork and cooperation.

	2. "It wastes time and resources."	
Employees are measured not only by functional goals and standards but also by how much they contribute to the overall success of the company.	1. "Such measurements are too complicated and too confusing."	1. Learn about the benefits of new ways of measurement and the costs of continuing with the old methods.
Administrative policies and procedures encourage a wide view of the company's business.	1. "Policies and procedures are already so complicated that rewriting them will only add to the confusion."	1. Learn about the costs and benefits of continuing with the old versus starting with new, focused policies and procedures.
	2. "Employees need to focus on their own jobs. This will only scatter their focus and cause worse results."	2. Learn about other companies' experiences with similar programs before judging worth of the effort.

- Employees learn that whatever else they do, part of their job is to move those numbers in the right direction.
- Employees have a direct stake in the company's success.

The last point, "employees have a direct stake in the company's success," reinforces the earlier point that if you want to ensure that employees will follow new directions, measurements and rewards for those employees must be tied directly to those new directions. Without this tie-in, employees will rightfully ask: "Why bother?"

Open-book management is part of the solution to overcoming functional myopia. Employees must also understand the company's basic business processes and its internal and external value chains, as well as how their individual and collective work fits into those processes; only then can employees work toward improving individual, group, and company performance.

CREATING AND SUSTAINING EFFECTIVE LEARNING TEAMS

Teamwork, within and across functional and organizational boundaries, has become a key element of many companies' renewal efforts. The only real purpose for putting people together on a team is to enable them to *learn from each other*—to learn how to get better results for the company than if they were working separately. But teamwork doesn't just happen—people need to learn how to work as part of a team. And company policies, procedures, and methods, along with proper training and coaching, must make effective teamwork possible.

Your company has effective learning teams in place if:

- Teamwork is viewed as a common way of working rather than as an exception to normal work practices.
- Measurement and reward systems recognize the value of teamwork and not just of individual achievement.
- The company has a comprehensive plan for team development, including formal training programs and ongoing coaching.

- Empowered, self-managed teams are eliminating the need for some managers.
- Teamwork has resulted in significant business results, such as reduction in time, costs, or defects.

Building Teams at Sun Microsystems

The process of building and sustaining cross-functional work teams at Sun Microsystems falls under the umbrella of SunU, the company's training organization. According to Lew Jamison, a group manager within SunU, the company has developed an inventory of 13 skill and attitude measures that are applied to newly formed teams to assess their readiness to work together (see Table 6.4).

This initial assessment allows SunU personnel to tailor instructional and coaching activities to the specific needs of a particular team, not forcing everyone to go through a complete training pro-

Table 6.4
SunU Team Competencies

- To establish and communicate clear team goals.
- To assess the team's technical skills to do the job.
- To cooperatively take action towards accomplishment of the goals and mutually communicate / cooperate in and out of meetings.
- To handle difficult or dominant team members.
- To consider options and innovative ideas and reach team consensus.
- To resolve team conflict.
- To listen and get feedback on progress.
- To monitor and control work in order to stay on track; to manage changes and disruptions.
- To recognize accomplishment of goals.
- To display leadership.
- To communicate to others outside the team; to attend to customers.
- To create and commit to plans, guidelines or ground rules for achieving goals.
- To ask for and utilize resources.

Source: Used by permission of Lew Jamison, SunU.

cess if some of the necessary factors are already in place. Depending on the needs identified by the assessment, individual team members, or the entire team, may be led to specific learning activities, may be coached individually by SunU staff, or may be given team exercises to accomplish in order to build skills necessary for the team to function effectively.

Overcoming Deficits in Teamwork

Table 6.5 lists indicators by which you can judge whether this foundation is present in your company.

Some Thoughts on Teamwork

For most Americans, teamwork is not part of their upbringing. At home and at school, we are raised on the ideal of individual achievement rather than team achievement. Our primary views of teamwork come from sports—football teams, baseball teams, hockey teams, and so on. The major goal for these teams is to win games, to beat their opponents. At the end of the season, we declare a championship team for each sport—the one that has won the most games. Ties are not generally tolerated (except in some college sports where cochampions may be named).

In business, you have to watch out that the teams you create also have the goal of winning. But in your company, you do not have to have losers in order to have winners. The opposition must not be other teams within the company—everyone must be focused on being part of the larger team, the company team, and ensuring that the company is the winner.

To make the company a winner, the teams within the company must measure themselves against the company's goals, such as:

- Improving profits.
- Speeding new products to market.
- Higher rates of quality.
- Improving customer satisfaction ratings.

Table 6.5

Assessing Learning Needs for Foundation 4: Building and Sustaining Effective Learning Teams

Desired Behavior	Indicators of Deficit	Knowledge /Skill Requirements
Teamwork is viewed as a common way of working rather than as an exception to normal work practices.	"We're too busy doing our own work to start working on teams and explaining what we do to others."	Learn about the benefits of teamwork for individuals, functions, and the company as a whole.
Measurement and reward systems recognize the value of teamwork and not just of individual achievement.	"My people work hard and excel at what they do. I'm not going to tell them that their salary reviews are going to depend on what other team members do."	Learn how team incentives, properly designed and implemented, can help both the individual and the company as a whole.
The company has a comprehensive plan for team development, including formal training programs and ongoing coaching.	"Our people are good at their jobs. We'll just put them together on a team and they'll do fine. We don't need to waste time and resources training them."	Learn what it takes for a team to function well and how a good team development plan can facilitate outstanding teamwork and team results.

(continued)

Table 6.5
Continued

Desired Behavior	**Indicators of Deficit**	**Knowledge /Skill Requirements**
Empowered, self-managed teams are eliminating the need for some managers.	"I've worked long and hard to get to the (management) level I'm at, and I'm not about to give up my power and responsibility to a team of people who are below me in the hierarchy."	Learn about new management styles and alternative roles for middle managers. Learn how a good team manager can have long-lasting effects on the company's success.
Teamwork has resulted in significant business results, such as reduction in time, costs, or defects.	"There's nothing a team can accomplish that we can't do ourselves."	Learn to view teamwork as a learning experience, where team members improve products, services, and processes by learning from each other and together.

- Improving product or service performance and ratings.

One of the earliest literary efforts devoted to team performance in a company was a book entitled *The Soul of a New Machine* by Tracy Kidder.[11] It was a remarkable book about the trials and tribulations of creating a new computer design by Data General. When I first started working for Digital Equipment Corporation, a major competitor of Data General, my manager told me to read the book because DG's product development process closely paralleled that at DEC. Looking back on that book, you will see that it more closely follows the sports analogy than what I would recommend for today's company.

Ask yourself whether the following characteristics of the "Soul of a New Machine" team are the same ones you want to operate in your company:

- Separate teams work on different approaches to the same problem with it being made clear that one would win and continue and the other would lose and be dismantled.
- Team members work literally around the clock, with the expectation that some members will drop from exhaustion.
- Although the team manager worked to ensure that the members of the winning team got some financial reward (in the form of stock options), the main reward from winning was the chance to play again.

In today's business environment we need to set up not win-lose situations, as in *The Soul of a New Machine*, but win-win situations, where every team member, every employee in the company, can see how his or her individual and collective efforts are affecting company results, and every employee is rewarded based on contributions to the overall health of the company. As we will see in Chapter 10, Action-Oriented Teamwork, the challenge is not only forming teams but also giving them real improvement goals and the tools and training they need to achieve their goals.

MANAGERS AS ENABLERS

Traditional management styles where managers *controlled* their employees have given way to new styles where managers *enable* their employees to get their work done. In the sport of curling, where players push a large stone down the ice, the team captain (known as the "skip") skates in front of the moving stone, sweeping its path so that each player's effort gets the maximum effect. This is the new role of manager—sweeping obstacles out of the way so that employees get the maximum effect from their efforts.

Agreement with each of the following statements indicates that your company has already made the transition to managers as enablers:

- The company has redefined management jobs, making managers more responsible for the development of their employees.
- The company provides training and development programs to help managers learn new skills, such as coaching.
- Managers view their new roles as teacher, team builder, and coach positively.

Assessing Management Skills at PPG Industries

PPG Industries' Training, Development and Education (TD&E) Group invested a great deal of time and effort developing an excellent *Professional Development Sourcebook*. This book covers a wide range of professional development activities. In later chapters we'll look more closely at how the sourcebook was developed. Here let's look at how the sourcebook addresses one of the key skills needed for the "managers as enablers" model—coaching.

In the section on coaching, the sourcebook addresses the following topics (the full text is contained in Appendix B):

- Effective Behaviors.
  1. For Competent Employees Confronting New Situations (describes desired behaviors).

2. For Employees in Need of Corrective Action (describes incorrect or problem behaviors).

- Sources of Information.
- Developmental Suggestions—specific methods of acquiring and mastering the needed knowledge and skills, both for those confronting new situations and for those who need corrective action.
- Readings—books employees can read on the topic.
- Training Programs—offered by PPG TD&E.
- Ways to Practice (and get feedback and coaching).

PPG's approach lays out the basic measures for many areas of skills and knowledge required by employees and gives managers methods of assessing whether their employees already meet the requirements or require development.

Management Assessment Centers

An approach used by many companies to help validate the skills needed to succeed in particular management jobs is the "assessment center." Assessment centers use "a variety of testing techniques designed to allow candidates [for specified jobs] to demonstrate, under standardized conditions, the skills and abilities most essential for success in a given job."[12] These centers evaluate individuals using standardized testing and such methods as:

- In-basket exercises.
- Leaderless group discussion.
- Simulations of specific tasks.
- Structured individual interviews.
- Oral presentations.
- Business games.

Assessors are typically individuals one or two levels above those being evaluated and receive extensive formal training in the assessment methods. Studies over the past several decades have validated that the assessment center methodology provides excellent predictors of future success in specific, usually supervisory and management, jobs.

The use of assessment centers was begun by the Office of Strategic Services during World War II. The first major application in industry was by AT&T in the 1950s. Assessment centers are used in approximately 25 percent of American companies today and a slightly higher percentage in the United Kingdom, where more than one-third of *The London Times* Top 1000 use assessment centers for hiring, promoting, redeploying, and developing their employees.

The reason for using assessment centers is to avoid the problems and costs inherent in hiring, promoting, and training people who later wash out of middle- and senior-level jobs. Because the evaluation methods have been standardized and validated, they also help companies avoid discrimination lawsuits.

Some American companies, such as Northeast Utilities in Berlin, Connecticut, have placed a major emphasis on assessing the skills needed for specific jobs, with the goal of hiring and promoting people with the needed skills and, therefore, lessening both training requirements and job turnover. But Northeast Utilities, after several years of investment in the assessment process, has come to realize that the needed skills are not always readily available in the internal and external labor markets. Many must be developed through learning activities for their employees, and the company is now putting greater emphasis on management development.

In the UK, company development/assessment centers are designed to assess both the current status of individuals' skills, knowledge, and behaviors with respect to specific jobs and to provide advice, based on the findings, for developmental activities. The assessment process is a rigorous one, including standardized and customized testing, role playing, interviews, and other assessment methods, and can take as long as three full days.

Because assessment panels are typically composed of line managers as well as human resources personnel and, often, external consultants, these centers are a very expensive activity. But as one study concluded: "The evidence indicates that [assessment centers] predict future performance or success better than any other widely researched assessment tool."[13]

Overcoming Deficits in Managerial Practices

Several indicators of whether your company's managers have taken on these new roles are included in Table 6.6, along with pointers to the learning needed by managers to be effective in these new roles.

Managers as Teachers and Coaches

First-level managers and supervisors, whether on the factory floor, in service operations, or elsewhere, spend up to half their time training employees to do their jobs, helping them solve problems when they arise, and coaching employees for better performance. As managers rise in the hierarchy above that first level, the amount of time they spend in these activities tends to diminish. Unfortunately, in our society "teaching" is not a high-status occupation. In many companies, instructors in the company's training group have relatively low status. For example, if two engineers with similar educations and work experiences were to select two different career paths in the same company, one in the company's training function and the other in the design engineering group, you would generally find that the one selecting the training career path will, from the beginning and continuing throughout his or her career, earn less money and have less company status than the one choosing the design engineering career path.

If learning is the key to company renewal, learning activities and the people who can foster those activities, whether as a line manager or a training professional, need to be recognized as contributing at least equally to the company's success as others who have chosen career paths that are traditionally more glamorous. Managers must be goaled on developing their employees' knowledge and skills, for only by building these knowledge and skill assets can the company thrive in the future.

Table 6.6

Assessing Learning Needs for Foundation 5: Managers as Enablers

Desired Behavior	Indicators of Deficit	Knowledge /Skill Requirements
The company has redefined management jobs, making managers more responsible for the development of their employees.	"We built the company on a strong management style and have done very well with it. Why change now?"	Learn how company renewal requires new ways of working for managers and employees alike.
The company provides training and development programs to help managers learn new skills, such as coaching.	"Our managers are great people. We'll just tell them how we want them to change and they'll do it."	Just as employees will need training and coaching for new skills, so will managers. Managers need to learn the skills necessary to enable and facilitate the company's renewal process and, like employees, will need ongoing coaching and follow-through to ensure that they master these new skills.
Managers view their new roles as teacher, team builder, and coach positively.	"I worked hard to get where I am, and now you're asking me change the behaviors that made me successful and to give up my hard-won power and authority to my employees. This isn't a new way of working—it's a demotion!"	Learn the value of new ways of managing and how managers can add value to the company and its people. Learn how new styles open up new career directions and new opportunities to contribute to the company's success.

Coaching the Coaches

One error that even more enlightened companies often make is not providing the ongoing support needed by managers who take on new roles as enablers. We often ask managers to change their entire style of working, to alter long-held work habits, to do things differently from every manager for whom they have ever worked, and sometimes we provide training for these managers on these new skills. But just as nonmanagers need opportunities to try out new skills and test new knowledge by applying them in a nonthreatening atmosphere, just as we are asking their managers to provide coaching and reinforcement of these new ways of working, we most often fail to recognize that managers also need coaching and reinforcement if we want them to be successful in changing the ways in which they work. Too often we assume that since we may pay managers more, because managers have more years of experience in the company, they can come out of a training program and start applying their new knowledge and skills flawlessly. This is a poor assumption.

TAKING YOUR VITAL SIGNS

Whether in a medical emergency or for a routine physical examination, doctors prescribe no treatment without first taking the patient's medical history and current vital signs and performing both a routine examination and, if needed, more extensive diagnostic tests. Then, using the information gathered, the physician applies his or her knowledge of medicine to prescribe a treatment plan. Whether to treat a current ailment or to practice preventive medicine, the treatment plan is based on the physician's accumulated knowledge and wisdom. Where the physician is uncertain of the diagnosis or the treatment, he or she may require more tests to uncover clues to the diagnosis or may call for consultations with specialists who have a greater depth of knowledge in specific areas.

There is a lot of science, as well as a lot of art, in medical diagnosis. Many times a diagnosis or treatment has no easy answers, for a specific malady may present itself differently in different patients, and each individual may respond differently to similar treatments or pharmaceuticals. This is why doctors don't "do" medicine—they "practice" it. It is also why the physician's clients must be "patient."

Companies seeking to renew or transform themselves must similarly follow some set procedures to diagnose their ills and then begin a course of treatment. In other cases, companies seek to practice preventive medicine, hoping to prolong life and improve the quality of life, even if there is no current medical crisis.

Let's review the basic steps that Corning followed in developing its "innovation process," already described in Chapter 4.

INNOVATION AT CORNING INC.

When Corning vice president Thomas MacAvoy decided that the company needed to focus on how new products were developed and brought to market, he knew that although the company was in no imminent danger and that it had a lot of internal knowledge about innovation, much more needed to be learned to improve the company's "quality of life" and prolong its health into the future.

He started by bringing together a wide variety of knowledge resources—from Corning, from academia, and from other companies—in an open conference to discuss ideas and approaches. Further research was conducted through benchmarks at other companies known for their innovation, such as 3M. He recruited resources from within Corning to capture this knowledge and the ideas generated. The conference and the benchmarks helped the company develop its baselines, which could be used in its diagnosis and treatment of its own innovation processes.

With this knowledge in hand, Corning next started its examination of the patient; that is, it examined its current processes for developing new products and bringing them to market. This process involved all of the functions that took part in the development and marketing of new products. This examination pointed out where:

- Goals and processes within individual functions needed to be altered to reach the company's goals.
- Cross-functional goals and processes needed development or refinement to ensure alignment with overall company goals.

- Knowledge and skill deficits needed to be overcome to enable accomplishment of the new company goals and the facilitation of the new processes.

By combining the results of this examination with the knowledge of theory and other companies' practices, Corning was able to diagnose its own condition and to prescribe a plan of treatment, as was described in Chapter 4.

STARTING FROM THE MIDDLE

Ideally, top company management will drive the assessment process, just as they ideally will implement a comprehensive approach to transformational learning. But if this does not happen, there is no real reason that midlevel managers cannot accomplish significant results for their own functions or business units. The procedures are the same, only done on a smaller scale. Does your group have the five foundations in place?

- Does your function or group have strong, committed, visible leadership?
- Do your employees have the basic skills necessary for thinking literacy?
- Have you found ways of correcting the functional myopia within your own group?
- Are you using teamwork effectively within your group and in combination with your internal and external customers and suppliers?
- Is your management style to enable your employees to do their work?

The work of a functional or business unit leader will be more difficult if the transformational learning process is not being led by top company management, but it is still possible and can be done effectively if you build strong foundations within your group. If the company is not undertaking an enterprise-wide assessment to find its starting point, you can still do your own assessment on a smaller scale.

MOVING BEYOND THE FIVE FOUNDATIONS

The five foundations are prerequisites for a company renewal effort. Without strong foundations, transformational learning cannot take place, and company renewal efforts can be, at best, only partially successful. While I believe that the establishment of strong foundations can take you 80 percent of the way to your renewal goals, they are not in themselves sufficient to renew a company.

In the next three chapters, we will examine three concepts that can help you select the best paths for your company's renewal, can help to establish the type of learning culture necessary for that effort, and can provide the tools and resources needed to undertake transformational learning.

SEVEN

BUY, RENT, OR DEVELOP: KNOWLEDGE ACQUISITION STRATEGIES

Once you have discovered what knowledge and skills are needed by the company to meet its short- and long-term challenges, three basic strategies can be used to acquire them. You can *buy* them, *rent* them, or *develop* them or, more likely, use a combination of these strategies.

BUYING KNOWLEDGE AND SKILLS

The *buy* strategy is the simplest, but not necessarily the fastest, of the three: Find the knowledge or skills you need in the marketplace and buy them. This can be done in several different ways (see Table 7.1, which summarizes all three strategies):

- *Hire* people who already have the knowledge and skills you need and have them do the work you need done.
- Form a *partnership* with another organization that has the required knowledge and skills.
- *Outsource* a function to another organization that has the required knowledge and skills.

Table 7.1
Knowledge Acquisition Strategies

Strategy	Methods
Buy	■ Hire people who already possess the required knowledge or skills. ■ Form partnerships with organizations that have the required knowledge or skills. ■ Outsource a function to another organization that has the required knowledge or skills.
Rent	■ Hire a consultant. ■ Obtain assistance from a customer, a supplier, an educational institution, or a professional association that has the required knowledge or skills. ■ Subcontract work to organizations that have the required knowledge or skills.
Develop	■ Send employees to be trained outside the company. ■ Develop and deliver in-house education and training programs. ■ Hire outside trainers to do training in-house. ■ Spread the knowledge and skill resources that already exist within the company.

With each of these methods, the company is seeking the knowledge and skills it needs *outside* its own organization. By buying the resources, it is controlling how the resources are used and, it is hoped, how they will affect the company's overall results.

Buying Knowledge and Skills at Ace Clearwater

At Ace Clearwater Enterprises, Kellie Dodson bought a lot of the skills and knowledge the company needed by *hiring* a number of key personnel: a manufacturing director, a manager of materials and logistics, a chief financial officer, and so on. She knew that ACE needed these people immediately. There was no time to develop the knowledge and skills of current employees. If improvements were not made immediately, Boeing would cancel the contract. Hiring people from the outside helped her both with her immediate needs to meet the requirements of the company's contract with Boeing and to start building the overall knowledge and skill resources within the company. These people were hired to help solve the current crisis and to start educating her and the rest of the company's employees in order to build a better future.

Buying New Executives

In recent years, many well-known companies that have traditionally promoted from within have brought in new CEOs, not only from outside their own company, but also from outside their industry. IBM hired Louis Gerstner from RJR Nabisco. Kodak hired Kenneth Fisher from Motorola. In making these "buy" decisions, these and many other companies have not just been purchasing the traditional skills of a CEO, for they had internally developed many CEOs with these skills over the past decades. They were buying a set of knowledge and skills that these people developed in other companies and other industries and that they felt their companies needed but lacked. IBM was hopeful that Mr. Gerstner would bring his consumer marketing experience from Nabisco. Kodak looked on Kenneth Fisher as a person who could help them become more focused on the high-technology marketplace.

Buying a new CEO from the outside, especially when the company has a tradition of promoting from within, also sends a strong message to employees, customers, and investors: that the company is committed to change, that the renewal effort is real and not just "this month's new idea for saving the company."

Hiring new executives to help effect a new strategy is not limited to the CEO level. Lowe's Companies is a home improvement and building supply company headquartered in North Carolina. Traditionally Lowe's had focused on smaller showrooms (15,000 square feet). From its market research, it found that it needed to create larger, more attractive "superstores" to effectively compete with newer chains, such as Home Depot and Home Quarters (HQ). "To accomplish our goals, we had to go out and get the people we needed to make the bigger stores happen," says Cliff Oxford, vice president of corporate relations.[1] To get this expertise quickly, Lowe's hired Michael Rouleau as executive vice president of store operations. "Michael had senior positions with Target Stores, Dayton Hudson, Office Warehouse, Lechmere. He was the guy who knew how to put people and programs in place in big stores, and he helped orchestrate the whole shift into these large destination home centers."[2]

When to Consider Hiring New Talent

Companies buy talent when:

- They need an *immediate* infusion of new skills, knowledge, and ideas.
- These new skills, knowledge, and ideas are needed on a long-term basis.
- People with the desired set of skills and knowledge are available in the marketplace at a price the company can afford.
- They want the new resources not only to use their knowledge and skills to improve the company's situation but also to transfer their knowledge and skills to other employees.

Partnering—Using the Best Resources for Each Step in the Value Chain

In other industries, notably biotechnology, dozens of small companies specialize in one or a few aspects of the product development cycle. Some companies focus on basic research, others on commercializing the basic research, some on developing products that meet market needs, others on manufacturing methods, and so on. A few biotech companies, such as Biogen, are attempting to integrate the entire value chain within the company, but most are forming *partnerships,* allowing each company to focus its strengths and knowledge/skill resources on its own part of the discovery/development/commercialization value chain.

This approach is recommended by James Brian Quinn,[3] who suggests that companies examine each and every process in their value chain and do a separate make/buy analysis for each. Quinn's view is that the entire manufacturing enterprise can be broken down into a series of service activities and that each activity should be subjected to a make/buy analysis. With this approach, a company can become a true virtual enterprise; that is, a manufacturing company can design, develop, manufacture, and sell product without actually employing anyone or having any facilities for any of those functions, but only for coordination of the entire chain of activities.

In seeking out the best provider for each set of services within the value chain, companies are seeking the knowledge and skills required to do the best possible job at each step. The approach allows companies to identify their own core competencies, that is, those steps in the process where they excel, and focus their energies on building and maintaining a competitive advantage based on those competencies. They can then outsource other activities to companies that excel in those processes.

Outsourcing—Buying Expertise from Others

Outsourcing is a relatively new business practice where a company decides to buy specialized services from an external organization rather than perform those services for itself. A notable example was when Eastman Kodak decided that it was spending too much time and too many resources on its internal computing and telecommunications functions and decided to *outsource* those functions to other companies. It sold its equipment and facilities to other companies (IBM for computing and DEC for telecommunications) and arranged for those companies to hire Kodak employees working in those functions. In return, they signed multiyear contracts with those vendors to provide Kodak with the services it had formerly provided internally. More recently Dupont outsourced its entire management training function to Forum Corporation.

In each of these cases, the companies were seeking to improve the knowledge and skills applied to specific functions by buying that expertise from companies that focus on those functions as their primary business. This freed up both time and resources and allowed the companies to focus more effectively on their own core competencies.

The major difference between partnering and outsourcing, as the terms are being used here, is that partnering helps fill gaps in a company's knowledge/skill base and typically involves new—or newly discovered—needs. Outsourcing, on the other hand, involves the company's shedding a function that it has traditionally done itself and may involve the transfer of facilities, equipment, and personnel.

Short-Term and Long-Term Impacts

The short-term impact of a buy strategy can be very high, since it results in the company obtaining resources that already have the needed knowledge and skills and are ready to apply them immediately to solve today's business problems. In the longer term, the impacts of a buy strategy can range from low to high, depending on how effectively these resources are used. For example, if new hires hoard their knowledge to maintain status or for job security, the impact of their hiring will only last as long as they do. If, on the other hand, they actively share their knowledge and skills and help other company employees learn what they already know, their impact can last long beyond their personal tenure in the company.

Similarly, for partnering strategies, if nothing is done to transfer learning from the partners into the company, the impact will last only as long as the partnership agreements. If for any reason these relationships are severed, the company will be left in the same condition as before, that is, lacking the knowledge and skills it needs to succeed.

Outsourcing carries an even greater risk because by transferring facilities and personnel to the vendor, the company is losing its own stocks of knowledge and skill resources. If the outsourcing arrangement does not work out, the company will have no internal resources left to fall back on.

Cash Flows versus Knowledge Flows

The long-term cost of hiring new personnel will generally be less than the cost of renting or developing the needed knowledge and skills, but only if the people being hired stay with the company. If there is constant turnover of skilled employees, the costs of recruitment and orientation will mount, and the company will also suffer from gaps in the availability of the requisite knowledge and skills.

The costs of partnering with other companies to acquire needed knowledge and skills should come at market rates; that is, rates will be determined by the demand and supply factors within the marketplace. But partnering is an ongoing activity—the needed knowledge and skills will be available to the company only as long as the partnership lasts. This same relationship typifies outsourcing agreements—the flow of knowledge and skills from the selected vendor continues only as long as the contract. It should be noted, however, that one of the primary reasons that companies outsource entire functions (e.g., computing, telecommunications, training, etc.) is that they believe that they will reap substantial savings over providing those functions themselves.

Benefit Stream

With all three buy strategies, the benefit streams to the company will last only as long as the resources it has bought. The only way to extend the benefits beyond this point is if the people brought in help develop the knowledge and skills of company employees; that is, they transfer their knowledge and skills to other company employees. This is more easily accomplished when the company hires people. Partners and vendors may balk at training company employees because once they have transferred their knowledge and skills, why should the company continue to pay them?

Key Considerations in "Buying" Knowledge and Skills

In hiring new employees to bring to the company some new set of skills and knowledge, companies must be careful that the new hire "fits." The person may be hired because of specialized knowledge or skills, but the company is not buying just those skills but a "whole person." Do the person's other characteristics, for example, personality, knowledge of the company's industry, and management style, fit with the company's culture? Do the person's values fit with those of the company? Is the person willing to share his or her knowledge and skills with others in the company, or will he or she hoard them to provide job security?

Another consideration is that this key individual is typically hired to meet an immediate need for specialized knowledge and skills. Will the need persist, or is it temporary? As time goes by, knowledge and skills in any field will change. Will the individual being hired be able to keep up with the changes in his or her field?

Finally, do people with the needed knowledge and skills exist in the labor market? Can the company find the right person? At what price? What are the relative costs and benefits of hiring a key individual versus other alternatives, such as renting or developing the needed knowledge and skills?

In deciding to buy knowledge and skills, companies must consider not only the suitability of the resources being purchased but also the alternatives of renting or developing the needed resources (see Table 7.2).

Forming partnerships must also be undertaken with some cautions in mind. First, "partnering" implies a two-way flow of resources. The simplest arrangements are for the company to provide payment in exchange for the needed knowledge and skills.

A more complicated arrangement has a two-way flow of knowledge and skills, where the company and its partner complement each other's knowledge and skill bases. In these arrangements, care must be taken to ensure that the flows in both directions balance each other, that both partners feel that they are receiving sufficient value in exchange for what they are providing. When such arrangements get badly out of balance, resentment grows and may end up subverting the goals of the original partnership agreement. An example of this is how some large companies have tried to implement partnership arrangements with suppliers to support just-in-time (JIT) manufacturing. When these partnerships are properly arranged, it can benefit both companies' production schedules, inventories, and so on. But, in some cases,

Table 7.2
Key Considerations in "Buying" Knowledge

"Buy" Strategy	Key Considerations
Hire people who have needed knowledge and skills.	■ Do the person's other characteristics (besides the needed knowledge and skills) fit into the organization? ■ Will the person share his/her knowledge with others or hoard it? ■ Is the need for this person's specialized knowledge and skills temporary or long term? ■ Are people with the required knowledge and skills available in the market? ■ Will this person be able to keep up with changes in his/her field of knowledge?
Form partnerships.	■ What does the company need to give to its new partner in exchange for the needed knowledge and skills? ■ Is the trade-off cost-effective when compared with other alternatives?
Outsource to another organization.	■ Does the outsourcing agreement benefit both companies? ■ Will the companies' cultures, organizations, and work methods (along with their knowledge and skill bases) fit with each other?

large companies have simply shifted the burden of carrying inventory to their smaller suppliers, which, if anything, feel only greater burdens being placed on them with no rewards attached.

RENTING KNOWLEDGE AND SKILLS

Renting needed skills and knowledge is another way of filling a company's needs. Renting can be done in several ways (see Table 7.3).

Table 7.3
Key Considerations in "Renting" Knowledge

"Rent" Strategy	**Key Considerations**
Hire a consultant.	■ Is the consultant willing to learn about the company and adapt his/her methods to the company's needs? ■ Is the consultant willing to form a long-term relationship with the company? ■ Is the consultant willing to help company employees learn his/her methods? ■ Does the consultant really have the knowledge and skills needed to meet the company's needs? ■ Is the consultant willing to learn about the company's needs or is he/she just trying to sell his/her product?
Subcontract work to organizations with the required knowledge and skills.	■ Is subcontracting more cost-effective than other available strategies? ■ Can the subcontractor meet other company needs, e.g., schedule, quality, etc.?
Obtain assistance from customers, suppliers, colleges, or professional associations.	■ Do these resources understand, or are they willing to learn about, the company and its needs? ■ Do these resources have real-world experience? ■ Are these resources willing to form a long-term relationship with the company? ■ Are these resources willing to learn about the company's needs or are they just trying to sell their product?

- Hiring a consultant who has the needed capabilities.
- Subcontracting work to another company that has the needed skills and knowledge.
- Obtaining assistance from customers, suppliers, colleges, or professional associations.

With each of these methods, the *rent* strategy provides access to the needed knowledge and skills on a temporary basis in exchange for payment. These arrangements are typically on a fee-for-service basis and last as long as the work is needed.

Renting Knowledge and Skills at Ace Clearwater

At Ace Clearwater Enterprises, Kellie Dodson rented expertise from the California Manufacturing Technology Center (CMTC). The CMTC provided consultants to ACE to audit current manufacturing capabilities and to advise the company on needed improvements in plant layout, technology, worker skills, and so on. Her renting strategy was based on an immediate, short-term need to determine where the company stood and to help her plan for future development of company and employee capabilities.

When to Rent Knowledge

Companies rent talent when:

- They have an immediate, short-term need for knowledge and skills that cannot be filled by existing employees. In some cases, the only source of the needed talent may be a consultant, for example, where the consultant has developed a proprietary methodology that will benefit the company.
- The knowledge and skills are needed either on a one-time basis (e.g., for an audit) or to fill an interim gap while the company buys the knowledge and skills or develops them for the long term.
- The company wants to bring in someone with a wider base of experience to solve a problem or to validate an approach the company plans to take.
- The prestige of the consultant is such that his or her opinion will help reinforce an approach being advocated within the company by a person who does not have the clout to win the political battles. In these cases, the consultant is being asked to help influence a company decision.

Subcontracting

Companies subcontract work to other organizations when they feel that the other organization can do the work at lower cost, with better quality, or on a more timely basis than can the company itself. In some cases, the company decides that the skills and knowledge needed for a particular task do not exist internally, and, rather than develop the resources or invest in the needed plant and equipment needed to accomplish that task, it is more beneficial to subcontract the work to others who specialize in that task. This strategy makes sense if the task is not related to the company's core competencies.

For example, Whirlpool Corporation, in developing its latest gas range, decided not to develop the gas burner system itself but to subcontract that work to Eaton Corporation. As reported in the *Wall Street Journal,* Eaton "already makes gas valves and regulators for other appliance manufacturers. Whirlpool expects to get its new range to market several months sooner this way."[4]

Boeing Commercial Aircraft uses thousands of suppliers, tapping into their knowledge and skill bases. "We now realize that the people who make these components know a lot more about it than we do," says Ronald Woodard, Boeing's president of commercial airplane production.[5]

Assistance from Customers, Suppliers, Colleges, and Others

Many companies overlook the knowledge and skill assets that may be available from their customers and suppliers. Because of longstanding business relationships, a company's customers and suppliers may be very willing to share their knowledge and skills with your company. At Ace Clearwater, Boeing had a half dozen or more people working side by side with ACE employees at ACE's facilities. The primary reason for the Boeing presence was to ensure ontime delivery of defect-free Boeing parts. But at the same time, the Boeing employees were willing to share their knowledge with ACE employees. Honda of America has an outstanding program of training and consultation to help its suppliers.

Many large companies have developed extensive training programs for their own employees and are willing to share their knowledge with their suppliers, if only to ensure that the goods and services they are purchasing from those suppliers meet their standards.

Sometimes companies form consortia to help train their suppliers, as with the California Supplier Improvement Program, or The Consortium, formed by a group of high-technology manufacturers including Texas Instruments and Digital Equipment Corporation. In both of these cases, the consortia have developed training programs and then licensed those programs to community colleges, which deliver cost-effective training that meets the sponsors' specifications.

Professional associations, such as the Society of Manufacturing Engineers (SME), the American Banking Association (ABA), the American Society for Training and Development (ASTD), the American Production and Inventory Control Society (APICS), and dozens of others, offer their members consulting services, educational programs, publications, and other services and products to help them acquire the knowledge and skills they need to succeed.

Short-Term and Long-Term Impacts of Renting

The short-term impacts of renting needed knowledge and skills will be quite high, for an immediate problem will be solved. As will be discussed shortly, care must be taken to ensure that the resources being rented are well matched to the company's needs.

In the longer term, the impact of a rent strategy may wane—renting specialized knowledge and skills often comes at a high price, and if the company's needs for those resources continue on a long-term basis, it may behoove the company to pursue buy or development strategies to meet future needs.

Benefit Stream from a Rent Strategy

By its very nature, the benefit stream from renting lasts only as long as rent is being paid. If the company's needs are onetime or cover just a short period, the benefits from renting may meet company needs in a cost-effective manner. But if the company will require these resources on a longer-term basis, it may either rent for just long enough a period to allow for development of internal capabilities or, if negotiated up front, may ask the vendor to help develop the skills within the company, that is, ask the vendor not only to do some work in the short term but also to train company employees to do the work themselves in the future.

Many companies start out with a rental strategy and, if they find their needs to be ongoing and find the vendor suitable, work to transform the rental strategy into a partnership agreement. PHH Corporation, for example, started renting expertise from a number of training vendors to assist the company in developing skills. When a vendor proved effective in providing training, PHH training manager Tim O'Brien worked with the vendor to form a partnership agreement that covered a multiyear period and required the vendor to customize offerings to the PHH culture and specific company business needs.

Key Considerations in Renting Knowledge and Skills

There are many excellent consulting firms and independent consultants in the worldwide marketplace, but as with any purchase in the marketplace, companies must practice the principle of caveat emptor. In hiring a consultant, keep these considerations in mind:

- Is the consultant willing to learn about the company and adapt his or her methods to the company's needs? Too often, consultants peddle a package of services that may or may not exactly meet a company's requirements. "One-size-fits-all" solutions can be all right—if you happen to be the right size.
- Is the consultant willing to form a long-term relationship with the company? Especially with some of the larger consulting and training companies that employ professional salespeople, the salesperson may be more concerned with today's sale or making this year's quota than with developing a long-term relationship—although this seems to be changing according to some company executives.

- Is the consultancy willing to help company employees learn their methods? This may seem to be a self-defeating strategy to some consultants, but the more forward-looking see this as a way of establishing a longer-term relationship with the company: doing work to meet immediate needs, providing educational programs to help the company develop employees for the longer term, and then providing ongoing support and coaching to the company's employees on a long-term basis.
- Does the consultant really have the knowledge and skills needed to meet the company's needs? Many times consultants respond to every company need with "We can do that," and the company ends up paying the consultant to learn the subject, when they thought that the consultant already had the required knowledge and skills.
- Is the consultant willing to learn about the company's needs or just trying to sell products? An obvious clue to this will come from the initial meeting with the consultant: Is the consultant asking questions and trying to understand the company and its problems, or is he or she spending the time pitching what he or she has to sell?

In considering potential subcontractors, companies should consider these three factors:

1. Is subcontracting more cost-effective than other strategies? If the work being subcontracted is going to extend beyond a short period, would a partnership arrangement be better? Over the long term, will it be more cost-effective for the company to develop its own capabilities rather than to continue to rely on a subcontractor?
2. Besides the obvious need to produce a specific product or provide a given service, can the subcontractor meet all other company requirements related to quality, delivery schedule, and so on?

3. Are there ways in which the subcontractor can add value to the company's operations through sharing of its own knowledge and skill resources?

When a company asks its customers and suppliers for assistance, the company must be careful to ensure that the assistance being offered benefits the company as a whole and is not tailored to solely meet the customers' or suppliers' needs. Ace Clearwater Enterprises, for example, carefully examined Boeing's requirements and offers of assistance to make certain that they were in the company's best interests, not just in Boeing's best interests.

The same considerations applied to consultants, listed previously, should be equally applied to assistance being rented from educational institutions and professional associations. Additionally, when renting assistance from colleges and universities, companies may want to find out whether the consultants/instructors have real-world experience or are talking solely from a theoretical base.

DEVELOPING KNOWLEDGE AND SKILLS

The *develop* strategy assumes that a company wants its own employees to have the knowledge and skills needed for the company's success. Knowledge and skills are developed through a variety of learning activities, often through formal education and training programs but also through other activities such as working as part of a team, coaching and mentoring relationships, rotational job assignments, and so on. Formal education and training programs can be pursued in three different ways:

- Sending employees to external programs.
- Developing and delivering in-house programs.
- Bringing external programs in-house.

Companies often do not take advantage of the knowledge and skill resources already available within the company's boundaries. Companies must learn how to identify, capture, and disseminate the knowledge and skills they already have and to facilitate the sharing of these assets within the company.

Developing Knowledge and Skills at Ace Clearwater

At the same time Kellie Dodson was buying and renting knowledge resources to meet Ace Clearwater's immediate needs, she knew that the company's long-term success would depend on building the knowledge and skills of all company employees. She started building these resources for the future through a number of concurrent strategies:

- More than 150 employees participated in several weeks of training provided under the CALSIP program.
- She and her management team participated in more than 100 hours of the same training.
- She formed learning teams to address many of the company's most critical problems.
- She required her managers to act as teachers and coaches, to share their knowledge with other ACE employees.
- She created the position of "Director of Change" to act as a facilitator and coach for teams and individuals throughout the company.

She also recognized that in today's fast-changing environment, learning activities had to continue on a long-term basis, that continuous improvement depends on continuous learning.

When to Consider a Develop Strategy

Companies pursue the development of their employees when:

- They recognize that the skills and knowledge of their employees will be the primary source of competitive advantage in the future.

- The identified skill and knowledge deficits relate to the company's core competencies and will be needed by employees in the long term.
- The requirements for change within the company are based on the knowledge and skills of the company's employees.
- The costs of developing employees are lower than the alternatives of buying or renting the needed knowledge and skills in the marketplace.

Sending Employees to External Training

Literally thousands of education and training programs, seminars, and symposia are being given around the world in any month, and they all want company employees to attend. These programs may be sponsored by colleges and universities, professional associations, seminar companies, chambers of commerce, consultants, industry groups, and so on. Many have excellent content and instructors. If you subscribe to an industry magazine or belong to a professional association in any field, you are on their mailing lists and receive as many as a dozen program announcements a week. The programs cover every conceivable topic, from basic skills to the latest in industry research, from basic supervisory skills to leading an organizational transformation, from TQM to business reengineering. Sometimes, attending an external program allows the company to be exposed to a "leading authority" whom the company could not afford to hire as a consultant.

Another advantage of sending employees to external programs is that besides the subject matter being taught, they may have the opportunity to exchange ideas and experiences with people from other companies who have faced or are facing similar challenges. For example, if your company is exploring the idea of starting up a corporate university, you may send someone to attend an external conference that features speakers from a variety of companies and industries that have started similar programs and learn from their experiences.

Companies take advantage of these external opportunities when:

- The content of the external program matches a learning need of one or more individuals within the company.
- The number of people needing the subject matter is small. Otherwise, it may be more cost-effective to bring the program in-house.
- The timing and location are convenient to the employees who need to attend.

Developing and Delivering In-House Programs

No external program can be tailored as well to a company's specific needs as one developed in-house and delivered by the company's own employees. No external consultant or vendor can know a company's standards, practices, and culture as well as the company's own people. AMP, Inc., for example, has a very effective engineering education program where all development and instruction are done by AMP engineers. According to Dr. Joseph Giusti, AMP's associate director of global human resource development, the program is the company's major method of disseminating engineering standards and continuing to reinforce the company's engineering culture.

Bringing External Training In-House

The third option for the develop strategy is to bring external training in-house, hiring external consultants or trainers to bring the programs they have developed to your company and offer them solely to your company's employees, usually in company facilities.

Virtually any education and training vendor that offers public programs will be willing (if not anxious) to offer those programs within a company, usually at a lower per-person cost. Most of those vendors will also be willing to customize their existing programs or create new, company-tailored programs when offering them to a company's employees.

Companies employ this strategy when:

- They have a relatively large number of employees who need the program content.

- The knowledge resources needed to develop and deliver a similar program do not exist within the company.
- Using an external provider proves more cost-effective or timely than developing a similar program in-house.

Spreading the Resources That Already Exist within Your Company

Formal education and training programs, whether developed and delivered internally or externally, are only a subset of the wide variety of learning activities that a company may pursue. Often the knowledge and skill resources needed to meet a specific company requirement already exist within the company's boundaries, but not where they can have a direct effect on the specific challenges being faced. In a large, global company, these resources may exist anywhere on the face of the earth. The challenge to companies is how to identify the full stock of its knowledge and skill resources and how to make them available to the people who need them. We will discuss this at greater length in Chapter 9, Building a Knowledge Network.

Key Considerations for Developing Knowledge

Each of the four methods of developing knowledge just discussed can be effective in meeting employees' learning needs. In selecting any of these methods, the following questions should be taken into consideration (see Table 7.4 for a summary).

When considering whether to send employees to an external education or training program:

- Is the external training tailored to the company's needs? If you are sending an employee to an external program, it is unlikely that the program will have been designed with your specific needs in mind. But by researching a variety of programs from different vendors, you will be able to identify the one that is most closely matched with your learning needs.

Table 7.4

Key Considerations in "Developing" Knowledge

"Development" Strategy	Key Considerations
Send employees to external training.	■ Is the external training tailored to the company's needs? ■ Is the external training available at a reasonable price, in a convenient location, and at the right time? ■ Do the instructors have real-world experience, especially with the types of problems/challenges being faced by the company? ■ Is there a danger of employees inadvertently releasing critical proprietary information as they try to solve the company's problems in the class?
Develop and deliver in-house programs.	■ Does the company have sufficient knowledge resources to devote to the task? ■ Does the company have sufficient educational expertise to develop the needed instruction? ■ Will this strategy meet the company's needs on time? ■ Is this strategy cost-effective in comparison with buying external instructional resources?
Bring external training in-house.	■ Are the external resources willing to tailor their approaches and materials to company needs? ■ Do the external resources have real-world experience, especially in the company's industry and with the types of problems the company is facing? ■ Are the external resources willing to provide ongoing support to the trainees?
Spread the knowledge and skill resources that already exist within the company.	■ Do the needed knowledge and skills exist within the company? ■ Can you free up the people who already have the needed knowledge and skills to work?

- Is the external program available at a reasonable price, in a convenient location, at the right time? Few programs will meet all of these criteria, but the greater the number of programs you consider, the more likely it will be that you can find a cost-effective, convenient solution to your training needs.
- Do the instructors have real-world experience, especially with the types of problems or challenges being faced by your company? Some vendors use professional instructors who present the material very well but have little depth in the subject matter. Will the instructor be able to answer questions, or just repeat the materials that the vendor has provided? Has the instructor actually worked in solving similar problems, or is his or her experience limited to talking about problems and solutions?
- Is there a danger of employees inadvertently releasing critical proprietary information as they try to solve the company's problems in the class? This can happen when program participants are required to bring a real problem with them to work on as part of the program and are required to share their problems and solutions with the rest of the attendees.

When considering whether to develop and deliver programs in-house, consider these factors:

- Does the company have sufficient knowledge resources to devote to the task? If knowledge and skills related to the company's problems are in short supply (as they may well be if you feel the need to train more employees), can some of those resources be freed up to train other employees? This is always a difficult question.
- Does the company have sufficient educational expertise to develop the needed instruction? Even when subject matter experts exist, they may not have the skills necessary to develop and deliver effective training. When putting together an in-house program, you need both subject matter expertise and educational expertise.

- Will this strategy meet the company's needs on time? Even when the company has both the subject matter expertise and the required instructional methodology skills, the need for training employees may be so critical that it will be more effective to buy or rent the expertise in the short term to ensure that the need is met on time. In this case, the company may want to use the internal expertise to develop ongoing training, after the immediate need is met.
- Is this strategy cost-effective in comparison with buying or renting external instructional resources? This will depend on many factors, such as the number of employees needing training, the cost of developing the needed instruction, the cost of the external resources, the number of months or years the training will need to continue, and so on.

When evaluating whether to bring an external program in-house, consider these factors:

- Are the external resources willing to tailor their approaches and materials to company needs? Or are they only willing to deliver what they have already developed?
- Do the external resources have real-world experience, especially in the company's industry and with the types of problems the company is facing? Or are the instructors simply "talking heads"?
- Are the external resources willing to provide ongoing support to the trainees? Or are they simply interested in giving the program, collecting the fee, and leaving?

Finally, when considering whether the company can solve the problem by applying knowledge and skill resources that already exist within the company, consider these factors:

- Can you identify the knowledge and skills resources within the company's boundaries?

- Can you free up those resources from their other responsibilities to make them available to develop and deliver instruction?
- Are there other methods to help spread these internal resources that will not require taking people off their regular jobs?

BUY, RENT, OR DEVELOP?

Given all of the alternatives within the three strategies, and the many more combinations of methods, how does a company decide which path to select? Let's look at a process to make this decision.

Question #1: Do the Required Knowledge and Skills Already Exist within the Company?

In most cases, if the knowledge and skills are resident in the company and can be made available to help solve a problem in a timely, cost-effective manner, I feel you should do so, for the following reasons:

- Company employees are already aware of how the information will be used to solve company problems. They do not need to be trained on company methods—they already know them. Current employees can also tailor learning activities to fit into the company culture.
- By using company employees, you are creating a network of expert resources within the company, people who can be used not only to provide instruction but also to provide advice as problems arise as employees try out their new skills and knowledge.
- Being asked to share their knowledge and skills with other employees also is a way of providing recognition and status to current employees. These types of nonmonetary rewards are important in building employee loyalty.

Sharing knowledge and skills is not a problem in very small companies where everyone works together on a daily basis, where people know each other, and where any given problem will be known by everyone. In such small companies, people will volunteer their knowledge and skills if they think they can help solve a problem.

The difficulties arise in larger companies where multiple locations, business units, functions, and so on bar employees from knowing each other's capabilities and where problems being faced in one part of the company are not clearly visible to people in other parts. Although many companies have a computerized database that can identify every item in their physical inventories, regardless of location, few, if any, have similar databases to identify the company's stock of knowledge resources. In Chapter 9 we will examine tactics that companies can use to build their own knowledge network.

If the knowledge resources you need do exist within the company, you then need to ask the following questions:

- Are the internal knowledge resources sufficient to meet the challenge? Do the identified people have the depth or breadth of knowledge and skills to do the job adequately? How does their expertise compare with available external resources?
- Are the required people available to work on the problem? What priority does the new problem have in relation to the work currently being done by the people? Can the people be made available to solve the problem in the time frame required for its resolution?
- What are the relative costs of using internal resources versus looking outside the company to solve the problem? Are you going to spend more to develop your own solution than to buy a ready-made solution from the outside?
- Are there other benefits to be gained by using internal resources? Will it help protect proprietary information? Will it help further develop one of the company's core competencies? Will the new assignment help develop the designated employees for future assignments?

Question 2: If the Needed Knowledge and Skills Are Not Available Internally, Do They Exist Outside the Company?

If you cannot find the knowledge and skills you need within your own company's boundaries, you need to look outside. Start close to home, within the company's value chain—can you find what you need within your chain of suppliers and customers? If you already have good working relationships with these companies, it will be easier to work with them to solve the problem. If the company's value chain cannot supply a solution, then expand the search to other companies, consultants, colleges and universities, and so on. Or you might consider hiring people with the needed knowledge and skills.

In conducting your external search for the needed knowledge and skills, consider these questions:

- Are the needed knowledge and skills related to the company's core competencies? If they are, you should tend toward solutions that bring the knowledge resources permanently into the company, that is, buy or develop rather than rent. In an earlier example, Whirlpool decided that the technology needed for gas burners for its new range was not part of its core competencies and, therefore, had no problem in subcontracting the design of the burners to Eaton Corporation.
- Are the knowledge and skills needed on a long-term or a short-term basis? If they are needed on a long-term basis, you should consider a buy strategy or a develop strategy rather than a rent strategy. If needed only on a short-term basis, it may be more cost-effective and timely to rent than to buy or develop the knowledge and skills.
- Will the results of the project be proprietary to the company? If so, you should tend to use a buy or develop strategy. Despite nondisclosure agreements and promises of secrecy, work done outside the company can never have the total security of work done internally by the company's own employees.

- Does the work depend on knowledge of the company's culture, resources, methods, and so on? Consider how much time and effort it will take to get the external resources up to speed on everything they need to know versus how much time it will take to develop the needed knowledge and skills within the company.
- How well are the external knowledge and skill resources matched to the company's exact needs? If there is an exact match, and the external resource can meet the company's needs in a timely, cost-effective manner, then proceed. If the match is not exact, consider whether you should invest in developing the knowledge and skills of the external resource versus developing those of the company's own employees.

Question 3: What If the Needed Knowledge Resources Are Available Neither Inside Nor Outside the Company?

When your search for the needed knowledge and skills both inside and outside your company is not successful, you must either find another way around the problem or must develop the needed knowledge and skills yourself. For example, if the characteristics of a new engine being built by the company require a new type of lubricant and no current lubricant on the market meets your requirements, you can either try to develop the lubricant yourself or you can modify the engine design so that it can function with a currently available product. If you decide to develop the new lubricant, you will again have the choices of doing it totally within the company, of partnering with a lubricant manufacturer, or of totally subcontracting the job to the lubricant manufacturer. The decision should be based on the importance of the lubricant to your company's core competencies and on whether you have the needed skills and knowledge to undertake the job yourself.

EIGHT

LEARNING FROM THE BEST

No company, no matter how successful, no matter how modern its technology, no matter how excellent its employees and its training programs, no matter how many awards it has won for its products or services, can claim to be the best at everything it does. Even the most successful company in any industry, if it examines each of its business processes, both major and minor, will find other companies that outperform it on at least some basic time, quality, customer satisfaction, or financial measures.

Any effort to transform or renew a company must be based on the company's efforts to learn new and better ways of doing business. To become the best in any aspect of your business, from product design to service delivery, from warehouse logistics to financial management, from how you hire and train your employees to how you use technology, you must strive to learn from the best available resources.

BENCHMARKING BEST PRACTICES

> Benchmarking . . . is being humble enough to admit that someone else is better at something and wise enough to try to learn how to match and even surpass them at it.[1]
>
> David Ottenhouse
> International Benchmark Clearing House

Benchmarking and *Best Practices* have become watchwords in the business of quality improvement. Whether searching for best practices within your own company or outside it, these are *learning programs* where companies search out the best knowledge and skill resources on a given topic, learn how others have structured and implemented the same or similar business processes, and use that knowledge to improve their own performance. The process of *learning from the best* is outlined in Table 8.1.

ACKNOWLEDGING THAT OTHERS MAY KNOW MORE THAN YOU DO

No learning can take place unless the learner acknowledges that there is something to learn. Too often, when processes appear to be working, we ask why we should "rock the boat"—as the old saw goes: "If it ain't broke, don't fix it." At other times we are blinded by our own pride in the processes we have worked hard to develop over time, or we fear to admit that someone else may have a better idea.

> The director of clinical improvement at a large health maintenance organization tells how difficult it can be to get doctors to question their long-standing practices: "I went to a group of obstetricians and showed them that their rate of performing cesarean sections was 30 percent higher than the rest of their HMO colleagues and 20 percent higher than the national average. Their response was: 'That may

Table 8.1
Learning from the Best

1. Acknowledge that others may know more than you do.
2. Prioritize your learning needs.
3. Find sources of best practices.
4. Analyze best practices and compare with your own.
5. Choose your own course.
6. Implement changes.
7. Repeat steps 1 to 6 on an ongoing basis.

be true, but we only do C-sections when they are needed. There's nothing wrong with the way we practice medicine.' "

If your company has established a strong learning culture, if all five foundations are firmly in place, your employees at all levels will welcome the opportunity to learn from others and will already be in the continuous inquiry mode required to implement a "learn from the best" program. People throughout the company will be striving to discover their areas of unconscious ignorance, to discover what they "don't know they don't know." This requires a certain sense of humility, a sense that certainly wasn't present in the physicians just mentioned.

Overcoming Resistance

But what if your employees resist the idea that they can improve the performance of their business processes? What if they are so dedicated to the way they have been doing things that they show no interest in seeking better methods? If you face this situation, you can use two basic approaches to overcome this resistance:

1. Demonstrate the need for change.
2. Give employees incentives to change.

You can demonstrate the need to change, to improve performance, in several ways:

- *Use statistics* to compare current performance with industry or functional standards. Many industries publish statistics on basic performance measures, for example, average time for insurance claim processing, rates of cesarean sections, or owner loyalty statistics. In many cases, comparing your company's statistics with the industry averages will dramatically point out the need for improvement.
- *Use customer surveys.* Ask customers to compare your company's performance on key measures with those of

your competitors. The "voice of the customer" can provide its own mandate for change and improvement.

- *Read articles* in industry and professional journals and magazines to see how other companies are improving their own performance. These publications often do their own surveys and publish performance statistics. Many also feature stories about best practices and innovative approaches to common problems.

You can also overcome resistance to change by giving employees incentive to change.

- *Incentives* should be based on making improvements, with no distinction made between whether those improvements are invented internally or are learned from others. The "not-invented-here" syndrome, where employees fear that by admitting that others know more than they do or that others have discovered a better way of doing things, has kept many companies from needed improvements. Credit must be given for making improvements, no matter what their source.
- *Involve the people who need to improve.* Too often, companies that have discovered the need for improvement in a particular process or function immediately bring in external solutions without ever consulting the people who are currently involved. Too many companies assume that current employees either don't have any ideas about how to improve their work or that they cannot learn to make improvements. Involving employees in change efforts is, in many ways, more effective than other incentives. Ask them for their ideas. Give them subscriptions to professional and industry publications. Send them to conferences where they can hear of other companies' experiences.

My colleague Ed Deevy tells of a local bank that, in searching for ways of making the bank more user-friendly, hired a consultant to redesign the bank's lobby area. In the course of his work, the consultant asked several employees for their thoughts. One employee pulled out an old envelope and sketched a new lobby area on its back. The employees had already been thinking about what needed to be done. The consultant recognized that the sketch was a good response to the president's wishes. When asked why she had never volunteered her ideas, the employee responded: "Nobody asked."[2]

When Resistance Cannot Be Overcome

What if you have created a strong learning culture and have put in place incentives for improvement and given employees opportunities to share their ideas and to learn from others, and employees still are reluctant to acknowledge the need to change and keep defending the status quo? In those cases, you may have no choice but to replace the employees with people who are more open to new ideas. It is never easy to fire an employee, but at times there is no choice.

Sometimes employees' personal needs are so overwhelming that they cannot focus on their work. In these cases, you should attempt to help the employee—it is why so many companies have instituted employee assistance programs. But you must also keep focused on the need for improvement, and if the employee is totally resistant to the needed changes, you may need to change employees.

I had contracted with an instructional development group to develop a self-paced course on one of the company's products. The person assigned to the task was falling far behind schedule and making major errors with the content. Despite coaching from his management and referral to the company's employee assistance program, his performance was only getting worse. Finally, the project had to be taken away from him to meet deadlines and get the content correct.

Three months later it was discovered that the man had been suffering from the final stages of an inoperable cancer and, understandably, was totally focused on this, which he kept secret from his family as well as from his colleagues, and he died soon thereafter. Everyone who knew him was very saddened by his passing. But everyone involved also acknowledged that taking the project from him was the right decision.

PRIORITIZING LEARNING NEEDS

If virtually every business process within a company can be improved, where do you start? Can everything be changed simultaneously? Even if you could get everyone in the desired learning mode immediately, do you want to tackle everything at once? The answer is: "No, you can't change everything at once. You need to set priorities." These priorities should be based on:

- Sources of the company's competitive advantage and disadvantage.
- The company's core competencies.
- The interrelatedness of the company's business processes and internal and external value chains.

Sources of Competitive Advantage and Disadvantage

Unless your company has an ironclad monopoly in its market with no prospect of any other competitor ever entering that market (a virtual impossibility in today's global economy), there are particular business processes, certain aspects of the way in which your employees do their work, that help or hinder your performance in the market. These factors may include how quickly an insurance company settles claims, how customers perceive the quality of automobiles or appliances, the ambiance of a restaurant, the amount of leg room on an airplane, how long it takes to make an appointment at an HMO, and so on. Companies need to prioritize their "learning from the best" efforts on the factors that will make them successful. For example, in one company, the plant maintenance function undertook a TQM program and benchmarked with other companies with similar manufacturing plants and processes. The results of their efforts were impressive—reduced costs and improved maintenance—but would have counted for little if the company's products were not competitively designed and marketed.

So what are your company's sources of competitive advantage and disadvantage? Where do you want to improve processes so that you can stretch out your lead? Where do you need to catch up to your competitors? A lot of this information should be available from the planning efforts discussed in earlier chapters. You should be able to prioritize your learning needs based on what was learned in developing the company's vision and long- and short-term plans.

The Company's Core Competencies

In searching for ways of building competitive advantage, companies also need to identify and focus on their core competencies. Williams Companies, originally (and still) a gas pipeline company, built on its transportation core competency by stringing fiber-optic cables along its existing pipelines to create (in 1992) the fourth-largest telecommunications network in the United States. Sara Lee Corporation used its core competency in brand marketing to expand into packaged apparel.

As stated in a *Business Week* editorial: "Creating growth is often just a matter of identifying strengths and making an all-out commitment to build on them."[3] By focusing on core competencies, a company will strengthen the competitive advantage it has built and can extend that advantage into the future. The building and strengthening of core competencies must be given high priority for learning from the best.

The Interrelatedness of Business Processes and Value Chains

When changes are made in a particular business process, companies must also examine how those changes will affect other interrelated processes and parts of the internal and external value chains.

> A health care system developed a program to reduce the number of laboratory tests being ordered by physicians. It was felt that a lot of resources were being wasted in ordering unneeded tests and by ordering more expensive, state-of-the-art tests when older, more economical methods produced equally valid results. For example, in doing throat cultures for strep infections, the older testing method takes 24 hours for results and costs no more than a few dollars. Newer tests can provide results in just a few minutes but cost many times as much. In most cases, there is no harm in waiting a day for the lab results. But many physicians liked the new technology and the ability to diagnose a strep throat while the patient was still in the office.
>
> The campaign was successful, substantially reducing the number of tests ordered and resulting in substantial cost savings for the health care system. But because the system administrators had not examined the effects of the campaign on the entire value chain, a related but unforeseen problem arose—the productivity of the system's laboratories decreased sharply, and the lab administrators were called on the carpet.

No single business process can be changed without affecting other processes and other links in a company's internal and external value chains. These considerations must be addressed in *planning* the change efforts, not just reacted to when problems arise. By practicing fire *prevention*, companies can avoid having to spend a lot of time fighting fires.

Sometimes it is one of a company's suppliers or customers that can come up with innovative solutions to a company's problems. Collaborative problem solving can result in improved performance by both parties in a partnership.

> "Wal-Mart gave supplier Mead Johnson real-time access to product movement over electronic data interchange [EDI].

> Instead of responding to orders, Mead Johnson responds to need and ships appropriate goods. . . . It has meant a spectacular improvement in inventory turns—from under 10 to more than 100 at Wal-Mart; from 12 to 52 at Mead Johnson. Wal-Mart has cut hundreds of millions of dollars in inventory costs."[4]

Your company's examination of its business processes and its internal and external value chains, undertaken in building the five foundations, establishes the framework for seeking improvements throughout your own organization as well as in partnership with your customers and suppliers. Learning from the best should include your internal and external partners, for by learning from each other and together, you can improve your individual and collective performance.

FINDING SOURCES OF BEST PRACTICES

In searching for best practices, companies are well advised to look inside the company and within the company's value chain, as well as outside. No single company or industry can be the best at everything, and lessons can be learned from many sources.

Looking for Solutions Within

"Have you ever had a really good idea that you couldn't get heard? Have you ever known that you could help your company over some hurdle but were barred from helping because you were at the wrong level, in the wrong part of the organization, or because the person who owned the problem just wasn't open to others' ideas?"

When I have asked these questions of thousands of people in dozens of audiences across the United States and Canada, I have yet to see anyone in the audience who didn't start nodding vigorously. We have all been in this frustrating position, probably many times over the course of our careers. And for many of us, the continual rejection of our ideas has resulted in our being conditioned to keep our mouths shut, to keep our bright ideas to ourselves.

Companies seeking to renew or transform themselves must create an open learning environment where ideas are valued for their worth rather than for the level of their source. If your company's five foundations are solidly in place, you have already done a lot to create this type of environment. You have shown by leadership that new ideas are valued. You have given people the training and tools to develop their ideas and to bring them forth. You have created measurement and reward systems that encourage and reward good ideas, no matter where their source may be.

The most likely source for these good ideas originates with the people who are doing the work. As in the previous example of the local bank, many good ideas are never brought forth because "nobody ever asked." Ideas for improvements in customer service can often be found in the customer service department, coming from the people who daily face the challenges of meeting customer needs. Improvements in factory processes are just as likely to originate from the machine operators as from the industrial engineers. But you need to ask, you need to create an environment where people are open to sharing their ideas, where management is open to ideas springing from any and every source.

It is important to look inside for answers to company challenges for several reasons. First, even in companies that are not performing well overall, there may well be some "pockets of excellence"—places where an extraordinary group or individual is already doing an exceptional job, one that is as good as or better than you will find on the outside. Or it may be that a function you don't feel is performing particularly well compares favorably with similar functions in other companies.

Second, people like to feel included. Even if their particular groups or locations are not operating at a world-class level, they may be very proud of the work they are doing in their small piece of the company universe. In surveying internal best practices, it is important to include all relevant locations and groups in the survey—even if a particular manufacturing plant, for example, is the company's poorest overall performer, it may still include an outstanding logistics effort or plant maintenance effort or employee communications program.

Third, by finding and highlighting internal best practices, you are providing a very tangible, albeit nonmonetary reward to people who are excelling at their jobs. This recognition can come from publicizing internal best practices, giving outstanding performers an opportunity to train other company employees, as is done by Northern Telecom, or by giving employees a chance to present their work at internal and external conferences. All of these actions can help build pride in work and employee morale while helping to improve overall company performance.

How Dow Chemical Plants Learn from Each Other

Dow Chemical has established a series of technology centers whose job it is to conduct internal benchmarking for its major lines of business. According to one center director, William R. Knee: "They have a responsibility to know where our technology stands versus everybody else's, to look for new and emerging technology, to look for trends, and then to pull all that together . . . to help maintain the competitive edge of the company."[5] For example:

> A team of three or four people from a tech center attached to a Michigan plastics facility . . . might go to Germany for a week to talk to the staff of a plastics plant there about its manufacturing techniques. . . . If the German facility were to be found clearly superior, the tech team would bring back enough data from the staff so Dow headquarters in Midland, Mich., could conduct a cost-benefit analysis. And if the team gets the nod from headquarters, it would begin the transfer, coordinating research inquiries from the Michigan plant and otherwise seeing the transfer through to implementation.[6]

Learning from Others

When looking for external benchmarking partners, you are well advised to look for similarities between the challenges facing your company and those that have already been faced, and successfully resolved, by others. It is important that you benchmark against similar companies. A small company, like Ace Clearwater Enterprises (described in Chapter 2), does not have the resources to implement world-class technological solutions available to a General Motors or a Boeing. ACE needed to compare itself with companies with which it was competing, of similar size, resources, technology, and so on.

This does not mean that you have to benchmark with companies in your own industry; in fact, your closest competitors are probably the least likely to want to share information with you. When Xerox wanted to benchmark its customer services, it didn't go to another copier company but to clothing and sporting goods retailer L. L. Bean, long known for the excellence of its customer service.

Early in his tenure as General Electric's CEO, Jack Welch formed teams to find best practices within the network of GE companies. For many geographically diverse companies, practices for similar functions vary so widely among different locations and business units that a lot of good information on best practices can be found within the company's own boundaries.

Customers and suppliers within a company's value chain can also be valuable sources of best practices information. They may themselves have some exemplary practices to learn from. They also have contact with many other companies within their own value chains and may be able to provide pointers to other sources of information.

Health care systems in today's world of hospitals, group practices, clinics, HMOs, PPOs (preferred provider organizations), and so on have excellent opportunities to benchmark within their own bounds. Large health maintenance organizations often include dedicated clinics, relationships with many hospitals, thousands of physicians, and dozens of laboratories.

Finding Other Sources of Best Practices Information

In Chapter 3 we discussed a variety of sources of planning information that companies can use to formulate their long- and short-term plans. These same sources of information (see Table 3.1) will also yield many opportunities for benchmarking.

With the popularity of benchmarking, a variety of benchmarking information centers have been created to facilitate company efforts. One of these is the International Benchmarking Clearing House, a service of the American Productivity & Quality Center (APQC). Started in 1991 by a group of 87 companies, the center provides training, research, and information services to its member companies. Similar programs have been instituted by a number of professional organizations, such as the Continuous Improvement Center of the Institute of Management Accountants.

Most companies are open to benchmarking activities, especially if they feel that they also have something to learn from their benchmarking partners. Some, however, are not open to benchmarking inquiries.

> In researching this book, I contacted the director of organizational learning at a well-known manufacturing company. I explained what I was trying to do with the book and asked if I might come to talk with her, to learn more about the company's exemplary learning programs, so that I could include some stories about the company in this book. Her response: "We're flattered by your request. And we agree that we are doing some exemplary things with our learning programs. But we consider our approaches to be a source of competitive advantage, and we are not open to sharing them with anyone outside the company."

ANALYZING OTHERS' PRACTICES

Whatever benchmarking methodology you select, and many variations are described in the wealth of benchmarking literature, you must apply the methodology rigorously to both your own processes and those that you are examining. Otherwise, you will have no basis for comparison. You also need to focus on those factors over which you have control. For example, in examining how to improve warehouse performance, some cost factors are more controllable than others.

> "Warehouse costs are a factor of labor hours times wages, square footage times the price per square foot, and equipment investment times the capitalization rate. Warehouse

> managers have little or no influence on wage rates, price per square foot, or the capitalization rate, so the logical conclusion is to focus attention on the labor hours, square footage needs, and equipment needs.
>
> "Key performance indicators include productivity, accuracy, response time, storage density, level of automation (which may be dictated by the way product is handled—palletized, case or broken case)."[7]

The point of your search is to find similarities between other companies' practices and your company's needs. You need to be open not just to minor improvements but also to radically different ways of doing business. You may end up seeing ways of improving the company's current processes, or you may discover a totally new approach that mandates that the company scrap its current process in favor of a new one.

Benchmarking versus Business Process Reengineering

Business process reengineering (BPR) is one of today's hottest topics. The goals of reengineering are similar to those of benchmarking, that is, to greatly improve the performance of a company's business processes. The two approaches also have several major differences.

First, business process reengineering focuses primarily on the use of information technology in the company's business processes. Most of the companies selling BPR are information technology consulting firms. Benchmarking, on the other hand, is not limited to information technology but may include any business activity. Customer service, for example, may be improved by investing in information technology being used by customer service personnel. But customer service encompasses much more than technology. Benchmarking of customer service functions may also include human skills. Progressive Insurance, for example, greatly improved its customer service ratings and customer retention rates by putting claims representatives through "empathy training."

Second, with business process reengineering, a team of company personnel, often with the aid of consultants, start rebuilding business processes from scratch; that is, they ask, "If we started all over again, ignoring what we already have, how would we design this business process?" BPR can yield substantial results from these activities. But BPR limits possibilities to the abilities and imaginations of current company employees. It does not consider that the company may learn from others of new ways to improve the performance of its business processes that the company has never considered. BPR allows employees to learn from each other and to create a new future together. But by limiting possibilities to those created by current employees (and consultants), it may miss real opportunities that can be best achieved by learning from the best.

The third point is that BPR is a method of building a new solution from scratch. With learning from the best, companies may indeed choose to build a new process from scratch but may also find that another company has a process or technology already developed that can be purchased or adapted to provide a more timely or cost-effective solution.

CHOOSE YOUR OWN COURSE

After you have conducted your benchmarking studies and have found the best practices you want to emulate or adapt to your own company's business processes, you have to decide how you want to proceed. Do you want to reengineer your process? Do you want to replicate a practice or a system you found elsewhere? Did you find that you are already the best at what you do?

Committing to Improvement

Whatever course you choose, you must make a solid commitment to make changes that will result in improvements in a timely, cost-effective manner. Some years ago, while I was working for Digital Equipment Corporation, I participated in a meeting of trainers and organizational development consultants to discuss the selling of team-related training programs to Digital's customers. Some of the meeting's participants were part of formal customer training groups, others were internal trainers and consultants who were looking to improve their chances of survival by starting to generate revenue for the company. We had all just attended a team-building course given by a university professor, a course that had been developed with funding from Digital and that the university was offering to license to Digital for no fee. We had all agreed that it was an excellent course.

The disagreements arose because each of the parties represented in the meeting had all done some team-related training with somewhat different approaches. Each group wanted to take time to tailor the course to its own individual style and to incorporate some of its personal material and exercises into the course. After more than an hour of discussion and debate, I intervened.

"You have all said that you have customers waiting for you to train their teams. You have all agreed that the university course is excellent, even if it doesn't include your personal material. You have all agreed that you could pick up the university course and start teaching it tomorrow. Even if you could all agree on adding some other material or exercises, it will take several months, and thousands of dollars in development costs, to make those changes. In that time, many of your customers are going to find other vendors. If you really want to get into this business, you need to start now, and you have a course ready to go, which you have acknowledged as being excellent. It's time to put your egos aside and make a business decision. Do you want to get into this business or not?"

After several more hours of discussion, the group continued to agree to disagree. To the best of my knowledge, the university course was never utilized within Digital or by Digital with its customers. Most of the people who attended the meeting are no longer with Digital because, lacking customers for the services they wanted to provide, Digital decided not to be in this business.

If you want to renew or transform your company, if you want to be really effective in improving your individual, group, organizational, and company performance, you need to make decisions. You can't spend forever trying to find the "perfect" solution. You can't reject every reasonable alternative because it does not provide a "perfect" fit. You need to adapt the best solutions you can find, internally or externally, and do it quickly and effectively. The time you may spend haggling over a perfect solution to one problem can better be spent finding solutions to other problems. A 90 percent solution implemented today is better than a 100 percent solution implemented a year from now.

Factors Affecting Your Choice of Course

For the improvements you want to make from your learnings, should you buy, rent, or develop your solutions? Are these real core competencies for your company, or will you do better to buy or rent a solution from the outside? No single strategy will work for all companies—you need to plan your own course. (Many of the factors around knowledge acquisition strategies were discussed in Chapter 7.)

IMPLEMENT CHANGES

Your course is plotted. Now is the time for action. Benchmarking, learning from the best, is not an intellectual exercise. The benchmarking studies do no one any good sitting on a shelf or in a file cabinet gathering dust. The only purpose for all of the work done thus far is to enable you to take action, to improve your business processes, to undertake your company's transformation or renewal.

Your action plans will be determined by the path you have chosen, by your decisions to buy, rent, or develop solutions. It may include the introduction of methodologies, such as statistical process control (SPC) or quality function deployment (QFD), new training for employees, new systems, or a myriad of other options. In the implementation plans you develop, the focus must be on action. In Chapter 10 we will examine one method, action learning teams, recommended for implementing any change program you choose.

CONTINUALLY LEARNING FROM THE BEST

While your company is striving to catch up to the best practices you have identified through the process just described, those whom you are emulating are not standing still—they are improving on their own processes. At the same time, other companies are inventing their own solutions to similar challenges. Learning from the best is not a onetime activity. Just as continuous improvement is a watchword of the TQM movement, so continuous learning is a watchword of transformational learning. Learning never stops, and opportunities for improving your business processes never end. There is never time for a breather.

NINE

BUILDING A KNOWLEDGE NETWORK

Transformational learning to enable company renewal must use all of the knowledge and skills of all company employees. Often the exact skills and knowledge the company needs to succeed in its renewal efforts already exist within the company's boundaries but are never utilized. It is not that the people aren't willing but that the person, team, or business unit needing specific skills and knowledge doesn't know where to look for it. In other cases, one business unit may make major investments in developing a new approach to product development, customer service, or other business processes, not knowing that they already exist in another business unit or site that developed a similar process, or an even better one, in the recent past.

The purpose of a knowledge network is to ensure that all company knowledge and skills become part of the company inventory and can be accessed by any company employee, regardless of function, business unit, or location.

KEEPING INVENTORY

Many world-class manufacturing companies have a computerized, networked inventory system that can locate any part or raw material stock at any of the company's locations almost instantaneously. In these companies, if the part or material being sought is not in stock, the procurement function has a system that can locate a source and qualify that source on the bases of price, availability, quality, delivery, and so on, again, almost instantaneously.

Many companies, in both the manufacturing and service sectors, have spent years, and millions of dollars, developing systems that help them manage their stock of *physical* assets. Few of these companies have ever started to develop similar systems to help manage their *knowledge* assets.

Companies spend large amounts of time (not to mention money) buying, renting, or developing skills and knowledge that are already present within their current employee population because they have no way of identifying which employees have particular sets of skills and knowledge. This is especially common when the needed skills and knowledge differ from an employee's current job responsibilities or when the employee works at a site remote from that experiencing the need. The concept of a knowledge network is designed to help companies take advantage of the skills and knowledge they already possess.

By *knowledge network* I mean a systematized approach to:

- Inventory individual and organizational knowledge resources within the company.
- Provide pointers or access to external knowledge resources available to the company.
- Provide a database describing learning tools and resources available to company employees. (It may also provide on-line access to some of those tools.)
- Provide tools and databases that will help the company and its employees engage in continuous learning.

Conceptually, a knowledge network is not reliant on computer technology, but such technology can make the knowledge network easier to access and use. The discussion here focuses on the contents of the knowledge network rather than the enabling technologies. Dozens of computer-based applications can be used to build your company's knowledge network, and dozens more are being introduced each year. Rather than get bogged down in technology that will continuously evolve, let's examine why a company would want to build a knowledge network and what should be contained in that network.

Let's explore the concept of a knowledge network from the point of view of each of its four major components:

1. The Internal Knowledge Resource Database (IKR).
2. The External Knowledge Resource Database (EKR).
3. The Learning Resources and Tools Database (LRT).
4. Individual and Group Learning Facilitators (LF).

For each major component, we will look at what's available today and what a future knowledge network would contain.

THE INTERNAL KNOWLEDGE RESOURCE DATABASE

Just as many companies have inventory systems that can easily locate company stocks of parts or materials regardless of location, so they should be able to locate their stocks of knowledge and skills easily. Unfortunately, knowledge and skills do not come with readily available part numbers or bar codes nor can they be ordered in specific quantities for delivery on a specified date. The Internal Knowledge Resource Database (IKR) is designed to provide this type of inventory. The IKR database should be designed so that any manager needing to locate some particular knowledge or set of skills can search for them across all company employees, regardless of level, function, or location.

The IKR database has two major subcomponents—one that keeps track of personnel and another that tracks the company's intellectual assets.

- The human resources database includes resumes of company employees, a competency database, a training database, and so on.
- The inventory of company intellectual assets includes patents held by the company, processes, technologies, tools, equipment, and so on owned by the company or for which the company owns rights.

IKR Databases: Current Practice

Many companies today maintain a database containing the resumes of all company employees. In many cases, these databases contain the resumes that employees submitted to the company when they applied for a job, which have rarely, if ever, been updated. As with most resumes, these include educational history (degrees earned) and brief descriptions of precompany work experience. In some companies, the resumes are coded for major job classifications, for example, marketing or engineering.

Human Resources Information Systems (HRIS) also contain basic data about each employee, for example, date of birth, date of hire, job history within the company, compensation levels, benefits selections, attendance records, and performance ratings.

Competency databases are becoming very popular in many companies. Caterpillar, for example, maintains a very structured competency database for all factory workers, listing tasks for which each employee has qualified. The competency database is often tied closely to a training database, which contains each employee's record of training taken and competencies achieved. (Some debate exists as to whether these databases should be tracking competencies or performance; that is, having a competency does not guarantee the performance of the individual—you may have learned how to do a task, but that does not necessarily mean that you will do it well.) All in all, competency databases are a major leap over resume databases, but they require much more work—classifying competencies that employees need for particular jobs, tying competencies to specific training programs and other learning activities, assessment of each employee for each competency, and so on.

Consulting giant Booz Allen, for example, has created a system called "Knowledge On-Line" (KOL) to catalog employees' backgrounds and completed projects. KOL is designed to help any consultant in the firm tap the expertise and ideas of other Booz Allen employees, regardless of location or specialty.

> As long as he's got his laptop and a phone line, he can log onto KOL. One icon that appears on the screen is slugged Experts/Resumes/History; click on it and type a name, and

> up pops a colleague's resume; or type "customer service," and the system will deliver a stack of resumes of consultants who know the subject. Another icon is tagged simply Knowledge. Behind it are a number of databases. These contain about 1,500 documents (the number is growing rapidly), cross-filed by industry and topics such as reengineering, marketing, and change management. Our man in Jakarta can download oil-industry benchmarking studies, find journal articles, or copy a document, written for a client in another industry, that contains an especially good checklist of things to look for when reengineering customer service.[1]

More and more companies are recognizing the importance and value of their intellectual assets. These assets may include patents held by the company, company-proprietary systems and methods, company-developed tools and technologies, and so on, which the company feels give it some competitive advantage. Research-intensive companies, such as pharmaceutical and chemical companies, were among the first to recognize the value of these assets and to develop systems to inventory and control them.

It is also important to keep track of processes, tools, and technologies for which the company has purchased rights. Too often, for example, one group will go out and purchase a new technology, never knowing that the company has already paid for rights to a different, but perfectly suitable technology. Not only does this cost the company money, it often results in different but comparable groups using incompatible technologies. This incompatibility may not matter for the current project but may cause problems in the future when the two groups are required to work together.

IKR Database: Future Scenarios

Scenario 1A

A program manager reviews a request for proposal (RFP) from a major customer. She lists the skills and knowledge needed to undertake the project, including specific technical skills related to the job, knowledge of the customer's industry, experience working with the customer or bidding on other RFPs from the customer, language skills (if the project is foreign or multinational in scope), knowledge of other companies that will be competing for the contract, and so on. Entering the correct codes or keywords into the IKR system, she receives back a report listing company employees categorized by knowledge and skill requirements, experience level, location, current assignments, and so on. After contacting each of these resources by phone to check on availability and willingness to work on the proposal, she assembles her team and gets to work on preparing the company's proposal.

Scenario 2A

A self-managed production team learns that one of its members will need surgery and will be out for three to four months. The team examines the work being done by that team member and the skills and knowledge required. After determining which parts of that person's work can be assumed by other team members, the team finds that it will still need a temporary replacement with a specific set of skills. Entering the information into the IKR system, the team locates one employee in its own plant, three in other company plants, and two others in the company's field service group with the requisite skills. After making several phone calls, the team arranges for a temporary replacement.

Scenario 3A

A software company that has been developing products for a particular operating system discovers a new market for its products if it can convert them to work on another operating system. The company has no group of developers with responsibility for the new operating system. By searching the IKR database, the company finds several employees who have been taking courses at the local university on the second operating system. When management talks with those employees, it finds that one of them has already done the conversion as practice for his skills on the new operating system.

The IKR database of the future is designed to provide an inventory of the skills and knowledge of all company employees so that anyone in the company with a need for a particular set of skills and knowledge can quickly and easily identify employees who meet those requirements. Many times companies bypass opportunities or quickly spend money to buy or rent external resources when the needed resources are already available within the company.

To be able to find those resources, the IKR database must contain at least the following types of information:

- Competencies—These should include those that the employee brings from precompany work and those that the employee has developed off the job. The software company described in the preceding Scenario 3A saved itself a lot of time and expense by finding current employees who had developed the needed competencies outside their jobs.
- Employee Experience—Jobs held and types of work done throughout the employee's career. This category should be broader than technical skills or competencies and should include such items as languages spoken, time spent living in other countries, and industries in which the employee has worked.

  For example, an accounting firm received an inquiry from a large dairy farm looking for assistance with its financial record keeping. The firm had never worked with a dairy farm before. By using its IKR database, it located a junior employee who had grown up on a dairy farm and worked on it until entering graduate school. The company won the work from the dairy because it was able to show that it understood the dairy industry and that the person working with the customer spoke its language.

  The competencies listed in this section should not relate solely to technical skills but also "softer" skills. Has the employee had experience in working as part of a team or as a team leader? Has he or she acted as a group facilitator or as an instructor? Has the employee ever worked as a manager or supervisor? Has he or she participated in preparing a Baldrige Award application or been part of an ISO 9000 assessment team? These categories of experience are not always identified in listing formal competencies.

- Group/Company Experience—In larger companies, especially those that have decentralized operations or are part of a conglomerate, different plants or locations may have tried many different approaches to any given process or problem. It is important to capture the knowledge generated by these experiences. Have some plants used the Deming approach to quality management while others have followed Juran's advice and others have subscribed to the Crosby approach? What problems did each approach encounter in its implementation? How were these barriers overcome? What would those plants or locations recommend if they had to do it all over again? If another plant or location is exploring starting its own quality program, it can gain time and reduce expenses if it can share in the experience of others in the company, not to mention cost savings that may be gained by adding on to existing company licenses rather than negotiating a new license from scratch.
- Education—Subjects studied at any time in the person's career, including current enrollments. These should include not only company-sponsored or company-financed coursework but also subjects taken on the employee's own time, whether work-related or recreational. The fact that an employee has taken a course on a given subject, whether recently or long ago, is no guarantee that the person has the knowledge or skills the company may need at any point in time, but it gives the company a place to start.
- Areas of Interest—Most people have areas of interest that are far removed from their current job responsibilities. These may include new areas for career exploration or simply personal interests in a subject that the employee has pursued over some period of time. In-

cluding this category in the IKR database can help with employee career development and may yield fortuitous coincidences when the company must search for knowledge or skills in an area seemingly unrelated to the company's current business.

THE EXTERNAL KNOWLEDGE RESOURCE DATABASE

The procurement system that many companies have developed is a start for the External Knowledge Resource (EKR) database. These systems maintain a database of external suppliers for many of the parts and materials that the company purchases, including data on price, quality, delivery schedules, minimum order quantities, and so on. The EKR database is designed to provide a similar inventory of external sources of knowledge and skills.

The EKR database has two major components, one describing external resources (consultants, subcontractors, partners, etc.) that the company has utilized to meet knowledge and skill requirements that can't be met with internal resources, and the other describing potential sources with which the company has not yet worked but that company employees have identified.

EKR Databases: Current Practice

The few industry applications I have seen that match this scenario occur in the materials and logistics functions in manufacturing companies. These functions often maintain databases on suppliers and subcontractors for specific parts, materials, or manufacturing processes that the company typically outsources. In most companies, these "systems" consist of notebooks or personal files of the employees. In a few, they are formalized into an on-line database. In large, multisite companies, the databases tend to be local—who are the local suppliers or subcontractors? Few companies have a worldwide database. These few often have formal "vendor certification" programs for both materials and services. Few companies have formal systems for introducing new resources based on the experience of their employees, as will be described next.

This type of outsourcing practice is becoming more common as companies evolve toward becoming "virtual corporations." Two industries that have long practiced these principles are construction and motion pictures. In the construction industry, a general contractor takes responsibility for the total job and hires subcontractors to do most of the work. The general contractor keeps files (more likely a Rolodex than a database) of the various skills needed in typical jobs and which subcontractors have which skills. For example, the files may include several window subcontractors with notations that one is particularly experienced with high-rise construction and another is more experienced with windows for passive solar homes.

The motion picture industry is probably the premier example of the true virtual corporation, where a producer subcontracts with many individuals and companies to produce a movie. This is why you see as many as half a dozen companies listed in the opening credits and several dozen more in the trailing credits.

The EKR Database: Future Scenarios

Scenario 1B

The program manager has searched the IKR (internal) database and has found two specific requirements in the customer's RFP with which the company and its employees have had no experience. Switching to the EKR database, she enters the correct codes or keywords to see whether any of the company's partners or subcontractors can fill the bill. For the first requirement, she identifies two current subcontractors who have the needed skills. The database provides her with a report on the two, specifying other work they have done for the company, evaluations of that work, key contacts, and so on. After phone conversations with the two, she selects the one who is available to work on the proposal immediately.

The EKR database makes no match for the second requirement with any consultant or subcontractor who is currently working or has worked with the company. She does, however, find a note from a company employee who recently attended an industry conference and reported on two speakers who related their experience with similar projects. She contacts the employee, receives copies of the papers written by the presenters, and then contacts and later contracts with one to help the company with the proposal.

Scenario 2B

The self-managed production team is unable to find a match in the IKR (internal) database for the skills of the team member who would soon go on sick leave. Switching to the EKR database, the team finds the names of three contract employment agencies that have previously supplied the company with temporary personnel with the needed skills. After contacting the agencies, the team finds a temporary employee to fill the need.

Scenario 3B

The software company is unable to find any current employees with the skills needed to convert their application from the current operating system to a new one. Management checks the EKR database, but because this is a new requirement for the company, there are no entries for subcontractors with the needed skills. There are, however, several notes from employees about recent journal articles on the subject. Retrieving the journal articles from the online Learning Resources and Tools database (see the next section), the company calls the authors and gets referrals to several independent contractors with the requisite skills.

The EKR database is designed to enable employees to easily locate the knowledge and skill resources they need. If the company's needs cannot be met internally, through the IKR database, the queries are automatically forwarded into the external (EKR) database. The EKR database acts as a type of corporate memory, sharing resources that the company has previously utilized, along with evaluations of the company's experience with those resources. The database is worldwide, allowing employees to broaden their view of and access to resources that reside outside their local area.

As products, services, materials, technology, markets, and competition evolve over time, new requirements for knowledge and skills that the company has never before had will inevitably arise. Forward-looking employees, in trying to keep up with future trends, continually read professional and industry publications, take external courses, and attend conferences and symposia to try to keep up with developments in their fields and to prepare themselves for the future.

Too often the knowledge and skills gained through these activities have yielded benefit solely to the employees who have the subscriptions or have convinced the company to foot the bill for the conference. In a learning organization, this new knowledge must be shared to benefit other employees and the company as a whole. The EKR database provides opportunities for this type of sharing. As employees gather new information, they enter it into the database. The types of information may include:

- References to, and evaluations of, articles in professional and industry publications.
- Summaries and evaluations of presentations and papers from conferences and symposia. (Copies of presentations and papers will go into the company library system as will be described later in this chapter.)
- Pointers to potential knowledge and skill resources (consultants, subcontractors, etc.) identified through personal and professional networking.

THE LEARNING RESOURCES AND TOOLS DATABASE

Myriad learning resources are available both within and without companies. Many companies offer formal training programs on technical, professional, and managerial topics. Some go so far as to form "corporate universities." Others offer external courses at company facilities or pay employees' tuition to attend job-related, and often non-job-related college courses. If you subscribe to any professional journal or industry magazine, you see dozens of advertisements and receive a lot of mail from consultants, vendors, universities, and training companies that offer thousands of courses, seminars, and workshops per week across the continent.

But learning opportunities do not solely take the form of formal, stand-up instruction. People learn from each other in many ways, ranging from formal classroom settings to informal, nonstructured settings. On-the-job training, mentoring and coaching, reading, learning from a colleague, listening to an audiotape or watching a videotape, and taking a computer-based or multimedia instructional program are just a few of the ways in which people learn.

The Learning Resources and Tools (LRT) database is designed to organize information about the many learning opportunities available to company employees and make the information available to them in a timely, well-reasoned manner. It is also designed to provide employees with more than catalog descriptions by having employees annotate the descriptions with their own reviews and experiences in using a particular learning resource.

LRT Databases: Current Practice

Companies today provide their employees with information to foster their learning activities in a wide variety of ways. These include the sponsoring of internal training and development activities, provision of libraries of self-paced learning materials, information on local college and university courses, and information on other formal courses, seminars, and workshops.

Internal Training Opportunities

Many companies that have their own training and development departments publish catalogs and schedules of the courses they offer. These may include formal lecture/laboratory courses as well as paper- or computer-based self-paced training materials. Most often these are published as paper documents on a regular, typically quarterly, basis. Other times they are posted on computer-based bulletin boards and updated regularly.

The Company Library

Many companies maintain libraries containing marketing and technical materials, reference texts on a wide variety of company-related subjects, subscriptions to major professional, technical, and business periodicals, and a variety of instructional materials including books, audiotapes, and videotapes. At Digital Equipment Corporation, all company library catalogs are available on the company network. Employees can search the catalog from their offices and order materials, which are then delivered by interoffice mail.

Sun Microsystems has a similar library system, but its system also allows employees to search periodical and news databases and to read articles on their own workstations. Sun's system also allows employees to access computer-based instruction across the library network.

Other companies, such as Mercury Marine, provide learning centers where employees can go to access a wide range of computer-based and multimedia instructional programs and can borrow from a large library of audiotapes and videotapes. The learning center resources include work-related materials as well as general educational materials and other topics of interest (e.g., parenting skills) to company employees. Mercury Marine also provides confidential educational counseling and planning sessions using counselors from the local branch of the University of Wisconsin.

More and more companies are providing their employees with access to on-line news and literature databases provided across the Internet. These services allow users to create profiles of their interests using keywords, and continually scan news services and periodical databases for articles indexed by those keywords. The user can then scan the titles and abstracts of the relevant articles, select the ones of greatest interest, and read (or print) them at their workstations.

Some companies allow employees to do literature searches themselves. Other companies do the searches on major topics of interest and post what they find on network-based bulletin boards that can be accessed by employees. Price Waterhouse, for example, maintains electronic bulletin boards on more than 1,000 different subjects for more than 18,000 employees in 22 countries.[2] AT&T's Information Research Center worked with Dow Jones, Mainstream Data, Comtex, Reuters, Verity, and SandPoint to design and implement a "news alert" application for its employees.[3]

An interesting trend is that so many resources are becoming available over the Internet that employees, especially in technology-driven companies, are doing more and more of their own online research, thereby reducing the need for corporate librarians. Corporate librarians are finding that if they want to keep their jobs, they must shift their roles from doing research for company employees to teaching employees how to use these on-line services themselves.

College and University Courses

Some companies have arranged with local colleges and universities to offer college courses within company facilities. These programs usually get more publicity than other college programs that are not company-sponsored. Company human resources departments often receive catalogs and brochures on local colleges' continuing education and professional development programs. These typically get posted in one location or are circulated among various company departments, with no guarantee that the people who are most interested in the programs will ever see them. Some companies even sponsor "continuing education fairs" where local institutions can present their programs to interested employees.

Satellite Broadcasts

Some larger companies hold company-wide meetings and do multilocation training over satellite broadcast networks. With an uplink typically at company headquarters and downlinks at various company locations, these broadcasts provide one-way video, usually allowing for questions or discussion over telephone lines.

National Technological University (NTU) is a consortium of several hundred companies and several dozen universities, which provides a wide variety of seminars over its satellite network. Catalogs are published of seminar offerings, mostly technical subjects with a scattering of management topics, and members can enroll in those of interest. Subscribers can have live audiences or can videotape the broadcasts for subsequent distribution and use.

Other Courses, Seminars, and Workshops

Flyers and brochures about courses, seminars, and workshops offered by professional organizations, seminar companies, consultants, and other groups arrive at various locations throughout the company. These sometimes get posted or circulated but typically go no further than the person who receives them.

How Employees Discover Learning Opportunities

Employees seeking learning opportunities typically rely on the company training catalogs or on their own initiative in identifying external resources. If employees belong to a professional organization or subscribe to a professional or industry publication, they are generally inundated by program flyers and brochures. They also read advertisements from local colleges and universities and generally rely on word-of-mouth about which institution's programs are most suited to their needs.

LRT Databases: Future Scenarios

The future Learning Resources and Tools (LRT) database will contain virtually all of the features described in the previous section on current practice but will organize them for ease of use. It will also contain other features that will enable employees to identify and access more nontraditional learning resources. As technology becomes more affordable and capable, many of the capabilities for which employees must today travel to a specially equipped laboratory or learning center will become available on their desktops. Let's examine the future uses of the LRT database in terms of both current learning opportunities and nontraditional learning opportunities.

Current Learning Opportunities

The LRT database will provide an on-line catalog of all types of training available within and without the company. Besides company-sponsored training programs, the database will contain college catalogs, professional development programs from a wide variety of professional organizations, industry associations, consultants, and other training vendors. It will also contain schedules of satellite broadcasts, instructions for accessing available self-paced instructional materials, enrollment and cost information for both internal and external programs, and other relevant information. Employees seeking training will be able to search the LRT database on the basis of keyword descriptions, institutions, sponsors, or other criteria.

An additional feature of the LRT database will be the opportunity for employees to make annotations to program descriptions, describing their experiences with various programs or instructors, for example, "This is a terrific program to get a team started" or "Mary Jones, who teaches this course, is the best instructor I ever had" or "I took this course at College A and a friend took the same course at College B. From comparing notes with him, I think College B's version is much more practical." It will also include the names of company employees who have taken the course so that employees can seek out more information from people who have already experienced it.

The company library catalog will also be part of this database. Employees will be able to search the library and order materials that will be delivered to them over the network, where the materials are in electronic form, or by interoffice mail.

Many companies become part of regional business organizations, work with local colleges and universities on industry studies, become part of a local manufacturing consortium, or fund a research study by a local professor. In most cases, the results of these efforts (research reports, market studies, etc.) circulate only locally, sometimes not beyond the desk of the company sponsor of the program. Other times, one plant will conduct benchmark studies, as described in Chapter 8, and use them only for its own benefit. These reports are another form of knowledge that will be shared across the company by placing them within the company library system and by announcing their availability on the company's electronic bulletin boards.

The LRT database will contain bulletin boards on a wide variety of work-related topics. These bulletin boards will contain up-to-date news items from a varicty of news services, references to articles in professional publications, book reviews done by company employees, news on new additions to the company library, and so on.

Employees will also use the bulletin boards to post summaries of papers and presentations from conferences and workshops they have attended and will provide pointers to the full papers and presentations. The actual presentations and papers will be scanned into the database and added to the company library listings.

Employees will also have access to periodical databases so that they can do their own searches on topics of interest and will be able to retrieve copies of articles to read or print at their workstations.

Nontraditional Learning Opportunities

People learn in many ways, more often in nontraditional ways than in traditional training settings. Learning activities take place on a frequent, if not daily, basis. Many companies have stated a goal that all employees participate in 40 hours of training per year, and a few have set goals of 80 hours per year. For transformational learning to take place, this is not sufficient. Formal training programs may involve the employees for one or two weeks per year, but learning activities must take place continuously. Learning better ways to work toward the achievement of personal, group, and company goals must take a high priority in each employee's daily schedule.

Does this mean that employees must spend more time in the classroom, that they must spend three or four weeks per year in a classroom away from their jobs? The answer is that sometimes it may be necessary to have more formal training for employees, but in most cases, learning can take place in a variety of nontraditional, nonformal settings. Typically, people learn from each other. These types of learning can be facilitated by the LRT database and the other components of the knowledge network.

An employee who decides that he or she wants to learn more about a given subject may use the LRT database to discover:

- Sources of formal training programs, within and without the company.

- Library resources—books, articles, audiotapes or videotapes.
- Upcoming conferences or workshops on the topic.

The employee may also use the knowledge network to discover who else in the company has a background in the subject. With this discovery, he or she can contact the relevant people and ask their advice on how to best learn about the subject matter. In some cases, these learning resources may provide pointers to instructional programs or other resources. In others, they may tutor or coach the employee as he or she sets about learning the subject.

Other possibilities include finding the employee a developmental job in another part of the company to help the person gain skills and knowledge in the new subject. This might be a temporary or permanent job change.

People also learn from others by working as part of a cross-functional team. This type of "action learning" is the subject of Chapter 10.

For nontraditional learning activities to succeed, the company needs to have an open learning culture, where the company and all of its employees encourage and support a wide variety of learning methods. At Frye Computer Systems, a small technology company in Boston, employees are encouraged to share their knowledge with others by offering short seminars on their particular areas of expertise. Employees who volunteer to give such a seminar are given a $50 bonus for each seminar taught.

As people begin learning new subjects, they often require, or desire, an opportunity to discuss the subject matter with others who are pursuing similar learning strategies. In the next section, on individual and group learning facilitators, tools and technologies to foster these types of learning activities are discussed.

INDIVIDUAL AND GROUP LEARNING FACILITATORS

As with any new methodology or technology, the knowledge network will be successful only if it is easy to use. To foster an open learning environment, companies must provide their employees with tools, methods, and technologies that will enable and facilitate individual and group learning activities. These include not only the tools to access and utilize the knowledge network itself but also two other types of tools and technologies. The first is designed to make available training more accessible by bringing knowledge to the desktop, and the second facilitates the work of both individuals and groups, allowing them to learn from each other and to record their experiences to make them part of the group and corporate memory or inventory. The former category will be called "instructional tools" and the latter, "groupware."

Instructional Tools

More and more instructional programs become available every day in the forms of audio- and videotapes, computer-based instruction, and multimedia, CD ROM–based instruction. As computer technology becomes more affordable and capable, greater proportions of the company's employees will have multimedia workstations on their desktops, and these workstations will be connected to a high-capability company-wide network. As this happens employees will be able to access all of these types of media-based instruction directly from their offices rather than having to travel to a learning center or to order tapes that later get delivered by interoffice mail. Connections to the Internet will facilitate access to non-company-owned resources. All of this will facilitate "real-time" or "just-in-time" learning.

Employees will be able to watch a videotape on their workstations or copy an audiotape from the company library using their workstations and then listen to it in their car tape player on the way home. If they need to learn to use a new piece of software that has been loaded onto their workstations, they will be able to download the instructional program from the company library and take the course in their own offices. Satellite broadcasts will reach a plant's satellite dish and then be broadcast onto individual workstations across the plant.

As employees take these self-paced programs, they will be able to ask questions of instructors or subject matter experts using electronic mail, or the experts may announce "office hours" when they will be on-line to answer questions at specified hours each week.

The media-based programs will be continually updated by the subject matter experts to ensure that the version of the training being accessed by any employee at any time will be the most up-to-date version.

As capable as these types of instructional methodology become, they will never totally replace formal, classroom-based learning programs. Learning as part of a group, sharing the learning experience with others, and the group interactions that take place in more traditional educational settings can never be totally replaced by technology. But the goal of these new instructional tools is to provide "just-in-time" and "just enough" training.

Just-in-time training means that at the moment a learning need arises, an employee will be able to access the required training. Just enough training means that the employee will be able to learn what he or she needs to do the job and will not be required to sift through a lot of extraneous material to find what is needed.

Groupware

Groupware encompasses a wide variety of tools and technologies designed to facilitate the work of groups or teams. These tools and technologies can be classified by their major application areas:

- Communications tools and technologies.
- Database tools and technologies.
- Management tools and technologies.

I believe that all of these tools and technologies are in place for one reason: to enable and facilitate learning. Let's look at each of the three classes of tools and technologies (by general capabilities rather than technical descriptions or product names) and see how they can act as learning facilitators.

Communications Tools and Technologies

Communications tools are key to most groupware applications. Lotus Development CEO Jim Manzi writes:

> Today's evolving business practices are becoming less data-centric and more communications-centric. Each practice depends on teams of people having the tools to gain access, communicate effectively, act on a rich variety of information, respond to different people in different locations, coordinate skills and expertise, and accomplish common organizational goals.[4]

Communications tools are generally classified as:

- One-to-one communications—for example, telephone or electronic mail, where one person communicates or sends a message to another person.
- One-to-many communications—where one person sends a communication to many people simultaneously. This can be done with telephone/voice mail and electronic mail applications using distribution lists. It can also be done via computer-based videotext and bulletin board applications.
- Many-to-many communications—where many people can send communications to many other people. These applications often take the form of computer-based conferences or notes files, where many people can add information, submit a query, or answer a query in a database accessible to many other people. The advantage of this type of communications is that the sender does not need to know specific names or addresses of other interested parties, as with one-to-one or one-to-many communications methods. Also in this category are a variety of "meeting technologies" where people at different locations can participate together in a meeting. Meeting technologies range from computer-based applications where many users can "talk" simultaneously over the computer network, to telephone-based conference calls, to video teleconferences where people not only hear other meeting participants but also see them.

The purpose of communications tools is to enable people to share ideas, to ask questions and get answers, and to facilitate the sharing of knowledge. As part of groupware, these tools allow members of a group (a team, a functional group, a business unit, a company site, or the company as a whole) to more easily communicate with each other and to share ideas, knowledge, and skills.

Database Tools and Technologies

Databases are simply organized methods of storing information. This information comprises individual and group records of work that employees do within the company. Collectively, databases are the company's memory—of sales, financial information, employee records, customer information, product information, and so on. The knowledge network we have been discussing contains three databases.

Because databases contain so much information about so many different subjects, it is a major technical challenge to build databases that are compatible with each other and that provide easy access to the data collected. Too often, different functions within a company have built so many different database applications over the years that multiple classification schemes exist for the same data used by different departments. The result is major duplication of effort and costs, and the inability to keep all records current. These inconsistencies and incompatibilities are a major cause of the need for and the popularity of business process reengineering.

When databases are properly designed, and efficient tools are created for their use, it greatly facilitates individual and group work and learning. As consultant Dave E. Hoffman states:

> Questioners do not need to know who has the specific knowledge, they only need to know where to pose the question. Ideally, the system will make an answer available, even if the source resides across town, across the country or on the other side of the world. Thus, groupware can promote a faster exchange and synthesis of corporate knowledge, capital and experience.[5]

Management Tools and Technologies

This class of groupware gives teams and other groups the tools and technologies they need to manage their work. For example, some groupware allows members of a project team to simultaneously work on a customer proposal and automatically keeps track of revisions to the proposal document. Another groupware application tracks the development of a new product through its many stages, alerting the team manager when deadlines are being missed.

Some typical examples of groupware applications being implemented by companies include:

> Research Tracking (AT&T Information Research Center): "Working with the Human Interface Group, we set out to build an application that would maintain a library of client profiles, facilitate entering and assigning of new work, help manage team workloads, and provide data for customer satisfaction surveys. In addition, we wanted the application to automatically feed data into our internal charge-back system."[6]

> Management Applications (Price Waterhouse): "When Rick Richardson arrives at his office each morning, he gets a cup of coffee and turns on his PC. On an average day he receives 20 to 25 E-mail messages—not surprising, since he's in charge of all the work that Price Waterhouse . . . does with New York City Banks. Then he clicks the mouse to see news articles on topics he has given the computer standing orders to track. . . . Richardson calls up a board that holds messages about the firm's financial services business. A Washington staffer reports on an accounting regulation change; Richardson adds a comment for all to see. A manager in Miami needs Spanish-speaking consultants for an assignment in Buenos Aires; Richardson zaps him a name by E-mail. . . . [H]e reads carefully a query from Chicago soliciting CFO candidates for a client. Perhaps he'll call the sender later and suggest a name."[7]

> Underwriting Applications (Insurance Company): "The system manages and tracks the work flow of an insurance application from quote generation through policy issuance and endorsement handling. The insurer realized a quantum productivity improvement, while greatly enhancing re-

sponsiveness and the quality and quantity of information available to management."[8]

All of these, and thousands of other applications of groupware, enhance company productivity, make information and learning resources available to more and more people throughout the company, and retain information as part of the corporate memory/inventory.

BUILDING A KNOWLEDGE NETWORK

The technology for building a knowledge network, including all of the databases and related tools and applications described in this chapter, exist today. This does not mean that the job of building a knowledge network is a trivial one. The knowledge network includes a wide array of applications, and although they are obtainable as individual pieces of software, many of them are incompatible with others. The most popular approach to creating a common platform for these diverse applications, as of this writing, is Lotus Notes from Lotus Development Corporation. Other technology companies are creating many other products to accomplish the same capabilities. However you approach the building of your knowledge network, the cost will be substantial. But the benefits of creating this type of learning environment are that it can enable your company to undertake transformational learning—the knowledge network can be a key enabler of your company's renewal efforts.

The greater problem with the building of a knowledge network is getting people to use it. With the establishment of an open learning culture in your company (greatly facilitated by the building of the company's five foundations), the knowledge network will be welcomed as a method of sharing knowledge and facilitating learning for all company employees. Without such a culture, people will see the network as a burden, turning them into data entry clerks.

In a true learning organization, an energy, a charged atmosphere, is evident when you walk through the facilities, when you talk with people about their work. This type of enthusiasm can be enhanced by the provision of the tools and technologies that make up the knowledge network. And this enthusiasm is what companies need when they are seeking to continually renew themselves or to transform themselves from their current state into a world-class competitor.

The existence of a knowledge network in and of itself will not accomplish these goals. To be useful, the knowledge network must be used to solve problems, to respond to new opportunities, and to create a new and exciting future. In the next chapter, "Action-Oriented Teamwork," we will examine how teams can use the capabilities of the knowledge network to meet these challenges head-on.

TEN

ACTION-ORIENTED TEAMWORK

The June 1994 issue of Stephen Covey's magazine, *Executive Excellence*, was focused on teamwork. The cover of the magazine shows a picture of a racing yacht with the caption:

> High wind and waves make for tough sailing; rough interpersonal relations and expert international competitors only add to the challenge. In business, all hands are needed on deck; otherwise, environmental elements and competitive forces defeat your teams and take the wind right out of your sails.

Teamwork has taken the workplace by storm. In its 1994 competition for "America's best plants," *Industry Week* notes the following workforce strategies, all related to teamwork, that its finalists had in common:[1]

- Cross-functional teams for special projects 100%
- Employee cross-training 100%
- Employee involvement in benchmarking 84%
- Self-directed work teams 80%

- Financial rewards for team-based performance/results 76%

Why is industry so enamored of teamwork? Because many companies have reported major gains in quality, productivity, and cost savings and have given credit for these gains to the implementation of teamwork. For example:

- At Steelcase, teams have reduced manufacturing cycle time from three weeks to three days while reducing raw material inventories by 55 percent and work-in-process inventories by 26 percent.[2]
- At Lord Corporation, team efficiency has reduced the manufacturing cycle time for one product from 75 days to 7. Overall scrap and rework costs have fallen by 85 percent and productivity has increased 30 percent.[3]
- At the Kansas City Armco steel manufacturing facility, $5.1 million of cost savings was achieved just 10 months into their new "Team Works" program.[4]

So how are these companies achieving these great results from teamwork? Is there a single best approach? Or do companies use what I call the "photographic" method of teamwork: Throw a group of people into a dark room and see what develops. There is no lack of advice on building teams.

The June 1995 issue of *Executive Excellence* includes 17 articles by noted consultants and business executives, all relating to how companies should build and manage teams. Within those articles are the following lists:

- Five new realities (for teams).
- Tactical skills (for team leaders).
- Strategic skills (for team leaders).
- Five tips for team coaches.
- Ten questions to ask in advance of forming teams.
- Five principles for forming teams.

- Ten ways to build trust with team members.
- Three steps to winning teams.
- Eight critical team success factors.
- Five reasons teams fail.
- Five characteristics to enable executives to use teams optimally.
- Four dynamics of effective teams.
- Seven elements high-performance teams have in common.
- Five actions for team leaders.

Teamwork is a key element in most companies' renewal or transformation efforts. There is no lack of advice to be found or purchased. In the current edition of *Books in Print*, 75 titles begin with the word *team*. This does not count probably several hundred more currently available books where *team* is not the first word of the title.

The approaches to building teamwork are as numerous as consultants, not to mention the approaches taken by tens of thousands of companies and managers on their own. The 1995 edition of the *Buyer's Guide & Consultant Directory* of the American Society for Training & Development contains 193 listings just under the topic of "team building."

Will this book add another approach? Another list? No! What we want to discuss in this chapter is how effective teamwork should be viewed as a key element in the theme of transformational learning. To this end, we will start with a simple statement:

> ***The only reason that a team should ever be formed is so that team members can (1) learn from each other and (2) learn together, in order to meet individual, team, and company goals.*** (Do two items constitute a list?)

TEAMWORK AS A LEARNING ACTIVITY

Learning does not take place in isolation—people learn from each other. Even when an individual participates in some form of self-study, for example, by reading, listening, or watching, he or she has a partner in the learning activity—the person who created the learning materials. But even individualized learning is not synthesized until the learner has the opportunity to discuss and test ideas, concepts, and skills. Referring back to the learning model presented in Chapter 1, the learning materials represent *data.* If the learner finds these data relevant and of purpose, it becomes *information.* Only when the information is applied to a person's work can it be classified as *knowledge.* And the application of information to a person's work, the creation of individual knowledge, cannot take place in isolation, for *no single person's work in any organization can be totally isolated from the work of others.*

In building the foundation of "overcoming functional myopia," companies analyze their business processes and internal and external value chains to better understand how each employee's work relates to the work of others and to the company's overall business. With this broader perspective, all employees can understand how their work contributes to the achievement of the company's goals, how they can align their work with the company's strategic business directions.

As a part of the company's value chain, each employee's job can be viewed as having suppliers (those from whom he or she receives the ideas, data, or materials on which work is done) and customers (those who use the completed work). When the employee views his or her job in this way, when the employee communicates with (internal or external) suppliers and customers and seeks ways of improving the overall performance of the business process that they together control, the results will always be better than if each person focuses solely on his or her own piece of the process. This is the basic thrust behind teamwork:

> *When people involved in multiple stages of a business process or value chain learn from each other and learn together, they can improve overall performance.*

LEARNING TOGETHER AND FROM EACH OTHER

Working as part of a team is not the way in which most Americans have been raised. Because we have had it drummed into our heads since birth that the measure of a person is individual achievement, teamwork requires us to unlearn old ways and to learn new ones. If any team is to be successful, it must learn to function as a team.

Learning to become an effective, action-oriented team—learning together and from each other—can be a true transformational learning experience both for individual team members and for the company as a whole.

Learning Together: Basic Team Management Skills

How will team members work with each other? Who will run meetings? Who will resolve the inevitable conflicts? How will the team and its individual members be measured and rewarded? How will the team decide whether it can handle a problem itself or should seek outside assistance? All of these questions are matters of how the team manages itself, and the questions need answering early on if the team members are to function smoothly, to focus their energies on meeting their goals rather than squabbling with each other. Table 6.4, team competencies used by SunU, provides a good list of needed team skills.

As stated earlier, team skills are typically not part of the public school or college curriculum. They must be learned by team members, and they must be learned together (Figure 10.1). Whether there is a formal team manager or whether the team is designed to be self-managing, all team members must gain a set of internal team management skills if the team is to function smoothly and accomplish its goals.

Too often, in the rush to jump on the team bandwagon, companies tell employees that they are (instantaneously) to be organized into teams. The reorganization may be initiated because a manager leaves the company, and, in an effort to save replacement costs, the manager's former subordinates are told that they will now function as a team, without a formal manager. Or it may happen that a company executive will attend a conference, or read a new book, or hear that the company's major competitor has moved to team-based management and decide that this is just what the company needs. Then she announces the new team organization and tells people that she expects the same levels of quantum

Figure 10.1
Learning Together

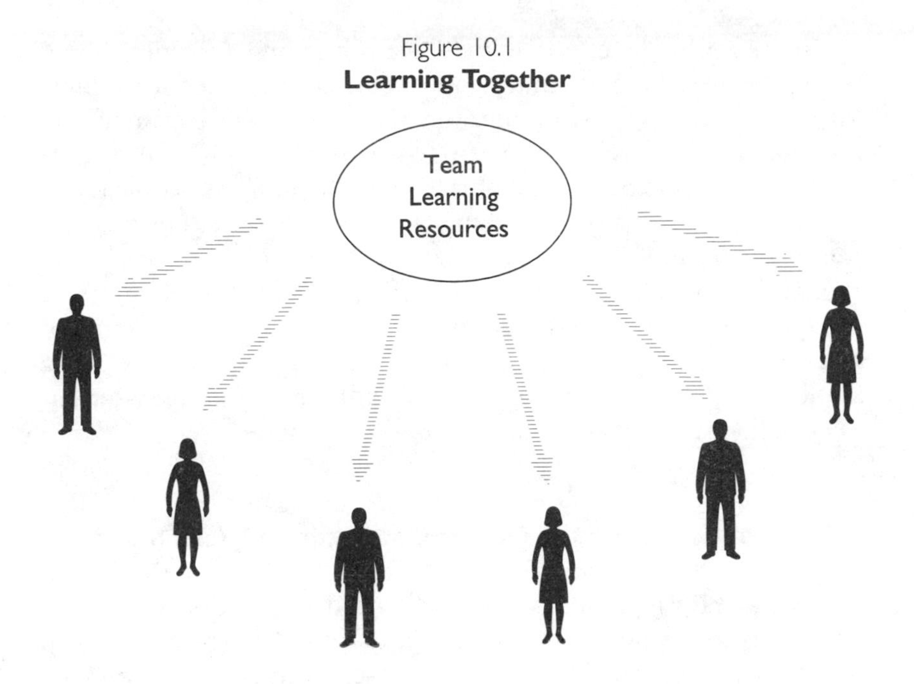

performance gain that was reported in the conference, book, or rumor.

It just doesn't work that way. Teams need to learn how to work as a team before they can even start to make any real progress toward team goals. As stated earlier, literally thousands of resources can be utilized in providing team learning opportunities. It behooves the company to study the major approaches and to select the learning resources that will best meet the company's needs. It is also necessary for company leaders to recognize that even when they provide some types of training up front, it will take time for team members to digest the training content, that is, to turn the information into knowledge by applying it to their work.

> Do you think for a minute that three days at team-building camp—or three months—is going to take away a culturally inculcated value around competition or a need for control?[5]
>
> Gloria Gery, President
> Gery and Associates

To be optimally effective, these team learning activities should be experienced by all team members as a group—the team must *learn together*. It is also important that follow-on coaching and reinforcement be provided to help team members get over the hurdles, to overcome the barriers that inevitably arise as people try to set aside lifelong ways of working to learn new ones. For this reason, team training cannot take the sole form of a single training program provided at the initiation of the team; training must be provided in easy-to-digest increments. In this way, as teams try out a first set of skills and begin to master them, they are moved along the learning curve to the next set of skills they will need—what EDS calls just-in-time and just enough learning.

Learning from Each Other: Cooperative Work Skills

Even as a team is mastering the skills needed to work together, it also needs to develop *cooperative work skills*. These are what help the team get its work done, to increase productivity or quality, compress time lines, improve customer satisfaction, or work on whatever goals the team has been assigned. Here is where team members must learn from each other (see Figure 10.2), learn about each other's jobs, how the work of each team member overlaps and affects the work of other team members. For example:

- In a production environment, cooperative work skills may involve cross-training of team members on each other's job tasks so that team members can fill in for each other or can shift tasks to even out work flows.
- In a product development environment, cooperative work skills may involve marketing, engineering, finance, materials, manufacturing, service, and sales members working together throughout the development process to reduce costs and time to market while improving quality and customer satisfaction.
- In a service environment, cooperative work skills may mean having marketing, sales, legal, and credit personnel working together to make it easier for a customer

Figure 10.2
Learning from Each Other

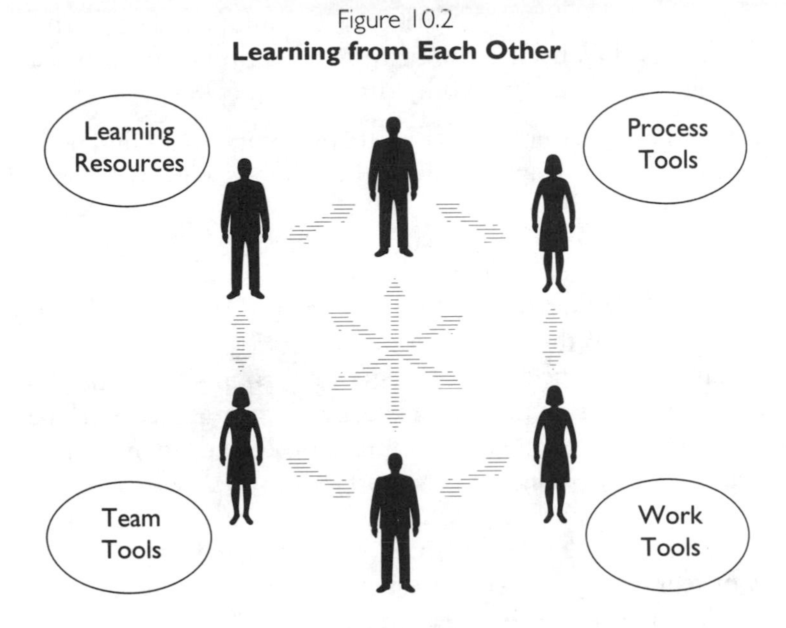

to obtain an insurance policy, an annuity, or a mortgage.

The basic idea behind cooperative work skills is that all team members strive to develop an understanding of the overall business process or value chain in which they are involved and to seek together ways of improving the performance of that process. This is why teams should be formed along the lines of those business processes and value chains—it is the people and functions that comprise the process or chain who will be closest to the challenges of improving performance and will be best able to affect that performance. For example:

- In the production environment, team members can discuss how each step in the manufacturing process affects the following steps and can seek ways of improving the overall process in terms of quality, scrap, rework, work flow, machine setup, and other production factors.
- In the product development environment, team members can negotiate how product features that improve

performance, but also increase manufacturing costs, can be balanced with customer requirements to meet both customer and company goals.

- In the service environment, team members can find new ways of making it easy to do business with the company.

The development of cooperative work skills can be enabled and facilitated by a variety of methodologies and tools related to both the functioning of the team and to the work it is doing. Some of these may fall into the generic category of groupware, as described in Chapter 9. Others will be very specific to the types of work being undertaken by the team. For example, a product development team may find use for Design for Manufacturing (DFM), Design for Assembly (DFA), or Rapid Prototyping tools; a service-oriented team may use work flow analysis or customer service tools. All types of teams may want to use benchmarking methodologies to ensure that they are "learning from the best."

Whatever tools or methodologies a team decides to use, it must first learn how to use the tools. Using the tools, and making discoveries about how they can improve the team's work processes, will also provide valuable learning. It may also happen that the team discovers that no team member has the right background to learn to use a particular tool or methodology, or that the amount of time it would take to develop the needed skills cannot be justified. In these cases, the team will need to search for the required knowledge and skills outside the team. This provides a perfect opportunity to use the features of the knowledge network, described in Chapter 9, to locate the needed resources whether they exist within or without the company.

Learning Together: Creating a Better Future

Once a team has mastered team management skills and cooperative work skills, once it is functioning smoothly and fully understands the business process or value chains it controls, it can start making the quantum improvements the company sought in first developing the team. By this time the members will no longer be a group of individuals assigned to work together but a cohesive team working together to meet and exceed specific goals. By learning from the best internal and external resources, by applying their knowledge and skills to the world they control, they can solve today's business problems and create new opportunities for the future.

> In the mid-1980s, Digital Equipment Corporation's Networks and Communications Marketing organization faced the challenge of addressing a totally new audience for its products and services. Traditionally, DEC's networking and communications products had been solely focused on data communications. With the advent of new technologies, the company was now to become involved in voice communications as well. This meant that the company's sales and sales support specialists would have to become familiar with the world of voice communications, that they would have to work with and sell to company telecommunications managers, who typically were part of a company's facilities operations, as well as to the familiar audience of data communications managers, who typically resided within the information services function.
>
> Since the knowledge needed to address this new audience effectively was not available within the marketing group, we teamed with Digital's internal telecommunications group. Digital was a multinational, geographically dispersed company and had a profile similar to many of its largest customers. The people who managed the company's own voice communications facilities already knew the company, knew the telecommunications subject matter, and were more knowledgeable about the interfaces with the data communications world than most of their counterparts in Digital's customer base.
>
> By finding the needed knowledge within the company, and recruiting people with that knowledge to become part of both the planning efforts and the eventual sales teams, Digital was able to save a lot of the time, effort, and resources that would have been needed if we had started to build these capabilities from scratch.

Finding the right knowledge resources to solve a problem, to take advantage of a new opportunity, is the primary job of the team. The needed knowledge and skills may reside inside or outside the team, within or without the company—the knowledge network can help the team locate the resources it needs. But this can only happen if the team is *action oriented.*

ACTION-ORIENTED TEAMWORK

"Of course our teams are action oriented," the executive avows. "Do you think we would bother creating teams, and all of the turmoil that entails, to have them be 'inaction oriented'?"

This statement is reasonable and understandable. But in many companies, teams have been put in place only to have business continue as usual. In fact, in some companies, the development of teamwork causes so much turmoil that results become worse! These are the companies that, in trying to reduce costs, have fired managers and told their employees to form teams and manage themselves. These are the companies that tell teams that they are to decrease costs, improve quality, and reduce customer complaints but give the teams no leadership, no training, no resources to undertake the task. These are the companies that say: "We have good employees. We'll put them into teams and they'll figure out what to do." These are the companies that have not taken the time to build their five foundations and, lacking leadership and direction from the top, cannot expect employees, whether organized into teams or not, to accomplish anything except business as usual.

Action-oriented teams exist in action-oriented companies—companies that have built their foundations, that have set challenging but attainable goals for the company and its teams. In these companies, teams are closely aligned with the company's strategic business directions and take direct responsibility for the success of the company's strategic business initiatives. They understand their roles in helping the company achieve its goals and have the will, the drive, the capabilities, and the resources they need to work toward achieving and even exceeding those goals. Action-oriented teams operate in a continuous-improvement, continuous-learning mode, seeking quantum improvements in current business processes and value chains on a daily basis.

Action-oriented teams have both a local, business process focus and a wider company focus. They are constantly learning, continuously scanning the horizon for new opportunities that may cross team and organizational boundaries. They use the company's knowledge network to find resources they need to succeed and to contribute to other groups' success.

Although in some cases successful, action-oriented teams have been formed on the initiative of a group of individuals who decide to work together as a team, in most cases, companies must jump-start the team development process.

JUMP-STARTING THE TEAM PROCESS

If your company's renewal or transformation goals depend on creating self-managed teams, you must realize that this cannot be accomplished by simply making team assignments and telling the new teams that they are to manage themselves. As has been discussed throughout this chapter, effective, action-oriented teamwork must have time and resources to foster its development. The best way of ensuring that this happens is to start teams out with a strong team manager.

The team manager is goaled on organizing the team, ensuring that the team gets the training and the resources it needs, and getting the team moving in the right direction. As the team learns both self-management skills and cooperative work skills, the role of the team manager diminishes until the team is effectively managing itself. The team manager then moves on to other responsibilities, for example, starting another team, taking a different management position, or joining a team as a team member.

To be effective in its work, a team must begin work immediately, even while learning the skills and acquiring the knowledge that will make it effective. The team manager, by making the early decisions, setting the early direction, telling team members what each should be doing from the start, can get everyone moving in the same, and correct, direction. As team members gain new knowledge and skills, they can begin making their own decisions, setting their own direction, and managing their own business, all the time being coached by the team manager.

People who are assigned to a team for the first time "don't know what they don't know." They need a strong manager to help them learn, either by providing training herself or by arranging for learning opportunities and ensuring that the lessons learned are applied correctly and effectively on the job. This type of continuous reinforcement and coaching will hasten the development of the team members' new skills and will ensure that the team can start working toward its goals, even as the members are learning to work together as a team. One way in which the progress of the team can be measured is by how well members learn each other's language and vocabulary, and the extent to which they develop their own, common language, which I call "team-speak."

Team-Speak

One of the most formidable barriers to effective, action-oriented teamwork is the lack of a common language and vocabulary. In our education, we learn the language and vocabulary of our professions and industries: engineering versus finance versus marketing, or insurance versus retailing versus manufacturing. Listening to people from different functions or different business units at their first team meetings more often resembles the Tower of Babel than an effective meeting of people with a common purpose.

> Bryan Lanahan, who was one of the key players in the creation and institutionalization of Corning's innovation process, says that a key to the success of the effort was the creation of a new, common language. The new language was used to overcome semantic differences among the vocabularies of the various functions represented on any given new product team.

Teams must address two levels of vocabulary: the language of the business and the language of their own professions, functions, or business units. In the first case, in order for any team to align its work with its company's strategic business directions, it must learn to speak the language of business leaders.

> The focus of my consulting work is helping training and development (T&D) groups and human resources (HR) or-

ganizations align their work more closely with their companies' strategic business directions. In company after company, in a variety of industries, I have reviewed plans that were written in very pure T&D or HR language. If you are a member of these professions, the plans are very clear and well written. But if you are a CEO or a business unit manager, the plans are gobbledygook.

Because the language and vocabulary of business managers is so different from that of the HR and T&D groups, who should be learning the other's language? The answer is clear: These groups were created to support the company's business, and they must cast their goals, their plans, and their programs in the language of the business rather than their own.

For example, one T&D group asked me to review its "planning process guide" designed for business unit managers to use in planning for the learning needs of their employees. In the section on "benefits of using this process," the first benefit was to make it easier for the business unit manager to justify spending money on training. I don't consider this a benefit for the business unit manager—it is a benefit for the T&D group. "What," I asked the T&D group, "is the primary purpose of your group?" After some labored discussion, mostly couched in academic terms, they finally came up with the right answer: "To help the business succeed." We then began examining ways of reworking the planning process guide with that purpose in mind.

Learning the language of the business is just the first vocabulary exercise. If a company has built its foundations properly, employees will already understand the language of the business, the company's major business processes and value chains, and how their individual work fits into the larger picture. The second lesson is learning the languages of the functions, professions, and business units represented on the team.

Different professions have different ways of measuring the quality of their work, and these sometimes conflict with each other. For example, a member of an insurance company's legal department may be measured by ensuring that the language of the company's policies is airtight, whereas the marketing department wants the language to be easily understood by potential customers. A design engineer may want to include the latest bells and whistles on a new product while manufacturing is trying to reduce costs by using stock parts and materials. Team members must first understand the vocabularies and standards that each team member uses to be able to reach the compromises that will allow the team to get its work done. To accomplish this, teams often develop a common vocabulary—team-speak.

There are many documented cases where twins, because they spend so much time together growing up, develop their own language, often referred to as "twin-speak." This language usually makes no sense to anyone else, not even the twins' parents, but provides an effective shorthand to facilitate communications between the twins. Similarly, teams that work closely together over a period of time often develop their own language, team-speak. Team-speak is essentially a shorthand method of communication that overcomes the differences in vocabulary that plague most teams as they start out.

> At a consumer products company, a new product development team had developed a set of four criteria for judging any new product idea. The list of criteria became so ingrained among the team's members that they referred to them by number. If someone proposed a new product but had not done sufficient customer testing, another team member might simply say "#2 seems weak," and everyone immediately knew what was meant.

Team-speak is also vital when you are dealing with cultural differences, as when you have an international team effort. Different cultures work on different paradigms, different body language, different meanings for common words. Malcolm Thomas, a vehicle line director in Dunton, England, puts it this way:

> If you judge people by what you have become used to in your environment, you can jump to totally wrong conclusions. For instance, if you're dealing with Spaniards, wearing a casual leather jacket to work is quite normal. But that

> could be construed as not taking the business seriously in some other circles.
>
> Don't assume the man from Texas is slow just because he talks slow. Don't assume the foreigner who is good with English is good at everything else. Conversely, because a foreigner has difficulty communicating doesn't mean he's not extremely good at his job.[6]

The development of team-speak not only can make the team operate more efficiently, by eliminating the need for long explanations but also is important in helping team members develop a "team identity." When a team has a high level of team-speak, it is a sign it is working as a cohesive unit rather than as a collection of individuals.

Creating a Team Identity

One of the great team success stories is that of "Team Zebra" within Eastman Kodak's Black and White Film Division managed, at that time, by Stephen Frangos. Team Zebra, encompassing all of the division's 1,500 workers and a host of external suppliers, turned the business around from losing market share and money to becoming a profitable, growing division for Eastman Kodak.

The identity of Team Zebra was portrayed by posters, stuffed animals, and other paraphernalia using the team name. But these types of gimmicks cannot alone make teams effective. The great motivator, according to Frangos, is successful performance: "You never see losing sports teams having fun. And if you just have fun and don't succeed, you won't be there long. Fun and performance go hand-in-hand. We were able to achieve both."[7]

Teamwork can also be effective in service industries. The fast-food industry, for example, is usually portrayed as providing dead-end jobs for inexperienced workers. But it doesn't have to be that way. Taco Bell uses local, store-based teamwork to provide a different work experience. According to CEO John E. Martin:

> For many young people entering the work force, Taco Bell represents their first work experience. Through a teaming

environment, they learn to accept responsibility and to establish a work ethic. We're lighting a spark among young people—one that is paying off with dramatically reduced turnover, greater morale, better profits, and more satisfied customers.[8]

TEAMS AS A USER AND SOURCE OF KNOWLEDGE AND SKILLS

Action-oriented teamwork can be optimally effective in a company's renewal efforts when developed in conjunction with effective benchmarking, as discussed in Chapter 8, and the creation of a knowledge network, as discussed in Chapter 9. These three program elements (Figure 10.3) must be layered on top of a company's five foundations and be used together as the basis for company renewal.

These three key elements feed on and supply each other. Teams use benchmarking, both inside and outside the company, to hasten their own learning, finding best practices that they can emulate. And even as they learn from others, they report their own experiences in the knowledge network so that others can learn from them. The knowledge network helps teams identify the learning resources they need, and as each team develops its own base of

Figure 10.3
The Three Key Programs

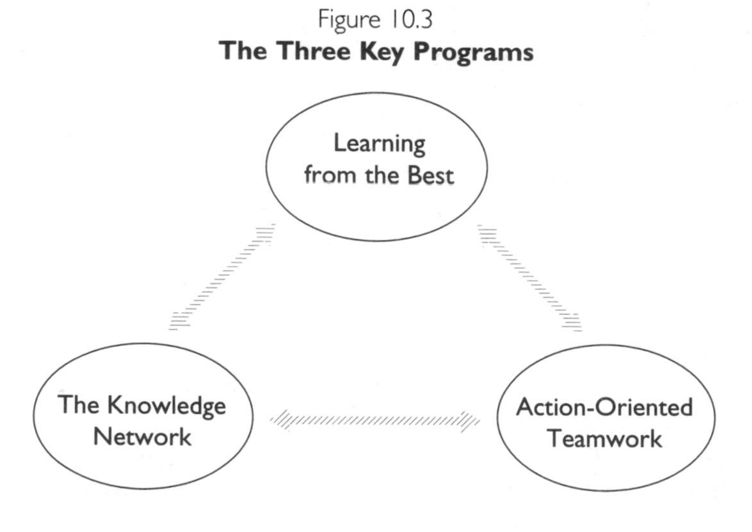

experience, the knowledge network makes those experiences available to others within the company. The result is an ever-increasing stock of individual, team, and company experience, knowledge, and skills that can be used to meet the new challenges that will inevitably arise.

ELEVEN

BRIDGING TWO WORLDS

Up to this point, we have been talking about business goals and how transformational learning can enable and facilitate a company's renewal efforts. The world of CEOs and business managers, of capital markets, of product and service development and delivery, is very separate from the world of training and development. CEOs generally don't understand what trainers in their companies do or how they might contribute to improving the company's business results, although they generally acknowledge that training is a necessary function (though perhaps not quite as necessary as research and development, sales, and service functions).

In the training and development world, trainers acknowledge that it is the business that funds their work and pays their salaries, but most trainers are more concerned with instructional design and learning theory and tend to focus on the needs of the individual learner rather than on the needs of the business.

The framework presented in this book, with the five foundations and the three-pronged superstructure of learning from the best, the knowledge network, and action-oriented teamwork, is designed to create a bridge between the two worlds (see Figure 11.1).

This bridge is not easy to construct and maintain, but it can be

Figure 11.1
Transformation Learning: Basic Structure

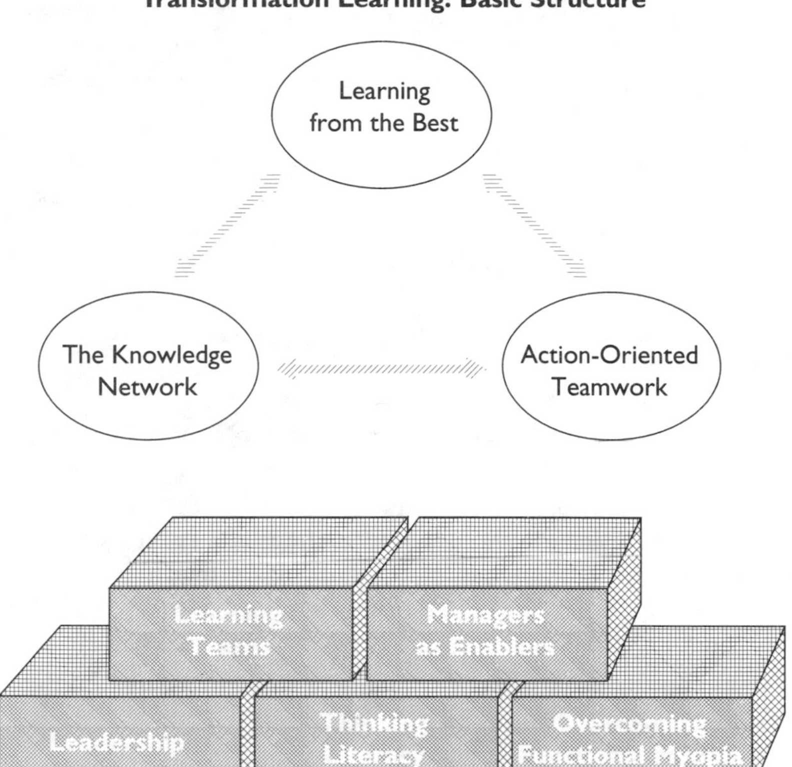

done. In most companies, attempts at bridge construction have been made on an irregular basis, usually resulting in one or both groups ending up in the river. Why haven't these attempts been successful? The fault lies on both shores.

- CEOs and other company leaders have not invested enough in understanding how to meet the company's human resources challenges.
- The training organization has historically been hidden away in a corner of the human resources organization, offering individual skills courses from a catalog, and has generally been invisible to the CEO and other company leaders.

- The training organization has been so focused on instructional methodology and learning theory that it has never been able to envision a role for itself in helping to meet company (rather than individual employee) goals.
- The training organization and the company's leadership may have met to discuss the challenges but found that they spoke such different languages that they could not understand each other.

Let's look at the problem from both perspectives.

EDUCATING BUSINESS MANAGERS

In the late 1980s, a large information technology company hired a well-known consulting company to conduct a survey of Fortune 200 CEOs. Senior partners of the consulting firm conducted the interviews, and the basic questions they asked the participating CEOs were:

- What are your major areas of responsibility and concern?
- In which of these areas do you feel totally competent, and for which ones do you seek outside assistance?
- What issues keep you awake at night?

The primary purpose of the study, from the sponsor's point of view, was the extent to which the CEOs became involved in the companies' information technology strategies. The results of the survey were very interesting. Almost all of the CEOs stated that their major area of responsibility was strategic planning, and they felt very comfortable with that role: "That's why they hired me."

The second most frequent area of concern surrounded governmental and environmental regulation. The CEOs generally felt that they could do little about these matters on an individual basis but were doing everything they could through industry associations, lobbyists, government relations programs, and so on.

Third on the list of concerns, mentioned by some 80 percent of the CEOs, was "human resources." This category encompassed such concerns as:

- Worker retraining, especially in light of rapidly changing technologies.
- Ensuring a continued supply of qualified employees, especially in view of the "poor product" being turned out by the public education system.

When asked how confident they were in their own capabilities to meet the human resource challenges, virtually all responded that they were stymied in trying to find solutions and would welcome assistance from any source, inside or outside their own companies.

The framework presented in Figure 11.1 is meant to help this business audience recognize how the knowledge and skills of all company employees will give the company its only sustainable source of competitive advantage. Other factors that control the corporation's destiny are often totally outside the control of the corporation—interest rates, competitors' tactics, and so on. Only by building a company that values learning, a company that invests in its most important assets, its employees, can corporate leaders succeed in the quest for corporate renewal.

If we have been successful in our arguments, where will the CEO and other business leaders look for the assistance they need to address these challenges? By charter and function, a company's training organization should help to meet these challenges. But it is not enough that company leaders are ready to build this bridge—the training organization must also be ready. A bridge cannot be supported from only one shore. And, in most companies, the training organization is *not* ready.

TRANSFORMING THE TRAINING ORGANIZATION

Before a company's training organization can start to help the company's transformation efforts, it must first transform itself.

Examine your company's current training efforts. Look at the structure presented in Figure 11.1. How many companies' training organizations have built their own strong foundations? How many training organizations regularly benchmark their activities against the best, have built their own knowledge networks, and have instituted action-oriented teamwork? Very few, if any, can claim to utilize all of these elements in their own organizations. And if they cannot do it for themselves, how can they do it for their companies? If training organizations want to build the bridge to their companies' business leaders, they have to start by shoring up the riverbank to support their own end of the structure.

Training in most companies today comes from a wide variety of sources and takes many forms. Let's look at the current state of affairs and then examine what training organizations must do to transform themselves.

Training Jargon

A lot of jargon appears in the training/development/education/learning literature. In various companies with which I have worked, I have encountered dozens of variations in the names of groups chartered to meet the learning needs of employees. A few common ones include:

- Training and Development.
- Education and Training.
- Employee and Organizational Development.
- Human Resource Development.
- Associate Development.
- People Development.

This is not to mention the names of specialized groups, such as:

- Organizational Development.
- Sales Training.

- Management Development.
- Executive Education.
- Performance Technology.
- (To quote the King of Siam) et cetera, et cetera, et cetera.

Colleges and universities, professional associations and journals, consultants and writers all coin their own phrases. People with new training-related responsibilities try to find impressive titles, often related to the latest trends, to put on their business cards. What do they all mean?

Some Basic Definitions

Training, development, education, learning—the terms are often used interchangeably, but they have different meanings. Let's use some basic definitions to keep them straight.

I have often been asked the difference between *education* and *training*. The easiest way I have found to explain the difference relates to my daughter's schooling. When she was in the fifth grade, she came home one day with a notice that her class would soon begin a "sex education" curriculum. My reaction to this news would have been very different had the notice announced a sex *training* program.

- *Education* involves *learning about a subject*—the acquisition of *information*. We talk about getting a "college education," where we receive a lot of information about a variety of subjects—the arts and sciences, social sciences, and so on.
- *Training* involves *learning how to do something*—the acquisition of *skills*. On-the-job training involves learning how to do the tasks associated with a job. Training may require some prerequisite education, for example, an electronics technician learns basic facts about physics and mathematics as part of her education and later

learns (is trained) to apply that information (to turn it into knowledge by making it relevant) to build or test circuits.

- *Development* is a more inclusive term. Employees develop the knowledge and skills they need through education, training, and a wider variety of development activities. In most companies, development implies preparing for a new role or an expanded set of responsibilities. Development activities tend to be experiential and may include serving on a cross-functional or multi-business-unit team, leading a United Way campaign, filling in for a manager on sick leave, and so on.
- *Learning* is the broadest of these terms and includes all of the preceding. Learning encompasses all activities by which the individual gains skills and knowledge.

The multiplicity of terms and titles often makes it difficult to even catalog all of a company's training-related efforts. In a typical Fortune 500 company, it is not unusual to find several dozen separate groups with one or more of these titles. And aside from these formal groups, business managers will be undertaking dozens or hundreds of separate training-related efforts.

Training's Functional Myopia

The training organization (used here as a generic, all-inclusive term) suffers from its own version of functional myopia. The great majority of training professionals have backgrounds in instructional design and learning theory or other specialties. Being true professionals, they tend to pay more allegiance to the standards of their profession than to the needs of their employers. They talk their own language, full of the jargon found in their college coursework and their professional journals. They measure themselves on strict educational criteria that often have little relation to the needs of their customers. When their companies tell them that they have to be more responsive to business needs, they pick up on the latest trends and buzzwords.

For example, the mission statement of a 50-person training organization supporting 30,000 employees in an international company reads:

> The [training organization] provides world-class industry education and development processes to continuously enhance the performance of people adding value to the global manufacturing and distribution enterprise.

What does that statement mean to a CEO or a business unit manager or anyone outside the training organization? The statement contains a lot of "three-dollar" words: *world-class, performance, adding value, global enterprise.* But what does it mean? If I were to write a mission statement for this, or any other training organization in today's corporate world, it would read:

> To provide or facilitate the learning the company and its employees need to succeed.

The reliance on their own professional methodologies and jargon is one of the primary reasons that so many training directors find that their work isn't appreciated by company leaders, that they can't get the ear of the CEO, that so many business units develop or buy their own training programs rather than utilize their corporate training resources.

For example, in another company, the training organization developed a "planning guide" to help business unit managers plan for their employees' training needs. It was a very well-developed, well-reasoned process, starting with the business unit's goals and taking the managers through a process to derive the skills and knowledge the unit's employees would need to reach those goals. But the planning guide was flatly rejected by business unit managers. Why?

- The guide started with the business unit's goals but quickly switched to training jargon that the managers did not understand.
- The process for planning of training needs had no relationship to the company's business planning process.

As one business manager complained: "I just finished months of work planning my business according to the company's guidelines. Now you want me to start all over, to go through an entirely different set of steps just to look at training? You're crazy!"

- In the section of the guide labeled "Benefits of Using This Process," the first benefit listed was: "More easily justify the money you spend on training." That is a benefit for the training organization, not for the business unit manager! The major benefit of using the planning process should have been: "To help you achieve your business goals."

If training professionals want to succeed in their companies, they cannot hide behind their professional standards and jargon but must learn about the business of the company:

- What are the company's business goals?
- Where does the company get its competitive advantage?
- What are the company's core competencies?
- What keeps the CEO awake at night?

Training professionals need to become part of the business, to be viewed as an integral part of the company's planning processes, to align their own goals with those of the business. To do this, they must be able to speak two languages—their own and that of the company's business.

Once they have achieved this broad stance, with one foot planted firmly in the training world and the other reaching into the business world, they must take responsibility for helping business managers achieve a similar stance, to bring one foot at least partially into the world of training and learning. This can only be achieved if the training professional speaks the manager's language.

Successful training groups make their agendas a key element in their company's transformation or re-

newal programs. They educate company executives to recognize employee and organizational learning as key elements in the company's future success.

The Results of Training's Functional Myopia

In one company, a business unit manager called in the corporate training organization to help solve a major business challenge. After finding a way to bridge the language gap, the two parties agreed on what needed to be done. The training director asked for a few days to put together a plan. Three days later, he presented the plan to the business manager and her staff. The "statement of problem" restated the business problem in business language. The rest of the plan was written in training jargon. At the end of the presentation, the business manager asked a series of questions:

Business Manager (BM): "How long is this going to take?"

Training Manager (TM): "We don't know right now. The needs assessment phase will take four to six months. Then we'll recommend a solution."

BM: "Come on. You have a lot of experience in your field. You have some idea right now of what the solution will be. Let's say that your gut instinct is correct, that the solution you have in mind right now is the one you will recommend. How long will it take to implement?"

TM: "I don't like being put into this position. We have a well-established, tested methodology to follow. But, if you insist, here's how I would see it happening. . . . The development team will take six to nine months to develop the needed training program. Then we'll pilot it with a couple of groups to validate our methodology. After revisions we'll go into production for the materials—allow two months for production. Then we'll train a group of instructors, schedule classes, and start the training."

BM: "We'll have about 800 people to go through that training. When will we be done?"

TM: "If we push everything to the minimums, we should be able to have everyone trained within 18 to 20 months."

BM: "I need it all done in six months."
TM: "It can't be done."
BM: "Then I'll hire an outside company to come in and do it, and I'll get it done in six months."
TM: "You don't understand our methodology and what needs to be done to do it right."
BM: "No, you don't understand the needs of my business. We don't have eighteen months. We don't even have the six months I offered you. We need a solution today, if not yesterday."

Professional standards—whether for training, engineering, medicine, or any other profession—were developed over time to ensure correctness and consistency, if not excellence. They were developed to protect the customer. But at times a pressing emergency arises, a business-threatening, if not life-threatening situation, where professional standards must be compromised. Too often this type of functional myopia, where a professional refuses to suspend the standards, stands in the way of a company's success. Training managers, and everyone else in a company, must work primarily toward achieving company goals. Refusal to compromise these standards may make the training manager feel good about his or her dedication to the profession, but it does nothing to help solve the company's problem. The training manager in this example will undoubtedly discover that the business manager did solve the problem with outside assistance, and she will find that the next time the business manager has a training-related problem, she will first look outside the company—rather than to the internal training organization.

Too often the very groups that train company employees how to be responsive to customers fail to respond to the needs of their own customers within the company.

Renewing the Training Organization

The blueprints laid out throughout this book for company renewal apply equally to the renewal of the company's training organization. The same steps that will lead the company's business leaders to corporate renewal through transformational learning will take the company's training leaders down their own path. But, to take this path, the training organization must recognize that it is a part of the business, just like finance, engineering, customer service, and other functions. And, as part of the business, the training organization must start by aligning its work with the company's strategic business directions and recognize that its local goals must sometimes be compromised to help the company achieve its larger business goals.

Only when the business world and the training world are talking the same language, when they are working toward the same goals, when they are working from a common set of plans, can the bridge between the two worlds be constructed. Once the bridge has been constructed, the role of the training organization will change significantly. Let's look at the role of the training organization in this new, conjoined world.

TRAINING'S NEW ROLE

The new role of the training organization will be *to enable and facilitate the employee and organizational learning needed to achieve personal and company goals*. This new role will be different from its traditional role in companies. Does it mean that traditional development and delivery activities will cease? Not necessarily. But the training organization's repertoire of methods will have to be expanded. Its standards will have to be revised. It will have to measure itself on its contribution to the company's success and not solely on the basis of traditional educational criteria.

Enabling Transformational Learning

To enable and facilitate transformational learning, the training organization will take on more consultative and coaching roles to:

- Help the company build and maintain strong foundations.
- Help business managers understand the learning needed to achieve their business goals.

- Help employees identify and access the learning resources.
- Help employees become knowledge resources.
- Coach employees as they work to master new skills and knowledge.

The model of transformational learning presented in this book does not necessarily eliminate the need for formal training but places it in a wider framework of learning methods. Expanding training's tool kit will open up a wide variety of learning options. At the extreme, it could destroy the training catalog.

Allied Signal Aerospace in Phoenix no longer publishes a training catalog. Traditional courses are still available, but where individual employees could formerly register for a course on their own, requests must now come from managers. A member of the training organization then meets with the manager to discuss the problem the manager is trying to solve. If after exploring the problem together they decide that it is a problem that can be solved by training, then a program is scheduled. Often, however, the discussion leads to the discovery that training is not the right solution.

The Canadian Imperial Bank of Commerce (CIBC) also destroyed its training catalog. Why did CIBC decide to take this radical approach? According to CIBC's Hubert Saint-Onge:

> Most companies can't tell you how much they spend on training. It took us six months to decipher—$30 million a year! And one penny out of a hundred hits the mark.[1]

Now CIBC's employees and their managers have been trained to identify learning needs, have been given access to many types of learning resources, and have been educated on a wide variety of learning methods. Individual employees, working with their managers, now determine their own learning needs and develop their own learning programs, using whatever internal and external resources they need.

New roles for training personnel in this framework include:

- Building the Knowledge Network—Whereas information technology specialists will be concerned with building the physical networks and databases, training personnel should take the responsibility for defining the content of the various databases, teaching employees how to use the knowledge network, researching resources to be listed in the databases, moderating bulletin boards and conferences, helping employees select groupware and other learning tools, and so on.

- Facilitating and Coaching Action Learning Teams—For the team development process described in earlier chapters to succeed, teams need instruction, facilitation, and ongoing coaching.
- Teaching How to "Learn from the Best"—Employees need to learn how to structure benchmark studies and how to translate them into action plans. Training professionals can help by (1) training benchmark teams, by (2) helping teams define the learning activities needed to implement their findings, and by (3) continually benchmarking their own work to ensure that the learning resources being used are the best available.

BUILDING THE BRIDGE

When business leaders and the training organization start speaking the same language, when the five foundations are solidly in place on both sides of the river, only then can the bridge construction begin. As stated throughout this book, the place to begin is with the company's goals, with its strategic business initiatives. The skills needed to start the company renewal process begin with the first foundation: leadership—leadership from both sides of the bridge.

Many companies have started investing more heavily in training activities over the past decade. But their efforts tend to focus on traditional training activities rather than on building the types of transformational learning opportunities discussed throughout this book.

A Focus on Training Is Good, But Not Sufficient

In recent years many companies have pledged that every employee will receive 40 hours (or sometimes more) of training per year or have decided to spend a specified percentage of payroll on training activities. These are positive moves but don't necessarily signify that the company understands the broader concept of transformational learning as a means of enabling the company's renewal efforts. Some companies have even gone so far as to organize a "corporate university" to demonstrate their commitment to employee training.

The Corporate University

Motorola University is undoubtedly the best known of the corporate universities, but there are many others: Hart, Schaffner, Marx University, PHH University, The Southern Company College, SunU, to name but a few. The formation of a corporate university usually has some benefits:

- It focuses the company's training efforts.
- It increases the company's training budgets.
- It gives training programs more status within the company.
- Typically, CEOs and other top company executives get more involved with the training efforts than they had earlier.

John Cone was one of the founders of Motorola University and is now president of Sequent University at Sequent Computer Systems in Oregon. According to Cone:

> The designation as a university has become a naming trend, but primarily it means something to the internal people running the business. It signals a change, suggesting much more than training: a broad focus, concern for complete development of all employees, research, connection to the larger academic community, and leading-edge thinking.[2]

Unfortunately, I believe that many training directors push to establish company universities because it adds status to their jobs without really changing the scope of the company's training efforts. I also feel that building a corporate university has some drawbacks:

- It places greater focus on formal training activities, often to the detriment of other types of learning.
- It stresses that learning activities should take place within the university structure, often reducing the focus on learning as part of daily work activities.
- It tends to tie training professionals more closely to the academic model than to being an integral part of the company's business.

This is not to say that excellent work has not been done by Motorola University and others. Many have produced outstanding programs and outstanding results. But the university structure tends to so formalize the development and delivery of training that development and delivery cycles often increase, and creative learning solutions are often left on the wayside in favor of more academically oriented programs.

Even with these new attitudes, even with the agreement to build the bridge, the actual construction requires a massive investment of resources (not necessarily monetary). In the next chapter, we will examine how companies are learning to value knowledge and skills, how they are sizing their investments, and how they are measuring returns on those investments.

TWELVE

VALUING LEARNING

What is this all going to cost? What returns will accrue to investments in transformational learning? How should knowledge and skills be valued? We'll attempt to answer these questions in this chapter.

BUILDING YOUR COMPANY'S RENEWAL PROGRAM

Think of building a company's renewal program as the redesign of an automobile. No matter whether the original model sold well but needs updating for the future or whether the old model never met expectations, the new model is important to the company's future.

As you think about the new model, there are many aspects of the design to consider: the power train, exterior styling, handling characteristics, passenger room, and so on. Each of these elements, major and minor, is part of a complex design, with all playing a role in the overall result.

Would you design this car without wheels and tires? Of course not. The car isn't going anywhere without wheels and tires. Think of the knowledge and skills of your employees as the wheels and tires of the new car; without investing in the knowledge and skills of the company's employees, your car won't fulfill its major function—to provide transportation, to take you on your journey to company renewal.

When an automobile manufacturer designs a new car, it doesn't question whether it should have wheels and tires. It doesn't ask the department in charge of wheels and tires to do a cost-benefit analysis to justify having wheels and tires on the car. The manufacturer knows that the car will not be complete, will not sell, without wheels and tires. So what does the manufacturer ask of the wheel and tire department?

- The *cost* of the wheels and tires must be in line with the overall cost of the car, for example, you don't put $300 tires on a Yugo.
- The *performance characteristics* of the wheels and tires must match the performance characteristics of the car; for example, you don't put snow tires on a convertible targeted for sale in Florida or Southern California.
- The *styling* of the wheels and tires must match the styling of the overall car; for example, you don't want fancy, cast magnesium wheels on a small economy sedan.

Just as many options can be explored in the redesign of your car, so your company's renewal effort can take many different forms. But no matter what design you select, knowledge and skills are the wheels and tires of that new design—the car, your renewal effort, isn't going anywhere without them. Nobody buys a new car to have it sit on blocks in the garage; no company invests in a renewal program to have business continue as in the past.

Just as knowledge and skills provide the means for moving your vehicle along your chosen path, so learning activities provide the fuel for the journey. Fuel is put into the tank and is used by the engine to power the transmission and send its energy to the wheels and tires to make the car move.

THE COSTS AND BENEFITS OF COMPANY RENEWAL

In redesigning a car, each piece of the car, each process in building the new car, is evaluated by its contribution to the new model. But when the manufacturer decides whether to proceed with the redesign effort, it makes its decision on the overall costs and benefits of the new model—will people buy the new model at a price that will prove profitable? A car is a complex piece of machinery. Its design and production involve thousands of parts, dozens or hundreds of suppliers, multiple manufacturing locations, distribution to thousands of dealers, and so on.

If the manufacturer demanded that each part, each process, each step in the value chain justify itself on a strict return on investment (ROI) basis, it might be possible to comply. But the time, effort, and costs involved in doing that much analysis would not only prove burdensome to the people at each step of the process, it would prove costly to accomplish, in dollars and in time—it would undoubtedly increase significantly the time to market for the new model. So the manufacturer sets basic guidelines and relies on the skills and knowledge of its employees and partners to make the right choices at each step in the process. And, in the end, the manufacturer makes its overall ROI calculations and decides whether to proceed with the redesign.

A company, even more than an automobile, is a very complex system. Companies begin to understand this complexity when they chart their major business processes and value chains, but the total system of the company can never be completely understood. Writing in *Across the Board*, Simon Caulkin explains the complexity in this way:

> Complexity says that long-term outcomes for a complex entity such as a company, a market, or an economy are essentially unknowable. This is because the relationships between actions and outcomes are nonlinear; through intricate feedbacks causes become effects and effects causes, so that in practice causal links can't be traced. And depending on initial conditions, apparently insignificant variations can be magnified by positive feedback into huge consequences.
>
> It may be that if atmospheric conditions are right, the heat from a jogger in Hyde Park will set off a hurricane weeks later in Florida—but no computer will ever be able to track the chain of causes.[1]

Because of this complexity, it is extremely difficult, if not impossible, to measure the benefits at a micro, piece-part, level. Benefits at the macro level are much easier to identify and quantify—they should flow directly from the manufacturer's original goals for the redesign effort, such as:

- Profitability of the new model.
- Market share within its class.
- Customer satisfaction and loyalty.
- Quality, as measured by initial defects and long-term warranty costs.

Similarly, the macro benefits from a company's renewal program should flow directly from its goals for that program. For a company that starts from a crisis, the primary goal may be survival (e.g., Ace Clearwater Enterprise's goal of saving the Boeing contract). For those starting from relative strength, the goals may be more ambitious, such as with Amoco's renewal program. Goals for a company renewal effort might include:

- Increased market share, for example, Jack Welch's goal that General Electric would be the #1 or #2 in each of its businesses.
- A refocused image that defines a new customer audience and gains its business loyalty, for example, Sears' renewal effort.
- Increased profitability.
- Entry into new markets.

When the goals of the renewal effort are correctly stated, they include the company's measures of success for the program. And, as stated earlier, the goals should be challenging but attainable.

WHAT'S IT GOING TO COST?

It is difficult to determine the costs of various learning activities, especially when learning becomes part of each employee's everyday work. Most companies, in trying to determine these costs, focus on training budgets, primarily because these costs are relatively easy to identify. They may include:

- The costs of running various training departments.
- The costs of the company's organizational development department or specialists.
- The costs of buying external programs and materials and bringing them in-house.
- The costs of sending employees to internal and external training programs.
- The costs of the company's tuition assistance program.

Many companies believe that a lot of the money they spend on these types of training is wasted—and they are right! To implement transformational learning, companies don't necessarily need to increase their training budgets but need to focus their spending on learning activities that support the goals of the company's renewal effort; that is, no money should be spent on training or other learning activities unless directly linked to organizational goals (or to individual goals that are directly linked to those organizational goals). Properly planned and implemented, the renewal program can even lead to reduced training costs.

Formal training is only a small part of what has been described throughout this book as transformational learning activities. A lot of what has been described is "cost-less"—it does not require direct expenditures of company cash. Let's examine each of the major learning themes described throughout the book and discuss the actual costs as well as the costs of not "investing" in each area. The areas we will examine are:

- Planning and alignment of goals.
- Building the "five foundations."
- Learning from the best.
- The knowledge network.
- Action-oriented teamwork.

PLANNING AND ALIGNMENT

To follow the recommendations contained in Chapters 3, 4 and 5 around planning and ensuring that all parts of the company align their own goals and objectives with those of the company's renewal effort, a company may need to change its long-term and annual planning processes. This may require some alteration in the company's current planning processes, may involve a larger number of people in the planning process, and may require more external research than has been common company practice. But the actual impact on the budget for company planning should be minimal.

To make these types of changes requires more leadership than cash. Minimal cash expenditures may be required to train people on new planning methods and to train the larger numbers of employees who will participate in the planning processes. The company will also be investing more of employees' time (and salaries) in the planning process, but these investments will pay dividends as people are able to start working immediately on the goals they have set, rather than waiting for orders to slowly filter down from above, and because they will be pushing themselves and their groups in the right direction from the start, thus requiring less corrective action later to get them back on course.

BUILDING THE FIVE FOUNDATIONS: COSTS AND BENEFITS

Training is a major expense item in building the five foundations. Many companies already spend considerable amounts on such topics as leadership training, basic skills training, and management training. By using the framework of transformational learning, many companies can find ways of reducing these training expenses or, more important, ensuring that the funds spent on these training activities will result in direct movement toward company goals. This can be accomplished by:

- Focusing training efforts to directly support the company's renewal program.
- Replacing some formal training programs with less formal learning activities.

- Ensuring that needed training is provided on a just-in-time, just enough basis.

The five foundations are prerequisites to any company renewal effort. Without the establishment of strong foundations, the goals of the renewal program can never be met. At the same time, it is difficult to assess the benefits of each of the foundations—benefits must be examined at the macro level, that is, at the level of the overall renewal program.

Let's take a brief look at the costs associated with each of the "five foundations."

Strong, Visible, Committed Leadership

What does it cost to develop strong, visible, committed leaders? In my earlier book, *Re-Educating the Corporation: Foundations for the Learning Organization*, I discuss a variety of options for leadership training. If your company is already doing some types of leadership training, implementing the recommendations of this and the previous book should help to focus those efforts. If a company is not doing any leadership training, some costs will be associated with starting this program. But once people have developed the necessary leadership skills, providing the needed leadership has few direct costs.

Basic Skills for Thinking Literacy

If a company has no idea of the basic skills needed by its employees and has never assessed the current skill levels of those employees, some investment is needed in these activities. But, especially in this category, many public resources (from school systems, community colleges, volunteer literacy groups, etc.) can be tapped at little or no cost to help with this type of assessment and to provide basic literacy education. Beyond functional literacy, companies will have to invest in other types of training, for example, communications skills, or basic business skills, to reach the full scope of "thinking literacy."

Overcoming Functional Myopia

If a company has never charted its basic business processes, if it has never examined its internal and external value chains, it will have to invest considerable time and resources in these efforts. These are true learning (although not necessarily training) activities—to improve business processes, you need to start with a basic understanding of what you are already doing. Overcoming functional myopia, like the other foundations, is a prerequisite to the company's renewal effort. Benchmarking activities, "learning from the best," cannot be effective unless the company knows its starting point, unless it has something to compare with others' experiences and practices.

The other major activity associated with overcoming functional myopia is the examination of the company's infrastructure of organizational design, policies and procedures, measurements and rewards, and so on, to ensure that all of these elements do not foster myopic views of individual and group work within the company. Again, these examinations and the resulting revisions are not training or learning activities but are necessary to the building and strengthening of this foundation, and they carry some costs.

Creating Effective Learning Teams

Since transformational learning is built on the ability of people to learn from each other and to learn together, the creation of effective, action-oriented learning teams is a prime prerequisite for a company renewal program. Certainly, training costs are associated with the formation of teams. Most companies already invest in this type of training. Just as important as the initial team training is the expense of providing ongoing coaching and reinforcement of team skills. This is an area in which company budgets will most likely need to be expanded.

Managers as Enablers

Most companies already invest in a variety of management training programs. The building of this foundation will not necessarily involve additional expense for more training but more the refocusing of existing programs on the skills needed by managers to enable their employees to do their best work. As managers at all levels master these skills and themselves find more effective learning methods, the costs of management training may actually decline.

LEARNING FROM THE BEST: COSTS AND BENEFITS

Benchmarking, whether internal or external, involves some costs. Books on benchmarking provide specific procedures for training benchmarking teams and the other costs of undertaking these activities. For companies in which this is a new activity, the associated costs will be incremental to existing budgets. But, as stated in Chapter 8, the resulting cost savings can be substantial by enabling the company to institute best practices, to eliminate waste and duplication of effort, to borrow ideas, systems, and procedures from others rather than having to develop them from scratch.

CREATING A KNOWLEDGE NETWORK: COSTS AND BENEFITS

Creating a knowledge network will undoubtedly be the most costly of all of the recommendations contained in this book. Expense will start with system costs, which will vary greatly from company to company, depending on their current levels of investments in information technology. The development of the various databases and the implementation of groupware technologies are not technologically trivial challenges. Training people to use these technologies will also involve some investment, but the greater challenge will be to change the culture so that people acquire the discipline to both enter information into the network and use the network on a regular basis.

If the prerequisites are met, if the five foundations are in place, the knowledge network has the potential to tie together all of the company's learning efforts, to enable true transformational learning, and to make the company's ongoing renewal efforts successful.

ACTION-ORIENTED TEAMWORK: COSTS AND BENEFITS

No costs are associated with action-oriented teamwork that have not already been covered by the foundation of creating and sustaining effective learning teams. Rather than being a cost, ensuring that teams are action oriented will provide savings to most companies. If all teams are required to be action-oriented, all team-related training will directly affect company results. Too often, in today's rush to implement teamwork, many teams are being created, at considerable expense, only to continue business as usual. The implementation of action-oriented teamwork will limit team development to those efforts that directly contribute to the achievement of the company's renewal goals.

OVERALL COSTS AND BENEFITS

Any company planning to undertake a company renewal program, any company that seeks to use transformational learning as the means to achieve its renewal, must be prepared to make some initial investments in building the five foundations, in developing the various initiatives described in this book. This may mean that, initially, training expenses will have to be increased. But the establishment of an effective learning environment—the ability for the company to tap the knowledge and skills of all company employees and to quickly identify and respond to individual and group learning needs—will be the major factor in the success of the renewal program.

Companies seeking to make this journey must start by setting goals for the overall program and then measure the costs and benefits of the renewal program on a macro level rather than to try to justify each individual expense item on an ROI basis. They must plan the entire automobile, ensuring that all of the necessary parts are included, before proceeding.

PERFORMANCE CHARACTERISTICS

In selecting wheels and tires for its redesigned model, the automobile manufacturer wants to ensure that their performance characteristics match those of the suspension, the steering, and other aspects of the design. Similarly, when planning learning activities to drive the company's renewal program, companies need to ensure that the performance characteristics of those activities match other components of the program.

This is where the company will work most closely with learning and other technologies. Learning can take place in many ways, from formal lectures to computer-based job aids to satellite broadcasts. The selection of methods should pay attention to:

- The company's resources; for example, it doesn't make sense to invest heavily in computer-based instruction if employees do not use computers regularly and have little access to them.
- The working styles of company employees; for example, salespeople who spend a lot of time in their cars generally find it convenient to listen to audiotapes as they drive from appointment to appointment.
- The speed at which learning needs to take place; for example, if the company plans to introduce new products in a six-month cycle, it doesn't make sense to select a learning method that requires a yearlong development cycle for learning materials.

Matching the performance characteristics of planned learning activities to those of the overall company renewal program will ensure that these activities will be made available in a timely manner and that employees will use them.

STYLING

A tremendous amount of literature is available on learning styles and how people with different learning styles respond best to various types of learning activities. Some people are visual learners; others prefer listening; others benefit most from hands-on learning. Although it is virtually impossible to create learning materials personalized to each employee's individual learning style (and too costly even if it were possible), it is important to learn about the different styles and to vary the modes of learning to accommodate a diversity of styles.

There is a great interest today in using technology to deliver training and to provide tools for what is commonly called "performance support." The professional literature is full of advertisements for the latest technologies and offers many stories that show how greatly some of these technologies have succeeded in cutting training costs. Everyone seeks to minimize costs, but it is important to remember that learning is a social activity—people learn from each other. And although the use of "performance technologies" and multimedia training may reduce out-of-pocket costs, it does not give people an opportunity to learn from each other.

> Last year, I gave a workshop for a chapter of the American Society for Training & Development (ASTD). The content of the workshop was based on my research, my writing, and my own two decades of experience in the field. But in that workshop, there were more than 200 years of experience in the field. And while I believe that I have some useful things to say, and some wisdom gained from my own experience, I could not totally match the breadth or depth of experience of the people in the audience.
>
> I could have made videotapes of my presentations for that workshop and sold the tapes to the participants. It would not have cost them much more than attending the workshop. But attending the workshop allowed the participants to gather information not just from me but from each other. *No matter how excellent the content of a training program, at least half of its value comes from the informal interactions of the participants among themselves.*

At Ace Clearwater Enterprises, as much value came from opening up communications between "the shop and the office" as from the technical content of the training. At Amoco, the new multimillion dollar business unit would not have been created without the opportunity for participants from different parts of the Amoco world to meet and discuss their ideas within the framework of the AMLC program.

Technologies can be very valuable as training and learning tools, and they can be very efficient means of delivering needed information, but they can never totally substitute for the informal interchange of ideas and experience that takes place when people gather together for a training program or other type of learning event.

SOME BASIC MEASURES FOR LEARNING ACTIVITIES

What about the fuel that goes in the engine? What about the learning activities that help people gain the knowledge and skills they need to make the renewal effort work? How do we measure those?

Again, the fuel, the learning activities, cannot really be measured on an ROI basis but must be considered a key element in the overall renewal effort, that is, they become part of the overall renewal program costs. But we can't just throw any liquid into the engine—we have to have some way of ensuring that the fuel contains the right mix of ingredients. The three key measurements for any proposed learning activity are:

- *Relevance* to the goals of the renewal program.
- *Adding value* to the renewal program.
- *Quality* of the learning activity.

Relevance

Too much training takes place in industry today that isn't really relevant to anything. Courses are given, learning tools are created, and people take time away from their jobs to repeat what has been done in the past without ever considering whether these programs are really relevant to company, group, or individual goals. In the April 1995 issue of *Training*, Edward Shaw writes that half of the $50 billion being spent on formal training is wasted—"squandered on training that's unnecessary, training that's aimed at non-training problems, and training that's doomed to fail by its poor design."[2] CIBC was spending $30 million annually on training, and only "one penny out of a hundred hits the mark."

Training programs and other learning activities must be viewed as relevant to the renewal program. If the objectives of a learning activity cannot be directly linked to the company's renewal goals, or to the group and individual goals that support the larger company goals, it should never be allowed to happen.

Adding Value

The second criterion for any planned learning activity is that it must *add value*. By this I mean that immediately upon completing the learning activity, the employee must be able to take the new knowledge or skill and do something differently, do something better—answer a question that he or she couldn't answer before, do a new task, or do an old task more efficiently or effectively, and so on. This is the concept behind "action learning," that learning must be tied to action, to making improvements.

One reason that so much of the training being done today does not add value is that companies create training without ever asking what the problem is that they are trying to solve. The fault for this lies not only with managers but also with training groups that are so happy to get a new assignment that they fail to ask whether the problem is really a training problem. For example, a product manager may come to a training group to ask that a new course be created on his product line, for which sales are not meeting expectations. The course may be just what is needed, but there may be other reasons as well that the product line isn't selling. For example:

- The product line may not be on the goal sheets for the sales force, that is, they may not be getting any rewards for selling the products.
- The products may be more costly than similar products available from other companies.
- Potential customers may have had such poor experience with previous products that they avoid doing business with the company.

This is the reason that it is so important to diagnose the problem before prescribing a solution—you must be certain that the proposed solution matches the problem.

In planning any learning activity, you must also assess the employees' starting point. Millions of dollars are wasted every year providing basic training to people who already have the required skills and knowledge. If you start every learning experience by reviewing the basics, you are not only going to waste many resources and a lot of valuable time, you are going to "turn off" employees before they get to the material that is of interest and value to them.

Quality

Quality is measured by the customer. Therefore, in planning learning activities, it is vital that you ask "who is the customer?" Training and development groups have traditionally looked on the participant or student as the customer. They have measured the participant's reaction to the training as the prime measure of quality. Training groups have traditionally used what are known as "smile sheets" as their primary means of measuring quality. From a learning theory point of view, this is the right approach. But if learning is to be the means to achieve company renewal, the customer is not the individual employee but the company.

Quality, in the context of a company's renewal effort, should not be measured by how well an instructor states the program's objectives, by how easy-to-read the visuals are, or how well the participant scores on a posttest. From the company's point of view, quality is measured by whether the employee, having completed the learning activity, is better able to meet the objectives of the renewal effort.

Too much time is spent by training groups on "window dressing" rather than on the content. Too much time is spent trying to dazzle students with the latest technology and the fanciest graphics rather than on ensuring that the content matches individual and company needs.

> One client sent me a new, computer-based testing program, designed to measure employees' knowledge about TQM. From what I was told before receiving the program for my PC, the client was very proud of this new program, both of the content and the fact that this was the first PC-based testing they had developed.

> It was a beautiful program. The graphics were outstanding. They had obviously spent a lot of time selecting the right color combinations, making certain that the text was easy to read. They made good use of learning theory, congratulating the employee when he or she selected a right answer and providing useful feedback when an incorrect response was received.
>
> The problem was that the content of the testing program was not well developed. Some correct answers received negative feedback. Other questions required the student to enter more than one answer but never advised the student to do so. And, generally, all of the testing material came from one book that the employee may or may not have read. The coup de grâce came when I completed the program and was told that I had answered "64 of 47 items correctly."

VALUING LEARNING

Many companies already have made major investments in training, developed "corporate universities" or other major training initiatives, offered employees many different types of training, established tuition assistance programs, and so on, only to find that many employees never participate in any of these activities.

> A training and development manager for a billion-dollar manufacturer commented: "We offer dozens of training programs, have learning laboratories with hundreds of self-paced, computer-based courses, have a library full of audio- and videotapes on every subject under the sun. We pay employees' tuition for all college courses, job-related or not. And with all of these opportunities, only about 40 percent of the company's employees use any of these resources in any given year. I can't figure it out!"

This is not an uncommon situation. But if transformational learning is to take place, if the company renewal program is to succeed, learning must be valued at all levels—by company leaders, by managers at all levels, and by individual employees. Even in companies that offer the most comprehensive set of training opportunities, many types of barriers to taking advantage of those opportunities also exist. Let's look at how all three groups (company leaders, managers, and individual employees) can demonstrate that they value learning and at the barriers each group typically erects.

Company Leaders

Company leaders are of prime importance in creating a learning culture throughout the company. The best way of leading this effort is by example—when leaders demonstrate that they value learning by themselves participating in learning activities, they make it clear that learning is valued by the company.

Another way that leaders can demonstrate the importance of learning is to make learning a key criterion in the company's program of rewards and recognition. When setting personal goals, employees tend to focus on those behaviors that will reap maximum rewards. If learning is to be a key in the company's renewal program, then learning goals must appear on every employee's goal sheet.

Company leaders are also the people who have the most control over the policies and procedures, the systems and organizational designs that can either inhibit or accelerate individual and organizational learning. Leaders need to direct the company's efforts to ensure that all of these factors are supportive of an action-oriented learning environment.

Just as leaders can accelerate the development of a learning culture by their actions, so they can also inhibit its development by erecting or maintaining barriers. Leadership cannot take the sole form of "lip service"—making a speech to support the company's new directions and then resuming business as usual. Amoco's vice chairman, in one year, spent a half day working directly with employees at the Amoco Management Learning Center—*each week for 40 weeks!* That's real commitment and real leadership!

Managers

Managers are more responsible for the death of many company renewal efforts than any other group. Too often, managers who have spent years fighting their way up the hierarchy are reluctant to share their hard-won power and responsibility with their employees. Knowing that knowledge is power, they hoard it, releasing just enough to each employee to enable him or her to get the day's work done.

If the company renewal program is to be successful, managers must also help to build an open learning environment by sharing information and by encouraging employees to be in a continuous-learning mode. Good managers hire people who are, and encourage employees to become smarter than they are. They align their work with company goals and encourage employees to see the larger picture. If the foundation of "managers as enablers" is built properly, this will happen. But many times leaders tell managers that they are to change but provide no help to them in making the necessary changes.

> At one time I was asked to develop and manage a course development group for my company's management education group. I used many of the principles I have described in this book, hired people with diverse sets of skills and knowledge, and encouraged them to work together to share ideas and experiences.
>
> One day my manager called me into her office. "Why," she asked, "are your people spending so much time in each other's offices? We are paying them to work, not to socialize!"
>
> This manager did not share my philosophy. Her management style was evident in other parts of the organization, where people did their own work, and spent very little time working together or learning from each other. It should be noted that my group turned out some outstanding programs that would not have been possible without the sharing of ideas, without the people learning from each other to create a better product than they could have individually.

Individual Employees

Not every employee wants to learn at work. Not every employee is vested in improving individual and company performance. Sometimes the employee's work is simply the means to earn income necessary to pursue outside interests or responsibilities. The concept of a person's "life work" does not always correspond to a person's "job."

If the foundation of "thinking literacy" is built, including the subcategory of "career and life planning," most employees will readily participate in learning activities, even if their primary life interests lie outside their jobs. They will view their jobs not just as a means of earning income but also as one means toward self-expression and self-actualization. When all employees are in a continuous-learning mode, when they daily seek new challenges, when they are sought out by others for their own knowledge and skills, a new level of energy will be evident throughout the company, an energy that will make people eager to come to work each day.

But this energy can easily be sapped by managers who discourage learning. How often has an employee offered a new idea only to have the manager reply: "That's a dumb idea," or "We tried that years ago—it will never work," or "I'm not paying you to think—just to work, so get back to work"? It doesn't take many of these statements to get people out of a learning mode.

TRANSFORMATIONAL LEARNING AND COMPANY RENEWAL

Company renewal in the context of today's global business environment is not a choice. To survive in this complex, competitive world, companies must continuously renew themselves, and the key to company renewal is learning— transformational learning that enables the company and its employees to continuously learn, adapt, and change.

When company renewal is the goal, learning becomes an integral part of all plans and becomes just as important to the renewal effort as wheels and tires are to a car. The question becomes not "do we need learning?" but "how can we best get the knowledge and skills we need to succeed?" The way to do this is to build a positive learning environment where employees at all levels are empowered to learn and to share their knowledge and skills with each other to meet their own and the company's goals.

When a company has built a positive learning environment, there are few obstacles that cannot be overcome. Whatever the goals of the renewal effort, employees will work together, will learn from each other and together from a wide variety of internal and external sources, to meet or exceed their individual, group, and company goals. The key to success is enabling employees and the organization to change, to see change as a positive step and not as something to be avoided at all costs. Whether as a company or as an individual,

You can't change without learning.
You can't learn without changing.

APPENDIX A

BIOGEN VALUES STATEMENT

BIOGEN

VALUES STATEMENT

Biogen's success is based on its people. Everyone here is a leader. The core of leadership is integrity and courage--characteristics we seek in every Biogen employee. These shared values describe how we aspire to lead and work together. They promote the most important organizational behavior patterns critical in building a successful company and should be viewed in the context of what is best for Biogen.

- Hire only the highest quality talent...Encourage each person's development...Recognize differences in people and look for the diverse ways they can contribute to our success...Treat each individual with respect and dignity.
- Communicate and then obtain alignment to our strategy and goals...Vigorously pursue the interdependent goals of world-class science and commercial success...Set aggressive, ever-increasing performance standards and hold people accountable for meeting them.
- Tell the truth, even when it appears to be discouraged, and expect nothing less in others.
- Face the facts, admit mistakes, accept criticism, learn from it and improve...Admit you don't have all the answers and learn from anyone, anyplace...Be intolerant of arrogance.
- Build teams...Play whatever role in your team is necessary to get the job done...Share information openly, up, down and across the company to help others...Help others succeed even at some cost to yourself.
- Forcefully resist adding layers, procedures and bureaucracy...Keep the matrix alive and fluid...Trust people with wide latitude and discretion.
- Assume your position responsibilities are a starting point, not a limitation...Take the initiative and have the self-confidence required to reach your goals...Strive for speed and quality in all that you do.
- Weigh the risks carefully but do not hesitate to innovate or to encourage and reward innovation and initiative...Accept that innovative approaches do not always succeed...Don't shrink from unpopular positions if you have passion for them.
- See change as an opportunity, not a threat...Recognize the need for flexibility...Be comfortable with ambiguity...Shift focus and priority with unwavering intensity and commitment.
- Serve and defend with equal energy our customers', our employees' and our shareholders' interests...The primary measure of our success as an organization is the value we create with our products.

APPENDIX B

"COACHING" SECTION FROM PPG PROFESSIONAL DEVELOPMENT SOURCEBOOK

SUPERVISION

COACHING:
Competent Employees Confronting New Situations
Employees in Need of Corrective Action

Effective Behaviors

For Competent Employees Confronting New Situations

Prepares for coaching situations by...
- Identifying situations in which employees need to be coached.
- Listing the specific skills the employee will need to handle the situation.

Coaches employees by...
- Describing the situation and detailing for the employee the importance of handling it well.
- Agreeing with the employee on the details of the current situation and on the expected outcomes.
- Identifying possible problem areas.
- Discussing alternative ways to deal with the problem areas.
- Agreeing on specific actions the employee will take in the situation when it occurs.
- Expressing confidence in the employee's ability and agreeing on a follow-up date to review what occurred.

For Employees in Need of Corrective Action

Prepares for coaching situations by...
- Identifying situations in which employees need corrective action.
- Identifying the deficiency in performance or work habit.
- Identifying the consequences of lack of improvement.

Coaches employees by...
- Describing the situation and telling the employee why correction of the deficiency is important.
- Agreeing with the employee on the details of the current situation and on the expected outcomes.
- Identifying possible causes of the problem.
- Discussing alternative solutions.
- Agreeing on specific actions the employee will take in the future.
- Explaining what actions will be taken if the employee does not improve (if this situation has been discussed before without improvement).
- Expressing confidence in the employee's ability and agreeing on a follow-up date to review what occurred.

Sources of Information

For Competent Employees Confronting New Situations

- Employees • Surveys • Peers • How employees handle new job assignments

For Employees in Need of Corrective Action

- Employees • Surveys • Peers • When employees have been performing poorly, does their work improve after coaching? • Do you need to take disciplinary action after coaching because the employee did not improve?

Developmental Suggestions

For Coaching Competent Employees Confronting New Situations

Preparing to coach...
- Identify situations in which an employee will be taking on a new task and try to determine what new skills are needed. Ask the employee to confirm that list.
- Ask a customer who works closely with your employees to identify a competent person who needs some coaching.

Coaching...
- Coach a competent subordinate in an area in which he/she is weak.
- Ask someone to advise you on how to coach.
- Observe a competent person coaching.

For Coaching Employees in Need of Corrective Action

Preparing to coach...
- Identify situations in which an employee is not performing as required.
- Write a description of a performance and work habit problem and ask your supervisor to review your description and make suggestions for improving its clarity and objectivity.

Coaching...
- Coach a competent subordinate in an area in which he/she is weak.
- Rehearse a coaching situation with another person in the role of the employee in need of coaching. Then ask the person who plays the role to give you feedback.
- Ask someone to advise you on how to coach.
- Observe a competent person coaching an employee who needs corrective action.

Readings

The One Minute Manager - Blanchard and Johnson
A Passion for Excellence - Peters and Austin
How to Motivate Today's Workers: Motivational Models for Managers and Supervisors - Rosenbaum

Training Programs

Dimensional Management Training I (Level 3)
Interaction Management - Various Modules (Level 3)
Interpersonal Managing Skills (Levels 1-3)
Leadership Through People Skills (Levels 4-6)
Leading For Performance Improvement (Levels 3-5)

Ways to Practice

These suggestions are effective both for: Competent Employees Confronting New Situations; Employees in Need of Corrective Action

Preparing to coach...
- Work with a new employee, make a list of that person's developmental needs, and coach the person on how to improve these skills.

Coaching...
- Choose a non-business setting where your skills and knowledge are needed and offer to coach someone who could use these skills.
- Coach someone who is a skilled coach and ask for feedback.
- Rehearse or role play with a peer, your manager, or a colleague.

ENDNOTES

Introduction.

1. Peter Dron, "Cab of Many Colors," *Car and Driver*, September 1992, p. 63.

Chapter One. The Art of the Possible

1. David Greising, "Quality: How to Make It Pay," *Business Week*, August 8, 1994, p. 54.
2. Celine Bak, "Lessons from the Veterans of TQM," *Canadian Business Review*, Winter 1992, p. 17.
3. Louis S. Richman, "The New Worker Elite," *Fortune*, August 22, 1994, p. 66.
4. Story paraphrased from "Sacred Cows of HR Are Barriers to Quality, Profits," by Joseph Bacarro, *HR News*, July 1994, p. 27.
5. "The Coming of the New Organization," *Harvard Business Review*, January-February 1988, p. 46.
6. Bruce Fern, "Gaining from Training," *Bankers Monthly*, December 1992, p. 38.
7. Greising, "Quality," p. 54.

Chapter Two. From Two Strikes to a Home Run

1. Perry Flint, "Partners Preferred," *Air Transport World,* February 1993, p. 59.
2. Quotation from "Boeing Gives Credence to Clearwater's Revival," by William H. Miller, *Industry Week,* January 17, 1994, p. 42.
3. Kellie Dodson, from a speech to the Boeing Supplier Conference, March 1993.
4. From NIST/California Manufacturing Technology Center, "Business and Product Description," February 1994, p. 4.

Chapter Three. Define, Then Align

1. Robert W. Mann, "A Building-Blocks Approach to Strategic Change," *Training and Development Journal,* August 1990, p. 24.
2. Ibid.
3. "Filling in the White Spaces," an interview with C. K. Prahalad (Univ. of Michigan) in *Across the Board,* September 1994, p. 35.
4. Ibid., p. 36.
5. Karl Albrecht, "The Power of Bifocal Vision," *Management Review,* April 1994, p. 46.
6. John H. Sheridan, "Paul Allaire Is Prodding Xerox Back into the Fast Lane of Technology Commercialization," an article from the *Industry Week* forum on CompuServe, December 1994.
7. Quoted by Michael A. Verespej in "New Responsibilities? New Pay!" *Industry Week,* August 15, 1994, p. 18.
8. Graham M. Palmer and Sherrill G. Burns, "Revolutionizing the Business: Strategies for Succeeding with Change," *Human Resource Planning,* February 1992, p. 82.
9. Sheridan, "Paul Allaire."
10. Carol J. Loomis, "Dinosaurs," *Fortune,* May 3, 1993, p. 39.
11. Quoted by Michael A. Verespej, "New Responsibilities?" p. 14.
12. Ibid., pp. 15–16.

Chapter Four. Forming the Partnership with Top Management

1. Carol J. Loomis, "Dinosaurs," *Fortune,* May 3, 1993, p. 37.
2. Ibid.
3. "The Savior at Sears," *Newsweek,* November 1, 1993, p. 42.
4. Ibid., p. 43.

Chapter Six. Finding Your Starting Point

1. *Re-Educating the Corporation: Foundations for the Learning Organization* (New York: John Wiley & Sons, 1994).
2. Srikumar S. Rao, "The Painful Remaking of Ameritech," *Training*, July 1994, p. 47.
3. Ibid., p. 48.
4. Ibid., p. 53.
5. "Job-Related Materials Reinforce Basic Skills," *HR Magazine*, July 1995, p. 89.
6. Ibid., p. 90.
7. Ken Blanchard, "Performance Appraisals," *Executive Excellence*, October 1994, p. 15.
8. Jack Stack with Bo Burlingham, *The Great Game of Business* (Doubleday/Currency, 1992).
9. John Case, *Open-Book Management: The Coming Business Revolution* (New York: HarperBusiness, 1995).
10. John Case, "The Open Book Revolution," *Inc.*, June 1995, pp. 29–30.
11. Tracy Kidder, *The Soul of a New Machine* (New York: Avon Books, 1990).
12. Dennis A. Joiner, "Assessment Centers in the Public Sector: A Practical Approach," *Public Personnel Management Journal*, Winter 1984, p. 435.
13. Victor Dulewicz, "Improving Assessment Centres," *Personnel Management*, June 1991, p. 51.

Chapter Seven. Buy, Rent, or Develop: Knowledge Acquisition Strategies

1. Quoted in Tim Noonan, "Seizing an Opportunity for Change: Lowe's Corporate Transformation," *Hemisphere*, January 1995, p. 36.
2. Ibid.
3. James Brian Quinn, *Intelligent Enterprise* (New York: The Free Press, 1992).
4. "Manufacturers Use Suppliers to Help Them Develop New Products," *Wall Street Journal*, 19 December 1994, p. 1.
5. Ibid.

Chapter Eight. Learning from the Best

1. "Making Benchmarking Faster, Cheaper and Easier," *CMA Magazine*, February 1994, p. 23.

2. Paraphrased from Edward Deevy, *Creating the Resilient Organization* (Prentice-Hall, 1995), p. 65.
3. *Business Week*, October 12, 1992, p. 178.
4. Perry A. Trunick et. al., "CLM: Breakthroughs of Champions," *Transportation & Distribution*, December 1994, p. 41.
5. Quoted in "Technology Transfer: Dow Chemical," *Financial World*, September 28, 1993, p. 54.
6. Ibid.
7. Perry A. Trunick et. al., "CLM: Breakthroughs of Champions," *Transportation & Distribution*, December 1994, p. 41.

Chapter Nine. Building a Knowledge Network

1. Thomas A. Stewart, "Mapping Corporate Brainpower," *Fortune* (CompuServe on-line edition), October 30, 1995.
2. David Kirkpatrick, "Groupware Goes Boom," *Fortune*, December 27, 1993, p. 99.
3. Mary Keselica, "The 'People' Part of Groupware," *On-Line*, March 1994, p. 101.
4. Jim Manzi, "Groupware: Future Prospects and Scenarios," *Telecommunications*, January 1994, p. 18.
5. Dave E. Hoffman, "Groupware Is More Than Just Glorified E-Mail," *Best's Review-Property-Casualty*, April 1995, p. 70.
6. Keselica, "The People Part of Groupware," p. 102.
7. Kirkpatrick, "Groupware," p. 99.
8. Hoffman, "Groupware Is More Than Just Glorified E-Mail," p. 70.

Chapter Ten. Action-Oriented Teamwork

1. John H. Sheridan, "Lessons from the Best," *Industry Week*, February 20, 1995, p. 13.
2. Charlotte Shelton, "Team Mania," *Executive Excellence*, June 1995, p. 9.
3. Ibid.
4. Ibid.
5. Gloria Gery, "A Rabble-Rousing Roundtable," *Training*, June 1995, p. 63.
6. Malcolm Thomas, "Forget Paradigms," *Industry Week*, March 6, 1995, p. 30.
7. Stephen Frangos, "Zebra Earns Its Stripes," *Human Resource Executive*, May 1995, p. 60.

8. John E. Martin, "Unleashing Power," *Executive Excellence*, June 1995, p. 6.

Chapter Eleven. Bridging Two Worlds

1. Quoted in Thomas A. Stewart, "Intellectual Capital," *Fortune*, October 3, 1994, p. 74.
2. Quoted in Marcia Atkinson, "Build Learning into Work," *HR Magazine*, September 1994, p. 60.

Chapter Twelve. Valuing Learning

1. Simon Caulkin, "Chaos, Inc.," *Across the Board*, July/August 1995, p. 34.
2. Edward Shaw, "The Training-Waste Conspiracy," *Training*, April 1995, p. 59.

INDEX

[28.004] In this chapter the law relating to the compliance with and enforcement of company law will be considered in the following sections:

[A] The Agencies of Enforcement and Compliance.
[B] Enforcement and Compliance – Criminal Sanctions.
[C] Registration-Type Offences.
[D] Non-Registration Offences.
[E] Restriction of Directors.
[F] Disqualification of Directors and Other Officers.
[G] Injunctions to Compel Compliance with the Companies Acts.

[A] The Agencies of Enforcement and Compliance

[28.005] Until the enactment of the CLEA 2001, the registrar of companies, the Minister for Jobs, Enterprise and Innovation and the Director of Public Prosecutions were the three agencies which shared the prosecution of offences under the Companies Acts. Since the CLEA 2001, the prosecution of company law offences and the enforcement of the Companies Acts are now shared by the following:

1. The registrar of companies;
2. The Director of Corporate Enforcement;
3. The Director of Public Prosecutions;
4. Private parties with *locus standi*.

The registrar of companies

[28.006] The office of the registrar of companies dates back to the Joint Stock Companies Act 1844, which first permitted incorporation *by registration*. Necessarily incidental to that momentous legislative decision to permit incorporation by registration was the creation of the office of the registrar of joint stock companies: the keeper of the register[11]. In *Business Communications Ltd v Baxter and Parsons*[12], Murphy J observed:

> 'Since the introduction of legislation permitting people to incorporate with limited liability, it has been recognised that the protection which this conferred on those taking advantage of the privilege has to be counterbalanced by statutory provisions to protect and safeguard the interests of those dealing with them. The original and essential protection to those dealing with companies incorporated under the Companies Acts from time to time was the creation of a registration office in which would be filed the essential information in relation to companies incorporated under the legislation so that outsiders would have an opportunity to ascertain the persons constituting the corporation and be in a position to form some estimate as to the assets which would be available to meet its liabilities[13].'

One of the original functions of the registrar of joint stock companies – now called the *registrar of companies* – the importance of which survives to today, is the receipt, evaluation and (if in order) the acceptance for registration of the documents lodged by persons desirous of incorporating a company. The registrar's primary function can thus

[11] See Ch 1, *The Private Company in Context*, at para **[1.080]**.
[12] *Business Communications Ltd v Baxter and Parsons* (21 July 1995, unreported) HC, Murphy J.
[13] *Business Communications Ltd v Baxter and Parsons* (21 July 1995, unreported) HC, Murphy J at p 15 of the judgment.

be seen as the statutory procreator of the artificial legal entity that is the registered company. The registrar's grant of a certificate of incorporation signals the birth of a company; s 18 of the CA 1963 providing that on the registration of the memorandum of association, the registrar 'shall certify under his hand that the company is incorporated'. The other three core functions of the registrar are: the receipt and registration of post incorporation documents; the enforcement of the Companies Acts in relation to the filing obligations of companies; and the making of information available to the public[14]. Notwithstanding the establishment of the office of Director of Corporate Enforcement, the registrar retains these four core functions.

[28.007] The Minister for Jobs, Enterprise and Innovation is responsible for the maintenance and administration of the Companies Registration Office ('CRO')[15] and for the appointment of the registrar and assistant registrars[16]. Section 368(4) of the CA 1963 provided that whenever any act is, by the CA 1963, or other statute, directed to be done to or by the registrar, 'it shall, until the Minister otherwise directs, be done to or by the existing Registrar of joint stock companies or, in his absence, to or by such person as the Minister may for the time being authorise'. It would appear that some doubt existed as to the validity of acts done to or by assistant registrars and others employed in the registrar's office. Section 52(1) of the C(A)(No 2)A 1999 provides that any act referred to in s 368(4) which, before the commencement of the C(A)(No 2)A 1999, was done to or by such persons:

> '… shall be valid and be deemed always to have been valid as if the Minister had directed under that subsection (4) that such an act was to be done to or by such an assistant Registrar or other such person (including in cases where the existing Registrar of joint stock companies (or his or her successor) was not absent).'

To put matters beyond all doubt, s 52(2) provides:

> 'On and from the commencement of this section, any act required or authorised by the Companies Acts 1963 to 1999, the Registration of Business Names Act, 1963 or the Limited Partnership Act, 1907 to be done to or by the Registrar of Companies, the Registrar of joint stock companies or, as the case may be, a person referred to in the enactment concerned as "the Registrar" may be done to or by a Registrar or assistant Registrar appointed under s 368(2) of the CA 1963 or any other person authorised in that behalf by the Minister.'

[28.008] The registrar is the person charged with securing compliance with the filing and registration requirements under the Companies Acts. The means of enforcement available to the registrar to ensure compliance (and to punish non-compliance) are: (a) the prosecution of companies and their officers for registration-type offences; (b) the imposition of on-the-spot fines[17]; and (c) strike-off of non-compliant companies[18].

---

[14] See the CRO website at www.cro.ie.

[15] Section 368(1) of the CA 1963.

[16] Section 368(2) of the CA 1963.

[17] See para **[28.041]** *post*.

[18] See, generally, Ch 26, *Strike-Off and Restoration*.

Chapter 26 Strike-Off and Restoration

(Thomas B Courtney)

Chapter 25 Realisation and Distribution of Assets in a Winding Up

(Thomas B Courtney)

Chapter 27 Investigations and Inspectors

(G Brian Hutchinson)

Chapter 28 Compliance and Enforcement

(Thomas B Courtney)

The Law of Companies

Third Edition

In memory of my father
Tom Courtney Senior
(1929–1992)

For Aileen,
Ally and Sophie